RED, WHITE, AND GREEN

RED, WHITE, AND GREEN

The Maturing of Mexicanidad
1940-1946

by

Michael Nelson Miller

SOUTHWESTERN STUDIES NO. 107

© 1998
Texas Western Press
The University of Texas at El Paso
El Paso, Texas 79968-0633

First Edition
Second Printing 2001
Library of Congress Catalog No. 97-062482
ISBN 0-87404-278-X

Texas Western Press books are printed on acid-free paper, meeting
the guidelines for permanence and durability of the Committee on
Production Guidelines for Book Longevity of the Council on Library
Resources.

Cover photo of María Félix c. 1943

This book is dedicated to
Ellen, Nelson, Sarah, and Dulaney
Hank Schmidt
Byron Baldwin and Tom Crofts
Jack Bristol, Bobbi Gonzales, Mary Anne Maier
Alison Riemersma, Jack Stotts, C. Ellis Nelson
Reg Baldwin and Connally McKay.

CONTENTS

Introduction 1

CHAPTER ONE
    Prelude: Cardenismo 11

CHAPTER TWO
    The Politics of Avilacamachismo: National Unity,
    Internationalism, and Young Intellectuals 25

CHAPTER THREE
    Avilacamachismo, Culture, and the Role of SEP 45

CHAPTER FOUR
    Radio 65

CHAPTER FIVE
    Film 87

CHAPTER SIX
    Art and Architecture 101

CHAPTER SEVEN
    Carlos Chávez: Avatar of Avilacamachismo 123

CHAPTER EIGHT
   Female Archetypes of Change 141

CHAPTER NINE
   Bodies, Visions, and Sounds: The Emergence
   of Mexican Women in Culture 159

CHAPTER TEN
   The Legacy of Avilacamachismo 179

Notes 191
Bibliography 211
Index 223

INTRODUCTION

The preeminent social, political, and public policy of the sexennium of Manuel Ávila Camacho (1940–1946) was called *avila-camachismo*. Historians generally have failed to understand the full dimension of avilacamachismo or its long-term importance. Almost no attention has been paid to the attempt of avilacamachismo to redefine and restructure the relationship between culture and state in Mexico in the 1940s. The value of this study is therefore found in its new interpretation of the Ávila Camacho era in the history of the relationship of culture and state in Mexico. Many Mexicanists have found the period to be one of convenient "transition" between the reformist sexennium of Lázaro Cárdenas and the era of industrialization and urbanization following the Second World War.[1] The failure to grasp the significance of avilacamachismo and to give it a rightful place in the development of the culture represents a serious lacuna in the writing of modern Mexican history.

Avilacamachismo was an attempt on the part of the state to create a mass media-based cultural nationalism rooted in loyalty to Mexican personalities who embodied the experience of their history in the artifacts of their creativity. Avilacamachismo was constructed at popular and high cultural levels ranging from radio, popular music, dance, musical theater, posters, film, and cartoon magazines to art, architecture, ballet, and classical music. Avilacamachismo inspired idealism. It appealed to the nation's youth and was aimed at Mexicans under the age of fifty. It was led by individuals in state positions who were often closer in age to forty than fifty and who were themselves active in the creation of culture.

1

Peter Berger pointed out in *The Homeless Mind* that ideas about "modernization" and "progress" in the writings of social scientists since the end of the Second World War, especially in relation to underdeveloped nations, have been too narrowly focused on economic development. Modernization and development have gone hand in hand, while only rarely have modernization and culture been discussed together.[2] In the public policy decisions of the avilacamachista state, modernization and culture were inextricably bound. The state endeavored to create a modern culture that Mexicans in every section of the large and historically disunited nation would find accessible and appealing. This approach to culture was rooted both in the Western idea of progress and in the philosophy of postrevolutionary intellectuals like José Vasconcelos and Jaime Torres Bodet. The Ávila Camacho administration advocated national policies that would move the nation toward unity, a pro-Ally internationalist policy, and industrialization. It expanded the idea of progress beyond the economist's mechanical measure of national growth, traditionally framed in terms of production and per-capita income, into the cultural arena, whose riches have rarely been calculated or esteemed.

A motivating principle of avilacamachismo was the development of both popular and high culture in order to undergird authentic national unity. Another major emphasis of the avilacamachista state was a commitment to internationalism in foreign policy. A third avilacamachista emphasis, which leaped forward in the circumstances of the war era from a lesser to an overwhelming position by 1946, was business and industrialization. Although industrialization was important from the beginning, it was not, early on, the primary emphasis of avilacamachismo. The infusion of capital generated by the war brought a dramatic change in the dynamics of avilacamachismo. Although economic development benefited commercial and political segments of the society, it also led to corruption that became worse in subsequent administrations beginning with Miguel Alemán.[3] It is clear that the explosion of the Mexican economy at this time has long overshadowed other important aspects of the era. In order to see the entire picture, especially those parts obscured by the brightness of the economic explosion, it is necessary to recover and document the original goals and policies of avilacamachismo. These original goals and policies, which were primarily concerned with national identity and national unity, may prove to be, in the final years of the twentieth century and in what may be the final years of PRI hegemony, of far greater historical and political significance.

Avilacamachismo funded a range of cultural activities that placed the Mexican state at that time among the world's leaders in the sponsorship of the arts. Between 1940 and 1946 it supported a national film industry, a national ballet, a national symphony orchestra, a radio symphony, several smaller symphonic and chamber orchestras, the national school system, public statuary, open-air art, and the mural tradition. Avilacamachismo sponsored art exhibitions, new museums, a national program to eliminate illiteracy, the publication of inexpensive books, the creation of a respected publishing industry, the founding of journals in art and music, the development of a recording industry that had worldwide sales, and the formation of a dynamic graphic arts industry. Avilacamachismo provided capital for the creation of new architectural forms and land for the construction of these new buildings. It paid for consultants to come together from health and architecture to design new hospitals. It brought teachers and architects together to create new designs for schools. Avilacamachismo supported with salaries, subsidies, commissions, and teaching jobs a large and diverse community of creative personalities, some of whom worked directly as officials of the state, while others served the state as "stars" of the emergent national culture.

The support of culture as a means to national unity was at the heart of avilacamachismo. Avilacamachistas used the word *desarrollo* to mean both cultural and economic progress, and sought to place the national culture on a par with the national economy. This approach to state-building was a direct outgrowth of the philosophical and political idealism of José Vasconcelos while he was education secretary under Alvaro Obregón (1920–1924) and was subsequently embodied in the youthful avilacamachista idealism of the early 1940s. Although by this time Vasconcelos himself had been eclipsed as a cultural leader, his influence, known as *vasconcelismo,* was pervasive throughout the Ávila Camacho administration. It was most apparent in the work of the powerful Secretariat of Public Education (hereinafter SEP), especially after 1943 when it was taken over by poet and vasconcelista idealist, Jaime Torres Bodet.

In defining culture it is commonplace to start with E. B. Tylor's 1877 statement that culture is "that complex whole which includes learning, belief, art, law, morals, custom, and any other capabilities and habits acquired by man as a member of society."[4] Since this initial usage, the term has acquired different meanings in various academic disciplines. In this book culture is defined as any artistic or didactic activity that represents some aspect of Mexican artistic creativity. This view is akin to the definition by Samuel Ramos that culture in Mexico is "any form of action inspired by the spirit."[5] Culture does not refer here to the behavior patterns of villages, families, sexes or groups, but to the creative actions of individuals who painted, danced, composed music, produced, directed or acted in films, sang or acted on the radio, taught in public or private institutions, or otherwise participated in the Mexican cultural experience. In this study culture will be treated in its "popular" and "high" dimensions.

From time to time in the narration Alex Inkeles's concept of "modal personalities" has been helpful.[6] This concept isolates key personalities as "signs" who represent focal points around which both cultural and political movements form. For example, in her book *Tinisima*, Elena Poniatowska explores the life of Italian expatriate Tina Modotti. As she looks at the many personalities surrounding Tina Modotti, a clearly defined circle of influence and friendship develops. This circle, a group of like-minded individuals surrounding and supporting a mentor with whom they also live an active social life, is called a *camarilla*. Tina Modotti's camarilla shared her interest in art, film, radical politics, and photography. Another classic example of the modal personality was Jaime Torres Bodet. Torres Bodet was a poet and teacher, and an heir to the camarilla of José Vasconcelos. Camarillas are important because they are the center from which some individuals break away. Although it may appear that some examples of modal personalities are somewhat randomly included, it will become clear in this extensive description of Mexican culture that deviations are significant. Francisco Javier Gaxiola, for example, began as a disciple of Torres Bodet and a young vasconcelista idealist. Lucrative business opportunities and corruption during the war years led him out of the Torres Bodet circle. He then became a modal personality who typifies the movement away from the early idealism of avilacamachismo and toward the subsequent corruption of the postwar PRI. The individuals who appear in this book, and their camarillas, are of critical importance in ultimately understanding the dynamic and complex changes that took place in Mexico between 1940 and 1946. The importance of the study of camarillas in understanding these changes in Mexican political life has been recognized by many, including Ricardo Pérez Montfort in *Estampas del nacionalismo* and Roderic A. Camp in his formative and innovative work on Mexican intellectual and political elites, *Intellectuals and the State in Twentieth-Century Mexico*.

Cliford Geertz has pioneered what has been called the semiotic interpretation of culture. One of his essays, "Thick Description: Toward an Interpretive Description of Culture," published in his book *Interpretation of Culture* (New York: Basic Books, 1973), has been especially helpful in formulating the overall structure of this study. Geertz, along with Irene and Thomas Winter, Paul Rincour and P. Bouissac, seems to suggest that culture is a vast communication network whereby verbal and nonverbal messages circulate along elaborate, interconnected pathways which, taken together, create shared meaning and community. One finds Bouissac's *Circus and Culture: A Semiotic Approach* (Bloomington: Indiana University Press, 1976) a good example of how cultural historians must look at personalities who use signs, symbols, and verbal and nonverbal messages to unlock the complex substructures of cultural history. In the semiotic approach, the study of culture is always interdisciplinary and must draw upon all areas of learning to achieve an accurate understanding. The study of one delimited area in the history of a culture, such as a study of Mexico in the sexennium of Manuel Ávila Camacho, requires a study of high culture (art, poetry, dance, film, and learned music) and popular culture (comic books, circus-inspired art, popular music, and folk dance) as well as more traditional areas of study such as politics and economics. Semiotics and modal personality theory work well together in setting forth personalities and symbols around which this complex culture unfolded between 1940 and 1946.

In looking at culture in the Ávila Camacho era, one finds a distinctive set of circumstances that David Brion Davis has called "the first and most abstract level of cultural history, which can be defined as a description of the characteristic styles, motifs, and patterns of a given period."[7] This uncovering of the connective points in the relationship of culture and state is what Jacques Barzun had in mind when he spoke of cultural history as a synthesis that attempts to convey the "intelligibility of the whole" by discovering and elucidating the relationship of the parts.[8] The tremendous variety of "parts" led to the problem of the proper selection of personalities and creative media for this study. The very comprehensiveness of the approach threatened to engorge the study with indigestible detail. To resolve this dilemma one must select a broad spectrum of artistic activity that is representative but certainly not exhaustive: film, radio, art, architecture, cartooning, classical music, musical theater, ballet, and public education. Central to the construction of this book is the literature available in English and Spanish on the history of Mexican culture in the 1940s. From these materials one can see the process whereby the state supported culture and cultural creators as well as the manifold ways in which the state directed culture by developing the film industry, radio, art, ballet, and public education. Helpful also is the work of Carl Bode, who argues that the historian of culture must live with a disturbing arbitrariness in the selection process, but boldly choose individuals whose lives, creative work, speeches, actions, decisions, interests, and friendships can reveal the relationship of culture and state. Barzun suggests that "articulate thinkers and conscious artists" tell us the most about what we need to know and argues that plain old "popularity" must also point us to the right people.[9] In the end the views of Barzun with his "cultural elite," Bode with his "popular artists," and Camp with his "intellectual elite" were influential in framing the standards by which the modal personalities in this study were selected. In addition, there is an anecdotal level that is developed gingerly. These stories are not substantive or significant by themselves, but taken together they form a series that capture symbolically elements important in cultural history: humor, tension, intrigue, and excitement.

The first two chapters outline events that led up to the election of Manuel Ávila Camacho in 1940.[10] Avilacamachismo was a political philosophy that formulated new plans derived from postrevolutionary idealism about culture and state, nationalism and national identity, and the role of the Mexican state abroad. The tension between the idealism of cultural avilacamachismo and the pragmatism of political avilacamachismo appeared slowly at first and then accelerated as the Second World War created new and unexpected economic and political opportunities. The complex mechanism for the infusion of wealth into Mexico during the war is fully explored in Steven Niblo's *War, Diplomacy and Development: The U.S. and Mexico, 1938–1954.*

Chapter three examines SEP as the heart and hands of avilacamachismo. This chapter begins with José Vasconcelos, who engendered much of the political and cultural idealism that bore fruit two decades later. It concludes with Jaime Torres Bodet, whose vasconcelista idealism shaped the cultural policies, programs, and praxis of avilacamachismo.

Chapters four and five look at the lives and work of singers, composers, film directors, and "star" personalities of the radio, film, and art worlds. The creation of a new national mythology of mass-media personalities was critical to the state's redefinition of culture. Radio music, for example, subtly reinforced the state as it encouraged a youthful and stylish redefinition of Mexican national identity. This new definition complemented and enhanced the new nationalism being built upon unity, internationalism, and industrialization. Mexican young people were encouraged to identify with popular cultural figures whose images reflected the modernity, national uniqueness, honesty, dignity, courage, and patriotism called for by Ávila Camacho and the avilacamachistas. These two chapters explore the mechanisms whereby the state sought to create a national mass culture responsive to an emergent, modern psychology of connectedness, identity, preservation, alienation, anxiety, adaptation, assimilation, and, among the young, peer pressure and popularity.

Chapters six and seven look at the fine arts in order to show how avilacamachismo made culture central to the state at every level. Artists and classical musicians of this period helped to shape perceptions and attitudes about such issues as a Mexican aesthetic, poverty, the past, industrialization, revolution, the future, the nation, life, and death. The focus here is not on art or art history per se but on the relationship of the art world to the state. It uncovers an identity of Mexican art beyond muralism as well as conflicts among personalities and artists. In chapter six the focus is on the architect Luis Barragán in the early stages of his career, being helped to fame by the avilacamachista state. Chapter seven examines classical music through Carlos Chávez, who was at the apex of his career and represented a Mexican with exactly the international status desired by the cultural avilacamachistas.

These two chapters shed light on the avilacamachista rationale for the support of high culture. This support remained constant even as the tensions of different commitments, values, myths, and symbols began to emerge within the state and between groups of artists. Avilacamachismo, after a struggle between its cultural and political components, came to accept the fact that high cultural creation could give symbolic expression to the inner strains of the nation, just as classical music might capture a theme alien to the goals of the state. These two chapters answer the question of why artists and composers were supported by the avilacamachista officials even when their work was critical of the state.

Two views of culture and its role emerged. One emanated from the conjunction of youthful groups within the state, including the president himself, and the art community. These young Mexican leaders, influenced by the fusion of politics and aesthetics advocated by Vasconcelos, believed that the development of culture was a primary function of the state. In addition, some believed that popular culture was as important as high culture and that the development of both was a prerequisite to the realization of national identity, unity, and prosperity. With the Second World War as a window of opportunity, avilacamachismo tried to become a large tent into which all artists would be welcomed or tolerated and given recognition, support, and space. The other view was held by avilacamachistas who found a use for art not in an idealism of culture and state but strictly in reaching political ends, causing, in fact, a diminution of idealism that may have contributed to subsequent historical misinterpretation of avilacamachismo.

Chapters eight and nine discuss a generation of Mexican women who were important in the avilacamachista iconography because they represented diversity among the leadership of a developing and inclusive national society. This choice was made because of the significance of these women as individuals and their symbolic importance to the state. These women were role models and change agents in the Mexico of the 1940s. These chapters consider the lives of these gifted individuals who all knew each other, were influenced by one another, and were, like President Ávila Camacho and many in his coterie, in their forties. None of these women worked directly for the state as members of the government, but all of them, even Tina Modotti, received some financial support from the state. None were as politically conservative as the government; in fact, several were members of the Communist Party. They were all independent, non-traditional women who embodied the sophistication of avilacamachismo as it unified and modernized the nation. Those who formulated avilacamachismo—a group that did not include everyone in the government—wanted to create a culture and state relationship that by the standards of the day was inclusive of women, youth, and native peoples, and tolerant of oppositional opinion and alternative lifestyles. It openly rejected repression, regionalism, mindless traditionalism, or violent anticlericalism. The seven women in these chapters reached the apex of their creative lives during these six years.

Research for this study began in 1985 in Santa Fe, New Mexico, with an interview with Lucienne Bloch, who gave me insights into the mind of Frida Kahlo. Research at the National Archives in Washington, D.C., revealed that the United States had a fascination with Mexican culture during the war years. The archives contain letters and reports indicating that much time was spent by the wartime embassy staff reporting on and no doubt enjoying Mexican culture in the Ávila Camacho sexennium. In 1990 and 1991, trips to Mexico City provided critical primary material from a number of sources, including the Archivo General de la Nación (AGN), located in the magnificently restored Lecumberi Prison on Calle Eduardo Molina. The Manuel Ávila Camacho collection contains 1,357 dusty boxes of materials. In Mexico the author conducted interviews, listened to music, danced in clubs, went to museums, and attended films and concerts. In Mexico City, San Miguel de Allende, Guanajuato, Tepoztlán, Jiquilpan, and Saltillo, the author interviewed people who lived through the era. These interviews were helpful in introducing me to the joy that this golden period of Mexican culture gave people, especially young people. A most important interview was with the art historian, art collector, and travel writer, Selden Rodman. Mr. Rodman, who now lives in retirement in Oakland, New Jersey, kindly provided me with helpful information on his friendships with leading Mexican political and artistic figures of the period.

This period in Mexican history has been overlooked and misunderstood. Only recently have historians begun to venture beyond the traditional interpretation. Clearly, any understanding of modern Mexico is impossible without reference to this era and this administration, and understanding this era is not possible without reference to culture. It is hoped that this effort will initiate a new interest in avilacamachismo and the dynamic relationship of culture and state that existed in Mexico between 1940 and 1946.

CHAPTER ONE

Prelude: Cardenismo

In the aftermath of the violence and the multi-sided struggle for power in the Mexican Revolution, the exact nature of the relationship between culture and state was unclear. At that moment there came forth a personality who would influence the individuals who later created cultural avilacamachismo. José Vasconcelos was the product of an important intellectual movement that began to emerge in the last years of the Porfiriato. According to Claude Fell, in the late Porfirian period a group of middle-class intellectuals disenchanted with the regnant positivism of the epoch began to meet.[1] Composed of José Vasconcelos, Antonio Caso, Alfonso Reyes, Martín Luis Guzmán, Pedro Henríquez Ureña, Carlos González Peña, and José Escolet, the group was first called the Sociedad de Conferencias.[2] In 1907 they read and discussed Henri Bergson's *L'evolution creatrice*, as they had the works of Nietzsche, Kant and Unamuno. [3] They were influenced also by the late romanticism of Justo Sierra. At the turn of the century, nearing the last decade of his life, Sierra published *México: Su evolución politica*

11

as an interpretive synthesis of Mexican history. Clear, balanced, critical of many people, even mildly of Díaz, yet optimistic about the future, Sierra's work was a paternalistic transition from the Porfirian era to the emergent intellectuality of the Sociedad de Conferencias. In 1910 they renamed their group the Ateneo de la Juventud. The Ateneo was the forum from which the group launched an intellectual attack upon materialism in general and positivism in particular.[4] Often called the Generation of 1910, the *ateneistas* began a humanistic reform movement that lashed out at the science-oriented conservatives who controlled the nation's intellectual life.[5]

In the first years of the postrevolutionary period the ateneistas became cultural heroes, founding, for example, the Universidad Popular Mexicana, a university for ordinary citizens where humanistic theories of social progress were taught. There is no doubt that the Generation of 1910 played an important role in the development of culture and state in the period leading up to 1940; but they were rivaled by the Generation of 1915, who, although also profoundly affected by the Revolution, had been too young to have directly participated in it.[6] This large group, which included Octavio Barreda, Narciso Bassols, Alfonso Caso, Ignacio Chávez, Vicento Lombardo Toledano, Jesús Silva Herzog, Daniel Cosío Villegas, Samuel Ramos, and Manuel Gómez Morín, among others, was also instrumental in shaping culture between 1940 and 1946. However, this group, extensively studied by Enrique Krauze, was more pragmatic about the state and less idealistic about culture than either the Generation of 1910 or the avilacamachistas. For a variety of political reasons, a significant few, such as economist and journal founder Jesús Silva Herzog and the Communist Vicente Lombardo Toledano, supported avilacamachismo two decades later. Others, like historian Daniel Cosío Villegas, seemed surprisingly indifferent to the goals of avilacamachismo. Some, like Manuel Gómez Morín, who founded the PAN, strongly opposed Ávila Camacho.

According to Fell, Vasconcelos was a major world philosopher in the early 1920s. In several chapters of this book, Vasconcelos's model for culture and state will be examined, primarily in light of his creation of an integrated, culture-centered school system. On 10 September 1921, while awaiting the reconstitution of the federal secretariat of education to which he had just been appointed head by President Obregón, Vasconcelos delivered a lecture that was a blueprint for his vision of a modern, unified national culture in Mexico. In "The Law of the Three Stages of Society" he outlined a philosophy of culture that placed aesthetics in a central role in building the postrevolutionary state in Mexico. The first stage of culture was tribalism, in which violence created a stable community. In the second stage, intelligence affirmed a superiority over brute strength. The highest level of culture and state, according to Vasconcelos, was a nation in which every member was encouraged to be an artist, a poet, a writer, a songwriter, a dancer, a reader, a learner, an artisan—that is, a cultural creator. This Greek view of society could be embodied in a nation where the role of the state would be that of enabling the people to build the state by creating the culture.[7]

In *La tormenta* Vasconcelos selectively remembered the process through which he arrived at his vision of a new Mexican state. He referred to his appointment as education secretary in 1914 by Eulalio Gutiérrez. In December of that year, however, he was arrested by Pancho Villa. While in prison, he learned that Emiliano Zapata had asked Villa to send Vasconcelos to him. Fearing that Zapata wanted him dead so that he could appoint his mentor, Otilio Montaño, as secretary of education, Vasconcelos escaped and fled into exile in the United States, where he spent much of his time in the New York Public Library. Every day he read the Greeks, looking for the missing piece to the puzzle of nation-building. At last he believed that he had found it. On a gray afternoon, at a desk in the reading room of the great library, he had a vision of Mexico as a nonviolent, united and prosperous nation where every Mexican, regardless of background, would read the classics, paint the walls of the nation with the colors of the earth and sun, and sing songs of the soul.[8] When he returned to Mexico as rector of the National University under de la Huerta and as secretary of public education under Obregón, he began to carry out his ideas. The seeds of vasconcelista idealism and his view of the relationship of culture and state grew to maturity two decades later in the administration of Manuel Ávila Camacho.

It is a necessary platitude to say that Mexico in the early 1920s, having undergone dislocation in the maelstrom of revolution, was a nation attempting to "consolidate the gains its people had struggled for since the waning of the Porfiriato."[9] Between the death of Alvaro Obregón and the accession of Lázaro Cárdenas, Plutarco Elías Calles dominated Mexico, first as president and then as the power behind Presidents Emilio Portes Gil, Pascual Ortiz Rubio, and Abelardo Rodríguez. To this day Calles remains something of a mystery. He assumed the presidency with a substantial agenda, announcing that he would balance the budget, reestablish credit abroad, shift the tax system from states to the federal level, establish a national bank and advance land reform. He also encouraged the labor movement and in 1929 organized the loose coalition of regional leaders into the Partido National Revolucionario (PNR). Historians give him credit in all of these areas.[10] His finest and most important decision may have been to proclaim that modernization and Mexicanization could, and should, go hand in hand.[11]

But there was another Calles, whom Vasconcelos called "a savage."[12] After leaving office Calles intentionally undermined the authority of his party, became increasingly corrupt, and used the party infrastructure to maintain himself as the center of power in the nation. If totalitarianism is an attempt at a radical cure for a fragmented and demoralized culture, then corruption is a cynical effort to exploit this disintegration. Calles's actions ultimately precluded the growth of honest and effective national government and retarded national identity. His corruption also provoked reaction among those who recognized in him the virus of *caudillismo* (dictatorship) with its deadly implications for the nation and its future.[13]

As the election of 1934 neared, it was obvious to Calles and his associates that a candidate was needed who could satisfy the growing opposition while remaining under the influence of his clique.

According to Luis Gonzáles, Calles himself picked Lázaro Cárdenas. Calles never said exactly why he picked him, but it seems that he did not know that Cárdenas was a charismatic leader with a potent vision for Mexico. In fact, Cárdenas was a modern and astute politician who would soon drive Calles from Mexico. Cárdenas's ideology extended to culture by incorporating the masses into the state, an action that underlies culture-state relations to the present day.[14]

In the campaign Cárdenas proved to be tireless, with a gift for remembering people. Almost every day he spoke to thousands, and weekly the crowds grew larger. Most impressive was his ability to listen with sympathy to the problems of the Indians, the stoop workers in the fields, and the dwellers in rural poverty or in the already sprawling *ciudades perdidas* (forgotten towns) on the outskirts of cities. This Mexico whispered softly but told him much of the misery of its millions. Cárdenas traveled 18,000 miles in the campaign, pioneering modern election tactics in Mexico.[15] During the campaign he used radio for the first time to reach large numbers of people in inaccessible areas of the country.

Radio would come to play a critical role in the culture-state policies of avilacamachismo. In 1934, still relatively new, it was quickly becoming a popular medium for culture. There were already radio "stars" with large followings. Jorge Negrete first sang on XEW in 1932, joining such personalities as Emilio Tuero, Chucho Martínez Gil, Juanito Arvizu, Gonzalo Curiel, and announcers Pedro de Lille and Alonso Sordo Noriega.[16]

Radio had begun officially in Mexico on 2 June 1923 when President Obregón ordered the secretariat of communications to regulate the development of commercial radio stations. By midsummer 1923 two stations were broadcasting.[17] The laws were somewhat vague, however, and in 1926 President Calles signed a bill called the Law of Electrical Communications. This set forth technical standards and guidelines for programming, and contained a clause that all stations must be owned and operated by Mexican citizens. The law defined a commercial station as one established for the purpose of broadcasting concerts, speeches, and news of general interest. One article in the law excluded any text that was against the national interest, that used poor grammar or profanity, or that expressed ideas contrary to national security or established customs.[18] In 1932 the law was rewritten again to allow the state to claim more air time on the seventy commercial stations then operating. Section 5 of Article 74 and all of Article 75 declared that every station licensed to broadcast in Mexico must carry government health bulletins, communiques about government services, and speeches "in favor of the public interest."[19] In addition to these commercial stations, in 1932 there were also at least ten stations owned by the state. These were called in the original 1926 law "official" stations. SEP, for example, went on the air in 1924 with station CEZ broadcasting from Mexico City. In 1923 the Secretariat of War and Navy went on the air with station JH, changed in 1928 to XFX. In 1937 this station became the voice of the Autonomous News and Publicity Department of the executive branch of the national government.[20]

In the election of 1934, Cárdenas used only commercial stations and was careful not to use language that might violate the laws governing radio broadcasting. Little work has been done on the impact of these radio broadcasts, an example of the early use of radio as a medium for the mass distribution of ideas, but undoubtedly it was significant. Never before had so many Mexicans at the same time heard a candidate speak.

These speeches by a young and idealistic national leader were broadcast all over the nation, some stations taking the feed over telephone lines, with others simply tuning a quality radio set to one of the 50,000-watt stations, like XEW in Mexico City, and placing a microphone in front of the radio. However primitive the technology, something powerful and new now entered the culture. In these broadcasts Cárdenas responded directly to the people he had listened to in his travels around the country.[21] In his speeches he set forth an agenda for the creation of five national programs, each designed to be understood by every listener and expressing Cárdenas's vision of the future of the nation. His plan included:

1. A program of agrarian reform based upon the primary nationalist ideal of "Mexico for Mexicans." Under the banner of this program, Cárdenas called for a dramatic redistribution of land to the landless poor of the nation.[22]
2. A program of national labor reform aimed at Mexican workers and designed to include collective bargaining, cooperative food programs, and free speech for labor and labor leaders.
3. A program of nationalist and socialist education with an emphasis on the construction of schools for rural youth in Mexico. The foundation of this new approach to national education would be "scientific."[23]
4. A program that would continue to reduce the power and influence of the church in Mexico.
5. A program of public works that would create new roads, dams, public buildings, and other public services.[24]

In these historic radio broadcasts and in his other speeches, Cárdenas conveyed what would become his central agenda as president. Implicit was the participation in a national culture of every citizen regardless of racial or economic background. Cárdenas's vision embraced national identity and pride, nationalism, land reform, labor reform, and progressive public education. This vision of national culture, rooted in the soil of *cardenismo*, would remain a vital influence in the administration of Manuel Ávila Camacho, even after many ideals and plans from the Cárdenas era had faded away, were dropped or transformed.

Cárdenas represented a new type of leader in postrevolutionary Mexico in that he was a break in the pattern of northern leaders. He was a nationalist with a vision that was authentically national in scope, significant in a nation in which regionalism had continually hindered national identity. His radio speeches were often couched in the language of solidarity, and he called for the reconciliation of conflicting viewpoints. Howard F. Cline has pointed out that for a while Cárdenas was even able to attract support from both anticlerical and church leaders. To Catholics he could sound like the lesser of two evils; when he turned against the most radical and outspoken of the anti-Catholics, the hated Garrido Canabal, he gained Catholic support.[25] Cárdenas also got the army behind him and most of the labor movement; and with this backing and the support of some Catholic leaders, he was emboldened to act decisively against Calles. Once Cárdenas was free of Calles and all that had gone with his corruption, he began to implement his programs.

Thus Cárdenas's first national success was in ridding the country of Calles and his clique. Moving in the direction of national unity and balance, he purged two leftist extremists from the party. Garrido and his "Red Shirts" from Tabasco were removed after they met in Coyoacán and let it be known that they would not support a government of reconciliation. Ousted at the same time was the communist García Tellez, who advocated that the schools teach children to say "salud, camarada" instead of "adios."[26]

The deportation of Calles and the removal of Garrido and García Tellez brought Cárdenas over 10,000 letters of support. Calles told the press when he arrived in Los Angeles that Cárdenas was "taking Mexico into Communism."[27] In fact, Cárdenas was establishing a unified state run by a government that would be, at least by the standards of Mexican political life in that period, aboveboard and honest. From the beginning Cárdenas had the support of individuals from a wide spectrum of political camps, including the two sons of Calles, Plutarco Jr. and Rodolfo, both of whom would serve in the government. Luis Gonzáles and nearly all historians of this period agree that between 1934 and 1940 Cárdenas created a nation that made significant progress. Gonzáles points to the way in which Cárdenas took over the PNR, reshaped it according to his goals for the nation, and then protected himself by giving the military rank and file a pay increase.[28] Carefully, Cárdenas created the structure for a powerful national party divided into four sectors: labor, popular, peasant, and military. This party was directed by a national executive committee. In 1938 Cárdenas renamed the PNR the PRM (Partido de la Revolución Mexicano).

In the end, Cárdenas fulfilled in large measure what Manuel Gamio called *forjando patria* (forging a fatherland). As president he saw that much of the population had not yet fully identified with the concept of nationhood. The poor, both Indian and mestizo, lived as an internal colony without civil rights, education, health care, or hope. Cárdenas believed that any action of a state built upon revolutionary political nationalism and seeking by that action to build national unity and national identity had to be a moral act. His nationalist philosophy held that all Mexican people had to share equally in the life of the nation. One feels that his use of radio to communicate his message is rooted in the notion that his government was for every locale, region, and class in the national social fabric. His approach to nationalism was inclusive and designed to reach beyond the limitations of traditional Mexican political activity. The nationalization of railroads and oil set a standard for economic nationalism that would not change until 1989.

His attempt to solve the longstanding social problems of the nation included a series of coalitions that often mixed elements of the left and right. Indeed, after his election Cárdenas continued to travel throughout the country. As the magazine *Hoy* reported in January 1940, Cárdenas was out of Mexico City for a total of 489 days from 1 December 1934 to 1 December 1939, visiting 1,028 cities, villages, and towns.[29] In these travels he met with church leaders, opposition leaders, and ordinary people, as well as his party supporters. Gonzáles describes the dramatic impact of his visit to the *municipio* of San José de Gracia, Michoacán, in 1940. President Cárdenas and the local priest gave each other the *abrazo* and "entered the village arm in arm along the road lined with people, through cheering crowds and handfuls of confetti."[30] He was, in the words of Gloria Gonzáles Atkins, an Odessa, Texas, woman who was a teenager in Mexico during this period, "a true champion of the people and a figure of immense popularity with the young people of the nation."[31] In addition to listening to and viewing the nation firsthand, Cárdenas became a master of strategic compromise through his preelection and postelection travels. It was this characteristic that led him to designate Manuel Ávila Camacho, with whom he remained close all of his life, as his successor.

As the election of 1940 approached, it fell to Cárdenas to pick his successor. He needed a man who understood the political system as it had been adjusted and customized by cardenismo. It is important that we outline the emergent Mexican political system as it had evolved under Cárdenas and passed to his successor. After 1935 Cárdenas had made some changes in the structure of the party. He released government employees from kicking back part of their salary to the PNR.[32] Although this was a move toward honesty, it also made the party dependent upon the government for almost all financial support.[33] With this arrangement Mexico had at last achieved stability, but at a price. The arrangement created a system that controlled many aspects of national life, and socioeconomic progress was tied to it. It also set the stage for the institutionalization of tolerance. Opposition to the government was allowed—as we shall see—but not in rivalry for power. In theory the president implemented his program "by decree and with the permission of congress."[34] The system meant, of course, that most issues were resolved in private meetings with coalitions of power groups. These groups were positioned by Cárdenas in the structure of the system. Labor, for example, was allowed to develop a strong voice, while the military was gradually reduced in power and influence.

The end result of the Cárdenas system, turned over to Manuel Ávila Camacho in 1940, was a powerful national political organization composed of moderate elements of the left, leaders of the industrial and traditional right, agrarian reformers, civil servants, enlisted men and junior officers, bureaucrats, and cultural leaders. Some groups were left out by design. Cárdenas was considered too left-wing by most of the upper ranks of the military; and in order to protect himself and his administration he had catered to the lower ranks by improving their schools, housing, and pay. After 1935 his Plan Sexenio Militar called for expanded education for military officers and for upgrading military institutions and facilities.[35] It was in this area that Cárdenas first observed Ávila

Camacho's leadership abilities. Already a Cárdenas supporter and party member, Ávila Camacho was asked to implement the Plan Sexenio Militar, which he did by encouraging the younger, idealistic army officers to join the popular, labor, or peasant sectors of the party. The army was thus divided into four political coalitions and given a focus beyond its traditional self-interest. He asked the rank and file to think of themselves as "armed auxiliaries" of the humble classes; and he joined Cárdenas in urging the army to become "less military and more civilian in spirit."[36] Ávila Camacho announced that the armed forces welcomed the president's call for a new version of the party in which the military would play a greatly reduced role.

These events produced anger and fear among officers and among individuals, politicians, and business leaders on the right.[37] There was no precedent in Mexico for nationalism without militarism, and Ávila Camacho was viewed as a stooge in Cárdenas's betrayal of Mexico. Some said he was not even a true revolutionary general because he had not received a field promotion.

In the two years before the election, tension began to grow in the north between these rightists and the party. In the summer of 1938, the CTM (Confederación de Trabajadores Mexicanos) in Sonora demanded the ouster of the governor, General Juan Yocupicio, who had become outspoken in his criticism of Cárdenas. Yocupicio called for the repudiation of the policies of Cárdenas and the party.[38] In Nuevo León another governor, General Anacleto Guerra, protested that his state was being bullied by the aggressive tactics of the CTM and threatened to "move against them with arms."[39] Cárdenas wanted a nonviolent solution to these northern problems and decided to send Ávila Camacho to negotiate.[40]

Cárdenas viewed Ávila Camacho as someone who not only understood the concept of nationalism without militarism, but who was also capable of dealing with those who stood against his leadership. He saw Ávila Camacho as honest, courageous, trustworthy, and cognizant of the dynamics of coalition and compromise. With men like Ávila Camacho, Cárdenas created a political nationalism that he believed was Mexico's best hope for the future. He also used their help to unite the nation, the party, and the government into a system that, while not easily understood by those outside of Mexico, slowly seemed to bring order and progress to the large and complex nation.

In 1939 Cárdenas faced the prospect of seeing his system destroyed by a renewal of civil conflict between left and right. He expressed to associates his grave concern that, unless he picked the right successor, someone who could preserve, protect and build upon his work, the nation would return to the cycle of political violence.[41] The newspapers speculated that Cárdenas might pick General Francísco Múgica, who shared strong ideological ties with the left.[42] Privately, others felt that Múgica would be the logical choice because Cárdenas could control him from behind the scenes, much as Calles had done with Portes Gil, Ortiz Rubio, and Rodríguez. The public speculation that Múgica would take over from Cárdenas terrified the opposition, and in early 1939 numerous antigovernment parties, all headed by angry generals, began to organize. Strongest in the north was PRAC, a semi-fascist party headed by Generals Pablo Gonzáles and Marcelo Caravelo. The strongest response, however, was the creation of PAN (Partido de Acción Nacional). Connected quietly to the Catholic church, PAN picked General Juan Andreu Almazán as its candidate. Almazán had wanted the government party nomination and believed that as the highest ranking officer in the army he deserved to be seriously considered. The party ignored him. Instead of turning to the left with Múgica or to the right with Almazán, Cárdenas picked a man who had faithfully served him, had a military background, was a moderate, a Catholic, and had the pragmatic, centrist political philosophy Cárdenas believed that the nation needed in 1940. Cárdenas himself named Manuel Ávila Camacho, his secretary of defense, as the official candidate.[43]

The choice of Ávila Camacho gave a boost to the Almazán campaign, for Ávila Camacho was not well known or particularly popular. In June 1939 Almazán resigned as commander of the Seventh Military Zone in Monterrey and began his nationwide campaign for the presidency. The campaign lasted a year and a half, covered tens of thousands of miles, and ended on one of the bloodiest election days in Mexican history, 7 July 1940. Troops were on the move all day, and few people knew exactly what they were doing. The atmosphere was tense, but the results came as no surprise to anyone since the PRM powers had ordained the winner. Ávila Camacho officially received 2,265,199 votes; Almazán 128,574.[44]

There was scattered violence for several weeks. In his last days in office Cárdenas prepared the way for Ávila Camacho by remaining true to his concept of coalition and compromise as the most effective form of political nationalism. Magnanimously, he invited all of the disaffected generals to return to their commands. He wanted them to rejoin the system, even offering them a pay increase and vacation pay for the time they were away plotting against him. The air force was given twenty-seven new planes.[45] Some have suggested that it was cynical of Cárdenas, perhaps even baroque, to reconcile the system and the dissidents by offering them what amounted to bribes. But it must be remembered that to Cárdenas, and later to Ávila Camacho, national unity and national identity were indispensable if Mexico was to survive. On 13 December 1940 Manuel Ávila Camacho was inaugurated as president. Violence had flared, and, significantly, it had been controlled. A man of the center, a nationalist, a follower of Cárdenas, a one-time military leader, and a Catholic who had announced during the campaign *soy creyente* (I am a believer) was in office.[46] Ávila Camacho became the president of a nation that had a tradition of government seizure by powerful and ambitious men. His first obligation was to establish himself firmly in the office or invite insurrection.

CHAPTER TWO

The Politics of Avilacamachismo:

National Unity, Internationalism, and Young Intellectuals

Manuel Ávila Camacho, born in Tezuitlán, Puebla, in 1897, was called by journalist Betty Kirk "the least aggressive and most balanced president Mexico has ever had."[1] An artist friendly to Ávila Camacho in the early days was the cartoonist Antonio Arias Bernal, who featured the president on the cover of *Hoy* during the inaugural week celebrations. He depicted Ávila Camacho throwing his whole weight against a door through which the four most famous leftists in Mexico were attempting to pass: functionary Narciso Bassols, intellectual Vicente Lombardo Toledano, labor leader Graciano Sánchez, and editor Alejandro Carrillo. The caption read with a play on the famous phrase from the Spanish Civil War, "*no pasarán*" (they shall not pass).[2] Centered, strong, and articulate, Ávila Camacho began to receive support from many quarters, even some beyond the party.

In his inaugural address he stated the intellectual foundation of his nationalist agenda by observing that "each new epoch demands a rebirth of ideas. The clamor of the entire republic now demands the material and spiritual consolidation of our social conquests in a prosperous and powerful economy. It demands an era of construction, abundant life and economic expansion."[3] In this speech he also declared that national disunity had brought only destruction and economic decline. He did not call for nationalism as much as for new vision. He knew that nationalism provided the integrative ideology of the Revolution, but he also saw it as a two-edged sword, with the forces of extremism also tapping its power and mystery. Ávila Camacho believed that in the postrevolutionary era new symbols were needed, and called upon the nation to grasp a visionary nationalism in which Mexican culture played a central role.

Although from the outset avilacamachismo meant more than simply political control of the nation, a measure of control was necessary in a nation with a recent history of political violence. The most effective means of control was the tax system. Most taxes were federal, and state and local authorities had to maintain a working relationship with the federal government in order to receive adequate financing. Local and state political bosses retained their power and money only by remaining loyal to the president and his government. Cárdenas bequeathed to Ávila Camacho this method of retaining national control of distant regions and caciques who might otherwise depart from the political agenda of the state.

The goals of avilacamachismo were lofty ones such as creating lasting national unity, developing the economy, and pioneering a successful role of Mexico on the international scene, especially in the Western Hemisphere. There is little evidence that the government had any interest in the oppression or exploitation of the Mexican people. Ávila Camacho held to the system developed by Cárdenas that James C. Cockcroft and Bo Anderson have called "co-optation."[4] They use this term to describe the process by which individuals or groups independent or powerful enough to threaten the PRN were traded concessions in exchange for dropping demands or reducing or redirecting their challenge.

Coalition and compromise were essential to avilacamachismo as it endeavored to create national unity and stimulate the economy. It was this ideology that led avilacamachismo to seek a positive relationship with the United States; and a pragmatic nationalism underlay Mexico's decision to declare war on Germany and Japan in 1942. The proponents of avilacamachismo believed that Mexico had much to gain from abandoning its longstanding suspicion of its northern neighbor and joining with the United States in the Allied effort. In both domestic and foreign policy, avilacamachismo was rooted in coalition and compromise.

As previously noted, from Cárdenas Ávila Camacho inherited a coalition of groups within the party representing the moderate left, industrial right, labor and agrarian groups, and the party bureaucracy.[5] His actions and his policies had to reflect a carefully scripted harmony of these groups and their needs and expectations. The most effective tool available to him, as to Cárdenas before him, was the tax system, whereby the federal government maintained control over the states. But it was not a final answer to the problem of national identity nor a key to the creation of a vibrant national culture.

Beginning with the Restored Republic (1867–1876), the Mexican state had used culture as a way of unifying the nation. The hard years following the 1910 Revolution drove large numbers of Mexicans from the traditions of village life; and the experience of being thrust into strange, urban settings created a feeling of anomie. In the villages, depopulation, mass-media cultural symbols, new schools, and improved transportation and communications fostered insecurity. Although the hierarchy of the church disappeared in large sections of the country, powerful vestiges of over four hundred years of Catholic morality remained intact. Conservative Mexicans found socialism and changing moral values intolerable. The radio brought songs that were shocking to many older Mexicans. The lyrics to many songs like Consuelo Velásquez's *"Besame mucho"* and *"Diez minutos más"* and Agustín Lara's lyric *"Aunque no quieras tu, ni quiera Dios, lo quiero yo"* brought demands for censorship of lyrics and films. Other songs declared immoral by conservatives included *"La ultima noche," "Tu ya no soplas,"* "Juan Charrasqueado*," "Aventurera," "El hijo desobediente," "Pecadora," "Toda la vida," "Frio en la alma,"* and *"Traigo mi 45."*[6]

By 1940 this disintegration of the old way of life was both a problem and an opportunity for the state. It was necessary to provide a sense of identity for a population for whom identity had always been defined by family, village, religion, and region, institutions seriously disrupted by the Revolution and its aftermath. Massive urbanization had begun, and there was a need for the reconstruction of elements vital to the social fabric. Here, then, was the moment to construct a new and truly national culture. Avilacamachismo—political nationalism devoid of militarism, teeming with vision and rhetoric and committed to the use of radio, music, and cinema—was an attempt to create a Mexican culture united and synergistic rather than fragmented and antagonistic. Ávila Camacho held firmly to this vision until he left office. In an interview on 11 November 1946, a few weeks before the end of his term, he repeated his inaugural call for a "new revolutionary cycle" led by "new men" with a vision for the future free of the images of the past.[7]

Yet it was World War II, not the Revolution, that hurried Mexico willy-nilly into the future. On 16 September 1942, the 132nd anniversary of the Grito de Dolores, an event took place that even to Mexican newspapers seemed amazing. On the balcony of the National Palace, six former presidents stood together in front of the nation and called for Mexicans to form ranks with them and unite with the world in the struggle against fascism. These men represented antagonisms, rivalries, conflicts, and violence going back to the early days of the Revolution. Even Plutarco Elías Calles had been invited to return from exile in the United States. He joined his old foes Lázaro Cárdenas and Manuel Ávila Camacho in linking arms with Adolfo de la Huerta, Emilio Portes Gil, Pascual Ortiz Rubio, and Abelardo Rodríguez in a presidential phalanx that symbolized significant changes. In the end, Mexico was the only Spanish-speaking nation in Latin America to become a combatant in World War II. The road leading to actual combat was, however, more important for the domestic agenda of the state than has been previously understood. Avilacamachismo, with its emphasis on national unity, national identity, economic prosperity, and internationalism, was at first assisted and then changed by the opportunities presented by the war.

As Steven Niblo has pointed out, it is generally forgotten today how massive was the Mexican wartime cooperation with the United States. When Ambassador George Messersmith arrived in Mexico City in 1942 there were between four hundred and five hundred people on the staff of the embassy there, and that figure grew to eight hundred at the height of the war effort.[8] Niblo observes that under Messersmith's leadership, "the two countries negotiated fifty-two or fifty-three major contracts covering all essential raw materials to support the war effort. Charged with implementing the maze of wartime regulations that touched Mexico, he produced a prodigious volume of correspondence and earned the nickname 'Forty-page George' from colleagues on the Mexican desk of the State Department."[9] Niblo also points out that with FDR in office, Messersmith's "position was firm and there was an open channel between Mexico City and Washington. The president made the importance of Mexico explicit to Ambassador Messersmith as he began his assignment: 'The outstanding example of national leadership which President Ávila Camacho is now giving to the Mexican people is a tremendously important contribution to our cause at this time.'"[10] According to Niblo, Messersmith's job was to administer Mexico's contribution to World War II. Moreover, since the Ávila Camacho government was following a high strategy of using the wartime cooperation to industrialize the country, "Messersmith's help with wartime regulations was wanted. No other U.S. ambassador ever held so many levers in his hands, and few others have been so laudatory toward their Mexican counterparts." Messersmith described the economic ministers Eduardo Suárez and Francisco Javier Gaxiola as "collaborating to the fullest extent possible." As he later reflected, "I do not recall a single instance when the Mexican government endeavored to take advantage of the war situation and enter into contracts providing for prices which were higher than those that should properly be paid."[11] Niblo concludes, "Messersmith was able to operate at a number of levels of Mexican society in ways that would be unimaginable for a U.S. ambassador today. He maintained contacts with labor and radical leaders and was welcome to give talks, from time to time, at the National University and the Universidad Politecnica. He maintained a cordial relationship with people with whom he disagreed, and even arranged for a member of his staff, Videl Poodevan, to spend her leave of absence assisting Diego Rivera, for which the great Communist artist was grateful."[12]

As early as July 1939, Mexico had been negotiating with the Federal Loan Agency of the United States for the sale of Mexican supplies of "critical materials" such as cobalt, copper, arsenic, cadmium, lead, manganese, tin, zinc, and tungsten.[13] On 10 July 1941 President Ávila Camacho issued a decree providing for the American purchase of all of Mexico's surplus war materials at prices favorable to Mexico. The sale of raw materials quickly placed the Ávila Camacho state on the strongest economic footing of any postrevolutionary government. It also fostered between the United States and Mexican governments a friendly spirit that within a year resolved numerous old problems. On 19 November 1941 Presidents Roosevelt and Ávila Camacho signed an accord that settled several agrarian claims, authorized reciprocal trade, and established a framework for negotiating bilateral problems related to the oil nationalization in 1938.[14] This was a government-to-government process in which both sides treated the other with utmost respect. The Mexican press reacted with enthusiasm, and the Mexican secretary of foreign relations was quoted as saying that the United States had "changed its attitude toward Mexico."[15] President Roosevelt, along with cabinet members Cordell Hull and Sumner Welles, declared the days of imperialism and brute force over, stating that in the future Mexico and the United States would cooperate as equals and "good neighbors." This, announced Ezequiel Padilla, was a moral victory for Mexico and for international law and cooperation.[16]

During World War II the principles of avilacamachismo became public policy. Mexico became united and internationally respected as it moved toward prosperity. In truth, Mexico had few options other than selling to the United States, since its exports to Europe declined sharply. Sales to Great Britain and Germany virtually ended. In 1938 Mexico sold 800,000,000 pesos' worth of goods to Germany; in 1941 sales were 400,000.[17] One can argue that there was a real desire on the part of the United States to develop a less imperialistic attitude toward Mexico. The United States could have secured the materials at a lower price, since Mexico had no other stable markets. But the United States wanted Mexico as an Allied neighbor and partner in hemispheric defense. Thus the United States deliberately aided the economic development of Mexico not only to acquire strategic war materials but also to win approval of the Mexican people, most of whom had no idea of the philosophy behind avilacamachismo and most of whom mistrusted the United States. American diplomats in Mexico saw that economic progress in Mexico, especially in the middle class, would translate into support of the internationalist, prowar agenda of Ávila Camacho.[18]

In the Ávila Camacho government there was virtual unanimity on the issue of cooperation with the United States, at least in the opinion of American Ambassador George S. Messersmith. With the exception of Francisco Castillo Nájera, who served as Mexican ambassador to the United States, and one or two others, Messersmith was convinced that the president and most of his leadership were ahead of the rest of the Mexican establishment in recognizing that the nation's future lay in an alliance with the United States.[19] He continually urged Washington to give tangible evidence of support in the form of trade agreements, educational projects for Mexican industry, travel grants, technical assistance, loans for medical and sanitation projects, cinematography and highway construction, and hundreds of similar projects.[20] These actions resulted in over $95,000,000 in United States loans to Mexico by 1945, mostly administered by the Office of the Coordinator of Inter-American Affairs.[21]

This office spent millions on promoting better mutual understanding between the United States and Mexico. It organized an exchange program between Mexican and American journalists and brought Mexican cartoonists to Washington and paid them for their art used in schools and public buildings. It hired Mexicans to translate American books into Spanish and paid for the books' distribution in Mexican schools. It encouraged American networks to produce programs on Mexican culture and history. It established scholarships for Mexican students to study in the Untied States. On the negative side, it also interfered with public policy, bribed, threatened, or manipulated people, and generally bought and bullied Mexican leadership throughout the war.[22] Nevertheless, friendship between Mexico City and Washington had never been better, and as a result a meeting was arranged for Roosevelt and Ávila Camacho in Monterrey in April 1943 to discuss economic and military cooperation.

This was the first visit of an American president to the interior of Mexico and only the second time that sitting presidents of the two nations had ever met. Mexican newspapers reacted with differing degrees of enthusiasm, but all were positive about the event. The oldest, *El Dario de México*, praised the "two wartime allies" meeting to plan hemispheric defense and economic development. The other large Mexico City dailies, *El Universal, Excélsior*, and *Novedades*, were equally laudatory. The government newspaper, *El Nacional*, pointed out that it was to both nations' advantage to defeat a common enemy and construct a lasting relationship.[23] *La Prensa*, at that time the most sensational of the papers, was positive but slightly more subdued than usual.[24] The Monterrey paper *El Porvenir* printed an extra edition with red headlines and a large photograph of Roosevelt.[25] There was little substance, however, in any of the articles. Ávila Camacho believed that in the relationship with the United States, Mexico must abandon the bitterness of the past and look to the future.[26] The following September, when national leaders gathered with an enormous crowd and a national radio audience to hear the president repeat the words of Father Hidalgo from the balcony of the National Palace, American General George C. Marshall stood beside the president and received the salute of 40,000 passing troops. In the parade were American-made trucks, jeeps, anti-aircraft guns and other war vehicles.[27]

Organized opposition to avilacamachismo came mostly from the far right. Acción Nacional, which soon was called PAN, was founded in 1939 by Manuel Gómez Morín and attracted Catholics, conservatives, and monied vestiges of the old aristocracy. It also had the support of conservative intellectuals who followed the philosophy of *hispanidad*, a form of traditionalism rooted in reverence for Spanish culture.[28] The most vocal right-wing group was the *sinarquistas*. Founded in 1937, they were overtly fascist and appealed more directly to Mexico's traditional xenophobia, hatred of bankers, anti-Semitism, anti-Americanism, and fear of atheistic communism. They had a strong appeal among the rural and urban poor who were marginalized in the growing economy and suffered food shortages throughout the war. Newspapers on 18 September 1943, only two days after the Independence Day parade in Mexico City, reported food riots in Durango and food shortages in other sections of the country.[29] From the early days of the war Washington was preoccupied with the sinarquistas.[30] Despite continued Mexican protestations that there was no real danger from Mexican fascism and that Mexico could be counted upon as a full partner in the war effort, the level of concern in Washington and in the American press remained high throughout the war. The specter of the sinarquistas as a "fifth column" was even raised in the American press during the "zoot suit" riots in Los Angeles in 1943.[31] Today, every indication is that the Mexican government was as correct as a cartoon by Antonio Arias Bernal appearing shortly after Manuel Ávila Camacho was elected, in which a resolute president was shown kicking over a column of rightists with the caption:

Habría que desterrar a la Quinta Columna (I will banish the Fifth Column). Sinarquismo declined; avilacamachismo succeeded.

Aside from the far right, there were objections by avilaca-machistas to what the magazine *Hoy* called the "foreign penetration of Mexican culture, magazines, books and radio programs" by zealous American cultural organizations associated with Nelson Rockefeller. This overkill, critics like Salvador Novo declared, worked against Mexican unity at a time when it was developing nicely. Logical as it was, Novo's criticism brought charges of disloyalty from the United States onto other high profile Mexicans. Accused of being pro-Nazi, for example, was Emilio Azcárraga, owner of radio station XEW and future television czar. The State Department file on Azcárraga is thick with investigations by the FBI and State Department. In the end he was cleared, but the heavy hand of United States power and money did not always serve avilacamachismo well.[32]

In spite of excessive and unnecessary interference from the United States, Mexico was indeed uniting around Ávila Camacho and the members of his government. In 1943 Ezequiel Padilla published a book that was quickly translated into English under the title *Free Men of America* with a preface by historian Carlton Beals. Padilla's point of view, similar to Torres Bodet's and Ávila Camacho's, was that the modern Mexican national culture should be rooted in vasconcelista idealism. Padilla also outlined an internationalist framework for avilacamachismo: (1) He held that the Western Hemisphere must stand together if the United States were to remain moral and the other nations were to remain free. If they stood together, he believed, they would be able to ensure for Mexico and all sovereign nations an international regime of imperishable peace.[33] (2) He believed that the central issue for the world was freedom. The economic systems of the Western Hemisphere needed to provide for a stable and modern economic system for every nation and thus remove the tyranny of slave wages and endemic poverty. Only then would freedom come to all of the nations of the Western Hemisphere.[34] (3) Finally, he argued that

Pan American solidarity was not a romantic myth but a reality, but could be so only if the Mexican people knew who they were and what they wanted. He believed Mexico had to accept an international leadership role in the creation of a family of democracies.[35]

Padilla offered an avilacamachista agenda that would take Mexico into a leadership role in the postwar world. Although some historians have argued that the advent of the Ávila Camacho administration was the beginning of the end of the Revolution, one can argue that the sexennium never lost its vision of a future based on the historic idealism of the past. For them, national unity and economic development would bring Mexico international respect, and culture would be central in the building of the state. The Ávila Camacho administration was consistent in moving toward its goals in nearly everything it did. In the fall of 1942, for example, President Ávila Camacho combined the Mexican military into a single unified command under the secretary of national defense. Disregarding American criticism, he appointed his friend General Lázaro Cárdenas to the new cabinet post. The obvious logic behind this appointment was national unity, for no one in Mexico was as deeply respected as the former president.

As Carmela Elvira Santoro observed, in a variety of ways, Mexicans "took their place along with the other allies in the fight against the Axis."[36] Shortly after Pearl Harbor, a semi-military training program was placed in the school system to teach young people patriotism and respect for the armed forces.[37] The state took every opportunity to create national unity by promoting the war effort. This included movie houses flashing civilian defense instructions and propaganda messages on the screens, postage stamps extolling the war effort, and newspaper advertisements reflecting war themes. American companies poured money into Mexican advertising. Ford, Republic Steel, Philco, Coca Cola, and dozens of others sponsored war-theme advertisements of Mexican-made products like radios, food items, and household products. Newspapers carried stories about Mexican citizens who joined the

United States armed forces in impressive numbers. The 6 January 1945 edition of *Excélsior*, for example, carried photographs of United States Army Corporal Luis L. de Guevara and his brother, Navy Seaman Arthur L. de Guevara, the sons of sr. and sra. Luis L. de Guevara of Mexico City.[38] By the end of the war 250,000 Mexican citizens had joined or been drafted into the American military. Nearly 15,000 served in combat units.[39] Mexican officers visited every theater of the war, observing and meeting Mexican servicemen fighting with units of the United States Army, Navy, or Marines. Also touring on behalf of the government were Mexican film and radio stars. The most famous was Rosita Moreno, who traveled the Pacific entertaining Allied troops and visiting Mexican soldiers.[40] On 16 November 1943 President Ávila Camacho, accompanied by Generals Cárdenas and Calles, spoke to the general command of the Mexican army. He said that the Mexican army was ready to send troops into combat under their own command and under the Mexican flag. Like the nation, the troops would have a clear Mexican identity and would not therefore be lost in the mass of Allied armies.[41]

By the spring of 1944 the Mexican air force had been chosen to lead the Mexican military into combat. Ávila Camacho made the announcement on 5 March 1944, and *Excélsior* printed the speech with the headline: *Posibilidad de que México envie aviadores a la guerra* (It is possible that Mexico will send pilots to the war).[42] In July 1944 a Mexican air squadron reported to San Antonio, Texas, for training; and in December the Mexican Senate passed a bill authorizing the squadron to be sent into combat. On 10 January 1945 Aviation Squadron 201, composed of 40 pilots, 350 ground crewmen, and a chaplain, left for the Philippines where they served with distinction. The fact that Ávila Camacho ordered a chaplain to be sent with the airmen is noteworthy in light of the church-state struggle in Mexican history. The chaplain conducted his first wartime funeral services at an American military chapel, when Lieutenants José Espinosa Fuentes and Fausto Vegar Santander were killed in the spring of 1945.[43] When the war ended in August 1945, an exhibition unit of the United States Army Air Force flew into Mexico City to show the P-47 Thunderbolts that Mexican pilots were flying in the Pacific.[44] A crowd of 300,000 attended. Squadron 201 returned to a nation-wide celebration, and the government retained the planes its pilots had flown alongside those of its Allies from Australia, New Zealand, and the United States. One of the Squadron 201 planes was purchased in 1980 from Mexico by the state of Texas for the Chester M. Nimitz Museum in Fredericksburg, Texas, and is today on display there.[45] World War II presented a unique context and atmosphere for avilacamachismo to unite the nation.

Most historians of this period have failed to note the preponderance of young intellectuals within avilacamachismo who made possible the pursuit of its lofty goals. In 1940 President Ávila Camacho was forty-three, and Jaime Torres Bodet was thirty-eight. Among the older members of the cabinet was Ezequiel Padilla, who was forty-nine.[46] The genial Ávila Camacho was known to have a youthful love of films, especially those of Jorge Negrete, María Félix, and Cantinflas. He had private film showings at the presidential residence, Los Pinos. He also appreciated music of all kinds, including youth-oriented popular music as well as classical music. The avilacamachista state was run by people of all ages and many viewpoints, but a significant number were young and, like Torres Bodet, were cultural creators.

For example, publisher and radio administrator Demetrio Bolaños Espinosa wrote novels and translated under the pen name of Oscar Leblanc. The former manager of a PRN-owned radio station, Bolaños Espinosa served as deputy from Oaxaca from 1940 until 1943, working hard for the avilacamachista agenda in Congress. He was a founder and editor of *Proa*, the first newspaper of the Mexican Congress, and also was editor of *El Universal Ilustrado*. Because he was related to a powerful PRN family in Oaxaca, and as a reward for his service in national unity and public education, he was named editor of the party newspaper *El Nacional* in 1946.

One of the most effective campaigners for Ávila Camacho in 1940 was the twenty-nine-year-old intellectual, Roberto Guzmán

Araujo. A native of Guanajuato and a Universidad Autonoma de México (hereinafter UNAM) graduate, he traveled the country speaking to young audiences on behalf of the presidential candidate. In 1941 he was appointed assistant attorney general of the Federal District. He also served as a director of the magazine *Revista America* and with Pablo Neruda founded the anti-fascist magazine *Nuestra España*. Guzmán Araujo wrote plays, novels, and books on history and philosophy as well as speeches and policy statements for the president. After Ávila Camacho left office, Guzmán Araujo served as senator from Guanajuato and continued to write for the rest of his life.[47]

One of the most important groups of avilacamachista intellectuals was the camarilla of Jaime Torres Bodet. Its members included Francisco Javier Gaxiola, Luis Díaz Garrido, and Rafael de la Colina, all forty-two years old in 1940, as well as José María de los Reyes, thirty-eight, Celestino Gorostiza, thirty-six, and his brother José, thirty-nine. Gaxiola exemplified those in government who were profoundly influenced by the economic changes of the period. He was born in Toluca and was an outstanding student, eventually becoming a prize-winning scholar at the Escuela Libre de Derecho. Elected governor of Baja California at thirty-two, he was appointed secretary of industry and commerce from 1940 until 1944. In 1942 Ávila Camacho picked him to be his personal representative to President Roosevelt for their meeting in Monterrey. He was a friend of Torres Bodet through his brother Jorge, who was Torres Bodet's personal adviser. He spoke fluent English, was the founder of the Mexican Bar Association, and had close connections with banking and industrial leaders, to whom he turned initially for support for avilacamachismo and later for personal investments. Gaxiola was close to former president Abelardo Rodríguez, with whom he organized a chocolate candy company called La Suiza in March 1943.[48] In 1944 Gaxiola resigned from public office. That same year he joined Rodríguez in organizing Pelotera del Noroeste in Guaymas. Other wartime businesses of Gaxiola and Rodríguez included a film distribution company and the famous soft drink and mineral water company, Peñafiel.[49]

As Steven Niblo has pointed out, the infiltration of American capital into Mexico spurred extensive economic development. The very abundance of hard cash threatened to subvert avilacamachista goals of national unity and international status. In the last three years of the administration, many government officials moved into private business arrangements, forming hundreds of companies. There was money to be made, and members of the government participated openly in the economic boom. By 1943 business began to outweigh culture in political priorities. Gaxiola, a dynamic speaker, was chosen to explain avilacamachismo to a nationwide radio audience on *La hora nacional* on the night of 14 December 1941.[50] As secretary of industry and commerce, he proclaimed that every Mexican could hope for a better economic future once the goals of avilacamachismo became national reality. This was certainly true for him. He became a wealthy man and a partner in more than a dozen business ventures.

The Mexican state has always struggled with authoritarianism and corruption. The classic example of this problem in Ávila Camacho's administration was the president's brother, Maximino. He was six years older than Manuel and served as secretary of public works beginning in 1941.[51] Many saw him as the power behind his mild-mannered younger brother, although this was not the case. By 1945 Maximino was a multimillionaire with questionable business relationships in sports, railroads, highway construction, and air transportation.

Maximino and Gaxiola were by no means the only apostates from the generally youthful, idealistic group of intellectuals who formed the core leadership of avilacamachismo. More typical, however, were the scholars who served the Ávila Camacho state faithfully, such as Luis Díaz Garrido, who was founder of the Mexican Association of Universities and Institutions of Higher Education, economics professor at the UNAM, and rector of the University of Michoacán. A close friend of Torres Bodet and the author of many books, he was employed in the Secretariat of Foreign Relations under Cárdenas and became director of Seguros de México during the war years. He resigned to become rector of

UNAM. Another example of the young intellectual and the state was Rafael de la Colina, a career diplomat who attended the National Preparatory School with Vicente Lombardo Toledano and Alfonso Caso. He was consul general in Washington until 1943 when he was given ambassadorial rank by Ávila Camacho. An expert in international relations, he was assistant secretary-general at the Inter-American Conference in 1945.[52] He continued in diplomatic service after the war, advocating a strong leadership role for Mexico in world affairs.[53]

José María de los Reyes was an innovative teacher who created the National Preparatory Night School. He was brought into the Ávila Camacho government by Torres Bodet as director of the Office of Cinematography and National Films for SEP. There he used his knowledge of Mexican geography, which he taught for thirty-five years, to produce patriotic films for use in schools.[54]

Perhaps the best example of Torres Bodet's intellectual friends in the service of avilacamachismo were the Gorostiza brothers, Celestino and José. José was first a literature professor at UNAM and then a professor of modern history at the National Teacher's College before going to London as first chancellor of the Mexican embassy. He returned to Mexico to join Torres Bodet in SEP under José Vasconcelos. In the following years he held a series of diplomatic and academic posts until 1944 when he entered the Ávila Camacho government as director general of political affairs in the Secretariat of Foreign Relations. He was a strong supporter of national unity and expanded Mexican influence in international affairs. He attended the San Francisco Conference to create the United Nations in 1945, and was an adviser to the Mexican delegation at the first meeting of the United Nations in New York. Like de la Colina, he believed that Mexico should chart an independent course and remain out of the emerging cold war. Like Torres Bodet, he was a serious poet and member of Torres Bodet's literary camarilla, the Contemporáneos.[55] His younger brother Celestino was also a member of the group. He remained in Mexico City as a teacher throughout his professional life.

Five additional government figures, three men and two women, who were intellectuals, proponents of high culture, and writers for Mexico City newspapers and magazines illustrate the quality of the individuals involved in avilacamachismo. Among the Generation of 1915 who supported Ávila Camacho was Jesús Silva Herzog, a businessman and intellectual who served as undersecretary of the treasury. One of many young intellectuals influenced by Vasconcelos, he taught literature and English before he went to work in SEP in 1932, and then held a variety of government positions ranging from director of the Department of Libraries to ambassador to the Soviet Union. In 1942 he founded the journal *Cuadernos Americanos*.

Roderic A. Camp has observed that *Cuadernos Americanos* was one of the few Mexican journals to publish Marxist and non-Marxist articles together. Also unusual, according to Camp, was its policy of publishing foreign scholars, especially from Latin America. He points out that between 1942 and 1971, one of every three articles was written by a foreigner, including many from the United States. Thus *Cuadernos Americanos* affirmed the avilacamachista principle that Mexico should be a unified, internationally respected leader nation open to a world of ideas. Silva Herzog's willingness to present all viewpoints and especially to develop the voices of other Latin American nations in the context of a Mexican magazine symbolized the avilacamachista commitment to a new, mature, modern form of nationalism.[56]

Another close associate of Ávila Camacho and a respected intellectual advocate of his programs was Luis Chávez Orozco. A native of Irapuato, Guanajuato, he entered government service after teaching at UNAM. His career is similar to those of Silva Herzog and Torres Bodet. He joined SEP in 1933, became head of the Department of Public Libraries in 1935, and became the undersecretary of SEP in 1936. Ávila Camacho picked him to head the Department of Indian Affairs in 1940. In 1944 Ávila Camacho asked him to head the Mexican and Russian Cultural Exchange Institute. He was the first general secretary of the National Teachers Union after it was unified by Torres Bodet. He wrote a column for *Excélsior* and often expressed the positions of avilacamachismo on various issues. He was the author of a twelve-volume history of Mexico, which was one of the few left-leaning books used in the reorganized public school system under Torres Bodet.[57] Once a militant anticlerical, Chávez Orozco is an example of a person for whom avilacamachismo represented a common ground for national reconciliation and recovery. He held the principle that authentic national unity could only be achieved if all Mexicans were willing to compromise.[58]

Antonio Armenáriz was another academic who entered public service while continuing to teach and write. After receiving his law degree, he taught sociology at UNAM and practiced law in the dual job structure of most Mexican college professors at that time. In 1945 he entered the Ávila Camacho government as director general of public education and served until the sexennium ended. He supported the avilacamachista positions on unity and cooperation with the United States. He was also editor of *Comercio Exterior*, the official publication of the National Bank of Foreign Commerce. Well connected in business, academia and government, he was an ardent spokesperson for avilacamachismo.[59]

Marta de Andrade was one of the many young women who were attracted to avilacamachismo. She took her first teaching appointment at Actopan, Hidalgo, when she was twelve years old and only much later received a degree from the National School for Teachers in Mexico City. She was one of the youngest members on the youth committee that favored the selection of Manuel Ávila Camacho as successor to Cárdenas. She was named head of the Department of Policy Inspection for the Confederation of Mexican Youth in 1937 and head of the Department of Feminine Action of the Youth Activities Section in 1939. With a government scholarship she went to the United States in 1941 to pursue graduate studies at Claremont College. When she returned, Ávila Camacho appointed her head of the Nursery Department of the Secretariat of Public Education.[60] A lifelong feminist, she authored several books on the role of women in Mexico and has been active in politics and a candidate for office on several occasions.

Another avilacamachista was Amalia Castillo Ledón, the first woman to address the Mexican Senate on the subject of women's role in government. At the age of thirty-eight in 1940, and with degrees from a teacher's college in Tamaulipas and UNAM, she was appointed head of the Bureau of Educational Activities in Mexico City. In 1945 she was named Mexico's delegate to an international conference on the role of women in the postwar world and went as a delegate to the San Francisco United Nations Conference. She wrote several successful plays and published a history of Mexican theater.[61]

Although not every supporter of Ávila Camacho affirmed his policy of culture and state, at the heart of cultural avilacamachismo were the young intellectuals who understood the goals of national unity, national identity, internationalism, and economic progress. They rallied around Torres Bodet and brought cultural nationalism to a new level.

CHAPTER THREE

Avilacamachismo, Culture, and the Role of SEP

It was not until the violent phase of the Revolution ended in 1920 that the institutional reorganization of education could begin. In 1921 under José Vasconcelos, SEP struggled to start schools, raise educational standards, and train as many teachers as possible. A variety of innovative schools were created, including the "House of the Indian" schools. These schools were designed to integrate young Indians into modern Mexico while at the same time emphasizing the preservation of native heritage. At the conclusion of Vasconcelos's term in 1923, there were 1,039 federal rural schools, 1,194 teachers, and 65,000 students.[1] Progress had been made toward a nationwide school system. Most schools were centered on a single priority: to teach Mexican rural children the values of the Revolution. These schools were called regional peasant schools or cultural mission schools.

Under Plutarco Elías Calles and his SEP undersecretary, Moisés Sáenz, policy shifted to the integration of Indians and the mestizo rural poor into mainstream Mexican society. But Calles also brought his anticlericalism and secularism into the struggle for control of the schools. He charged SEP with enforcing the provisions of Article 3 of the Constitution of 1917 that made it illegal for the church to have any influence in the education process. As a result, during the 1920s education became increasingly politicized, as Calles, Sáenz, and others implemented a divisive education policy. In this conflicted environment SEP had five heads between 1928 and 1934.[2] The political confusion and violence surrounding the schools caused teachers' morale to plummet. The situation was especially grave during the Cristero Rebellion (1926–1929), a bloody, primarily religious conflict.

From the beginning of the Vasconcelos period, the three basic problems facing education were poor pay, community violence, and lack of teacher preparation.[3] To cope with this situation two teachers' unions were founded: the National Confederation of Teachers (1924) and the Mexican Teachers' Confederation (1925). As the culture-state policies of the Vasconcelos era faded, the unions fought over programs, promotions, and power. Into this situation came leftist Narciso Bassols as the head of SEP for thirty turbulent months between 1931 and 1934.

The attraction of Narciso Bassols for many was the clarity of his education philosophy. He advocated a forthright Marxist social analysis of Mexican culture. He saw the nation's problems as primarily economic, not cultural, and sought to use education to transform the nation in four basic areas. First, he believed that better health care and better teaching about personal health and public sanitation would strengthen the nation's workers. Second, economic advancement could only result from the application of technology to production methods. Third, modern Mexican culture had to be socialist and based upon science and technology rather than art and music. Lastly, Mexico could only progress socially by rediscovering its aboriginal past.[4] These goals were in conflict with traditional and Roman Catholic elements in the educational establishment, and in the late 1920s and the early 1930s, the issue of public education became increasingly problematic.

The culture-state policies of Vasconcelos had approached the construction of the education system from an idealistic position that ignored political questions. The period of confusion that followed Vasconcelos appeared to end with the clearly defined Marxism of Bassols, who demanded that social reform be accelerated and that socialist ideology become the basis for public education. By this time, however, his ideology was only one of many. The struggle for political control of public education now included the idealistic heirs of Vasconcelos, conservative and traditional elements of the government bureaucracy influenced by Marxism, moderate elements of the bureaucracy who held to nativist or Mexican nationalist forms of socialism, and the teachers themselves, some wanting public education removed as a political football and others favoring Bassolsian socialism.

In 1933 Article 3 of the 1917 Constitution was amended to make education socialist. In the Revised Decree of Incorporation, Mexican education became secularized and essentially socialist, a measure that increased violence in the countryside. The professional magazine for Mexican rural teachers, *El Maestro Rural*, reported that in the two years after the amendment, rural teachers were attacked repeatedly by opponents of the changes.[5] A shocking thirty-seven teachers were murdered during this period.[6]

Early in his administration President Cárdenas, feeling shaken by the violence over the school issue and fearing the renewal of the political strife of the Cristero era, began to look seriously for a solution to the problem. He visited the location of serious armed conflict in Gonzáles, Guanjuato, where nearly fifty people had been killed or wounded in fighting between townspeople and the staff at a cultural mission school. After this visit, a saddened Cárdenas came to the conclusion that the socialist approach to public education was unproductive for his administration, and in 1936 he decided to abandon it.[7] At this point he moved toward the vasconcelista position, with education in the culture-state nexus of earlier years.

This decision subsequently became central to the development of avilacamachismo. When Ávila Camacho came to power, he continued removing public education from the political arena and giving it a constructive, rather than a destructive, role in the life of the nation. Under avilacamachismo, SEP came to play a major role in culture-state policies that reflected the vasconcelista philosophy of education. It is helpful here to compare the approach of those who favored socialist education to the approach taken later under Cárdenas and Ávila Camacho.

In the 1930s two of the main problems of education for the indigenous population were language and culture. The state and the "socialist" approach favored bilingualism but in fact produced teachers who could only teach in Spanish and had little understanding of the languages, traditions, or religious activities of native peoples. Many of the idealistic socialist teachers sent into the countryside during the administration of Narciso Bassols treated Indian culture as inferior and saw all religious activity as a useless vestige of the past. It was the notion of the young Bassolsian socialists who became teachers that redemption of the Indians would come only through assimilation and modernization, and that this could happen only if they learned Spanish. For this reason, the passage of the amendment to Article 3 calling for "socialist education" was seen by many Indians as an assault on all aspects of Indian traditional life, including native religion as well as Catholicism.

It was not until after Cárdenas decided to abandon socialist education that strong support for bilingual education developed once again. In 1937, when teachers from Indian areas in Latin America came to Mexico City for the Third Inter-American Conference on Education, Cárdenas attended some sessions and discussed bilingual education with experts. From this meeting there arose a public forum in which Mexican social scientists and educators could explain their ideas and programs in a nonpolitical way. The conference passed a resolution proclaiming that "bilingual education for the Indian is recommended in the firm belief that it will increase the effectiveness and ease with which we educate indigenes, thus affirming the cultural value of native languages as an extension of the national idiom."[8] This represented an important shift toward the reasoned and nonpolitical approach the educators brought to the issue. Searching for a way out of the national dilemma over the role of education and the violence it might precipitate, Cárdenas turned to the methodology set forth in the major paper of the conference, *"Ideario del maestro indoamericano: por el espíritu del indio se forjará la nueva cultural de América y su grandeza"* (Native teachers, native spirit and the formation of a great new American culture). Written by Ángel Corzo, the paper advocated the philosophy that all teachers, regardless of their political or religious views, approach native peoples with respect for their language, culture, and religion, and, in the process, attempt to learn as well as teach.

Central to the pedagogy of this paper was the notion that learning should take place in the language of the student, with Spanish added later. These ideas reflected the philosophy of Vasconcelos, who held that "Indianism" was a vital part of what made Mexico unique among nations. The work of Vasconcelos as secretary of public education in the twenties had called for the restoration of the Indian to a place of respect in the nation. However, idealism about the Indian had never been fully embodied in national policy. In fact, Mexican national identity was, at this point, according to Salvador Novo, still not fully defined.[9] The president's resurrection of this Revolutionary ideal, somehow forgotten by almost everyone including the socialists, had once again put before the nation the standard that all teachers should approach Mexican villages with respect toward their plural cultural and religious traditions. With the support of President Cárdenas, the First Inter-American Indigenous Congress was hosted by Mexico in his home state of Michoacán in 1940. Cárdenas's decision to end the socialist emphasis in public education and to depoliticize the issues related to the education of Indians set the stage for the policies of avilacamachismo.

The public education baton did not pass smoothly in 1940, however, as it was handed from cardenismo to avilacamachismo. The man whom conservatives urged Ávila Camacho to pick as the person who could end the socialist focus in public education, depoliticize the system, and promote cultural respect and diversity was Octavio Véjar Vásquez, a friend of Vasconcelos. Ávila Camacho resisted, his first choice being another cardenista supporter, Luis Sánchez Pontón. After a few months, Sánchez Pontón seemed confused and unable to perform the task, and thus resigned. After taking over as secretary of public education, Véjar succeeded in pushing out the socialists, but clearly failed in depoliticizing the issue and promoting cultural respect and diversity.

Véjar Vásquez was born in Jalapa, and, like Ávila Camacho and many others in the administration, he had just turned forty when he moved into his offices at SEP. At the time of his appointment he was attorney general for the Federal District and was considered bright, capable, and even progressive, having once been a professor of aeronautical law.[10] In his autobiography, however, Daniel Cosío Villegas remembered Véjar's ambition, always aggressively attempting to advance himself in University of Mexico politics. To Cosío, this was inappropriate, and he was delighted when Véjar was disciplined by Ávila Camacho in the only visit that Cosío remembered the president making to the campus.[11]

Under Ávila Camacho Article 3 was again amended, this time omitting every reference to socialism and stressing ideas compatible with the central themes of avilacamachismo. Article 3 now read that education should develop all human faculties harmoniously, including a love of nation and an awareness of international solidarity.[12] These themes linked education to culture and were subthemes of avilacamachismo, connecting national identity to the process of public education. From the nation's youth avilacamachismo sought an army of renewal, a vanguard educated to be the "new men" of whom the president dreamed in his speeches.

Shortly after he took office, it became obvious that Véjar Vásquez was more interested in driving socialists and communists from the schools than in promoting the goals of avilacamachismo. In fact his main agenda was, as at UNAM, the pursuit of personal political power. In his last months in office he announced the creation of "new schools" that he said would be "authentically Mexican." These new schools would be based on what he proclaimed as "the commonality of origin, spiritual and material interests, habit and customs" of a unified Mexico. But the emphasis in these schools was to be on Europe rather than Mexico, and here Véjar openly demonstrated that he was an enemy of bilingual education, a Hispanist, a fanatic anticommunist, and a political reactionary who had no sympathy with avilacamachismo.[13] He wore a gun and personally commanded an armed unit that closed schools considered to be communist. Soon he tried to influence the choice of teachers and programs at UNAM and the cultural programs of the state. Favoring European music, he hated the composer Carlos Chávez and tried to have him removed from his position as director of the Mexican Symphony Orchestra. He failed. In the process he angered the president, who was a friend of Chávez.

Véjar Vásquez at first had been supported by people who wanted to see the government move to the right. By 1943, however, he was far out of step with the administration and generating the kind of political conflict over public education that Cárdenas and Avila Camacho wanted to avoid. He had not depoliticized public education and, if anything, had made the situation worse. After being fired, he founded his own political movement, the National Independent Democratic Party.

It was now critical for Avila Camacho to find the right person to replace his second failed education secretary. He had the advantage of knowing that much of what he wanted to do in order to unite Mexico could only be achieved through SEP-funded programs. He saw that, in spite of the reactionary activity of Véjar Vásquez, the avenue for creating a unified national youth culture lay with SEP.[14] He knew that a leader was needed who understood the history of the secretariat and was familiar with the ideas of Vasconcelos in works like *La raza cósmica* and *Indologia*. In a stroke of genius, Avila Camacho found the perfect candidate in an intellectual and poet who had made public life his career. Almost as soon as Véjar Vásquez was fired, Avila Camacho asked the thirty-eight-year-old undersecretary of Foreign Relations, Jaime Torres Bodet, to become education secretary for the remaining three years of his administration. Torres Bodet was the very paragon of avilacamachismo.

Torres Bodet was known to be keenly interested in public education. He had written several articles on the importance of developing a national education program for the young combined with a national literacy campaign for older Mexicans. He was respected by all segments of the political spectrum and was seen as a moderate who could depoliticize public education and formulate an agenda that would bring constructive change. Avilacamachismo came to full fruition under Torres Bodet, who saw education as the most important area for the development of culture-state policy.

Almost from the moment he took office, Torres Bodet began implementing the goals of avilacamachismo that were, he announced in a series of speeches, vitally connected to public education. Unlike Véjar Vásquez, Torres Bodet listened to and quoted the speeches of Avila Camacho. It would be necessary, he believed, to eliminate the problems caused by poverty, insanitary living conditions, and hunger in order for people to have the strength and presence of mind to learn to read and write. He argued that illiteracy made it impossible to unite the nation in the constructive solidarity that avilacamachismo demanded. He called for new respect for the old traditions as well as new ideas to find the best way to carry out Avila Camacho's vision of national unity, prosperity, and international respectability.

Torres Bodet's first speech invited the renewal of dialogue between social scientists and public policymakers. Mexico's social scientists, who had been delighted to see Véjar Vásquez leave, were now excited to see Torres Bodet take the office. Alfonso Caso, director of the National Institute of Anthropology and History, immediately approached Torres Bodet with an idea for a literacy program, which became the basis for the Law for the Elimination of Illiteracy passed in August 1944.[15]

Jaime Torres Bodet, born and raised in Mexico City, was the gifted only child of Emilia Bodet, daughter of a French family who taught her son in both French and Spanish, and Alejandro Torres Girbent, a theatrical producer and businessman. As a youth Torres Bodet attended the National Preparatory School during several periods of Revolutionary street fighting. He hated the violence and the wearing of military uniforms required of the boys. In later years he remarked that it was during this period that he learned to hate war, and for the rest of his life Torres Bodet disliked all things military. He published his first poems at fourteen. In school he talked philosophy, religion, and poetry constantly with a group of friends with whom he would later found the review *Contemporáneos*, from which the name of his lifelong intellectual camarilla was derived. The membership of this group included Carlos Pellicer, José Gorostiza, Enrique Gonzáles Rojo and Bernardo Ortiz de Montellano.[16]

After graduation he studied philosophy with Antonio Caso at the National University. This was a formative period in his development as an intellectual and as a man of character. As the nation's most famous philosopher, Caso exerted a decided influence on the moral and intellectual growth of the young poet. At the age of nineteen, although he wanted to study in Paris, he took a position teaching literature at the National Preparatory School. In 1921 Torres Bodet was appointed secretary to the rector of the National University, José Vasconcelos, who would leave a lasting mark on him.

When Obregón made Vasconcelos secretary of public education, Vasconcelos appointed Torres Bodet head of the National Library Department. In this position Torres Bodet developed a program that anticipated his later work in the Avila Camacho administration. He oversaw the translation of literary classics into Spanish, organized traveling libraries, opened reading centers in industrial areas and rural villages, and distributed inexpensive editions of Mexican and world literature to every section of the country.[17]

While working under Vasconcelos at SEP, Torres Bodet learned firsthand that education was central to the culture-and-state philosophy of Vasconcelos. Two decades later, when he took the position once held by his friend and mentor, Torres Bodet's education programs were derived directly from those of Vasconcelos. Torres

Bodet's view of culture and state, therefore, represented a direct link between vasconcelistas and avilacamachistas. At SEP cultural avilacamachismo engendered an idealism about culture and state that was born with the ateneistas, matured by vasconcelistas, recovered by cardenistas, and brought to fruition by avilaca-machistas.

Torres Bodet was a functionary in the Mexican government for most of his life. He wrote in his autobiography that he never saw a conflict between his service to the nation and his creative activity.[18] There is no indication that administrative work slowed his output as a poet. While head of the National Library Department in 1922 he published *Canciones* and *El corazón deliriante*, and started a literary magazine. By 1928 he had published seven books of poetry, an anthology, and his first novel, *Margarita de la niebla*. In 1929 he went to Spain as a diplomat and then was assigned to Paris, The Hague, and Buenos Aires. He published *Cripta* and *Sombres* in 1937 while charge d'affaires in Brussels. He returned to Mexico in 1940 to join the Avila Camacho government as undersecretary of foreign affairs. He published *Nacimiento de Venus* in 1941. In 1943, when he was chosen education secretary by Avila Camacho, he was a respected poet and civil servant. Shortly, however, he was to emerge as the most articulate spokesman for avilacamachismo.

In the war-torn world of 1943, Torres Bodet, like Avila Camacho, saw the issue of education as critical for the future of Mexico. If the nation was to be unified, prosperous, and a viable member of a peaceful world order, it had to elevate the level of education in Mexico. In Torres Bodet's famous first speech, he said that "if the victory which the free nations hope for is to guarantee the ideas for which these free people are fighting, then the first task that these nations will assign to their educational systems will be the teaching of peace." The second task, he said, would be "the teaching of democracy" and the third "the teaching of justice."[19] In another speech he said that Mexican education had to be rooted in Mexican traditions, yet linked to universal human experience. In his speeches he often used the formulation that Avila Camacho did.

This progression of ideas always began with a call for a national unity rooted in self-esteem leading to economic development that would result in international respect.

In 1944 avilacamachismo declared war on illiteracy in Mexico. From his early days as a vasconcelista underling, Torres Bodet viewed education as vital to a healthy culture; by extension, he viewed illiteracy as a foreign virus making culture sick. Historically, the virus had interrupted the evolution of ancient Mexican iconographic and hieroglyphic language to phonetic language. The tragic events of conquest and repression made illiteracy the rule for the indigenous masses. Torres Bodet believed that the role of the state was to foster a culture in which all could read and write. Education was to be the link between the culture of the ancient past and the culture of the future. In this effort he had the support of the political avilacamachistas who were less idealistic and more pragmatic, but who saw education and the campaign against illiteracy as important in the creation of an educated work force and a necessary step on the road to economic prosperity.

Everyone over the age of eighteen and under the age of sixty who could read and write was drafted into a literacy army and ordered to teach one other person how to read and write. Every person in the nation who could not read or write was ordered to register his or her location with the village or neighborhood authority. It was a massive effort. The Mexican air force dropped leaflets in remote sections of the country. Torres Bodet ordered that several hours of radio time each week be devoted to the promotion of the project. Young people were encouraged to teach their parents, aunts, and uncles. The cartoon magazines contained pages prepared for the reader to use in order to share with a friend who might not otherwise be able to read it. If a literate person taught fifty illiterate people to read, he or she received a medal in person from the president as well as a chance to have his or her name drawn in a land giveaway.

The state also linked the literacy program to its promotion of popular culture. If a person taught twenty-five people to read and write, he or she received a free pass for a year to a movie theater. University students who taught fifty people to read and write received free tuition for a year. Each teacher received an instruction guide with hints for teaching someone to read. The manual also contained a section to be filled out by the teacher indicating the name of the person whom he or she taught to read and write. When this section was turned in, the teacher received a card necessary for the issuance of a driver's license, building permit, passport, or travel on certain bus lines in Mexico City.[20] Teaching materials were illustrated in the same style as cartoon magazines. Illustrations were simple and contained objects familiar to every villager, such as ducks, dogs, *metates*, or wells. Various government agencies volunteered their staff to teach people. The Department of Irrigation, for example, set a goal of 50,000 people whom it hoped to teach. It offered each student a kilo of corn for every session and installed sewing machines in the literacy centers to lure village women into the otherwise uninviting buildings.

States were funded so that they might give attractive prizes to the best teachers. Oaxaca set up over 3,000 instruction centers, many in converted cantinas, and offered villages that sent enough people to study prizes of radios and band instruments. Villages were then encouraged to turn out to hear the names of their participants announced on the radio. Special attention was paid to Indian learning centers. A task force was organized to train bilingual teachers in Tarascán, Maya, Otomí, and two dialects of Nahuatl. Each member then taught ten rural teachers who went into the villages to teach.[21]

Bilingual textbooks were made available to Indian schools as soon as Torres Bodet could have them printed. He hired artists, some of them well-known cartoonists who understood native traditions, to illustrate them with materials that would be familiar to Indian children. He announced that national unity must be predicated on respect for Mexico's remaining Indian cultures. Thus he articulated the avilacamachista cultural pluralism that recognized each group's right to exist and develop. On the subject of textbooks, Torres Bodet wrote:

What cohesion can a teacher of the Maya, Otomí, Zapotec or Yaqui child expect when, in order to establish in them the essential Mexicanness we propose, he wishes to teach him to read by using publications that do not touch the child's culture and are filled with examples taken from objects, people and landscapes he has never seen?[22]

The extent to which the literacy campaign was a success or failure is still being debated. The use of popular cultural emblems in a mass literacy campaign in which hundreds of villages were given new schools, band instruments, radios, movie projectors, record players, and cases of soft drinks, represents classic avilacamachista culture-state policy. The result was the enhancement of the national self-image, an increase in overall literacy, and a national cultural event involving thousands of citizens.

Another area developed by SEP during the Avila Camacho administration was the publishing industry, especially book production. Consistent with its campaign in popular culture, SEP published many books, pamphlets, and magazines. It also helped private publishing companies get started and granted them contracts to publish for the government. SEP books often sold for the equivalent of two 1940 pennies and were essential not only to the literacy program but also to the elevation of the reading standard of those who read at a marginal level. In addition to a series by United States writers, SEP also brought out a thirty-nine-volume series called the *Popular Encyclopedic Library*, with subjects ranging from mathematics to Mexican history and culture. The best Mexican scholars were hired to write the articles for it. One volume popular with the public was *La religión de los aztecas* by Alfonso Caso and richly illustrated by SEP artists with pictures reflecting indigenista nationalism. Another volume in the series was *Manuel José Othón: Poemas y cuentos*, edited by Miguel Bustos Cerecedo. This book explored the work of the nineteenth-century Mexican poet who anticipated the modernist movement, to which Torres Bodet belonged.

A number of private publishing houses were also founded during the Avila Camacho administration, several by Spanish

Republican refugees. Editorial Seneca was established by José Bergamín, a Spanish Catholic intellectual. Bergamín, who had resisted Franco from the beginning, held that Christianity and fascism were incompatible. He had published the works of García Lorca, Neruda, and Torres Bodet in Spain and was esteemed by the Avila Camacho administration. To establish his firm Bergamín was subsidized by Avila Camacho who believed that Mexico had an important role to play in the Spanish-speaking world now that Spain had become a fascist dictatorship. The president provided another subsidy to Bergamín to publish the works of Sor Juana Inéz de la Cruz and a volume of short stories by Torres Bodet's friend, Juan de la Cabada.[23]

With the support of Torres Bodet and Avila Camacho, composer and music entrepreneur Carlos Chávez worked with Spanish expatriate composers to publish their works. This led to the creation of Ediciones Mexicanas de Musica. In the same year, 1946, SEP also funded Spanish refugee Rodolfo Halfter's journal, *Nuestra Musica*, on whose editorial board were important composers and musicologists of the era like Jesús Bal y Gay, Blas Galindo, José Pablo Moncayo, and Carlos Chávez. The publication stated the avilacamachista goal of contributing to "the musical development of Mexico by focusing international attention on national achievement."[24] SEP funded the small music publishing industry for several years before it began to sell its editions beyond Mexico into the Spanish-speaking world.

When Torres Bodet took office he was quoted as saying, "I'm not going to be the secretary of education to serve one group. I won't compromise ideals. In the language of politics, I'm not really a politician."[25] With such statements he won the support of professional teachers. He organized the first "Institute for the Professionalization of Teachers in Service," a program to upgrade teachers' skills and sensitize them to indigenous contexts. This institute was successful and became a model for similar programs in the developing world. Mexican teachers began to admire the learned and moderate new secretary.

Under Avila Camacho and Torres Bodet SEP was the government agency that most advanced the professionalism of women. This was true in areas like social work and public health, but it was most important in the field of public education. Public school teaching during the Avila Camacho sexennium became a prototypical profession that served as a model for other types of professional development for Mexican women in the years that followed.[26] It was Vasconcelos who first issued the call for young female idealists to enter teaching in the early 1920s. During this period, for example, Marta de Andrade and Amalia Castillo Ledón, who were earlier noted as young avilacamachista intellectuals, became attracted to teaching as a profession. From 1923 until 1939 the number of women attending school increased significantly.[27] During the Cárdenas administration 14,000 new schools were constructed, with roughly the same number added between 1940 and 1946. With more schools and more children, especially girls, in school, the vasconcelista call for young women to step forward was echoed by both Cárdenas and Avila Camacho.

SEP was the governmental organization that embodied the culture-state ideology of avilacamachismo and diligently implemented that ideology. It was the agency that employed and directed the work of all the nation's teachers. SEP expected teachers to place cultural nationalism at the center of their work. Although it is not possible to measure the exact extent to which teachers fully understood and acted upon the culture-state agenda of avilacamachismo, it is possible to find examples of those who did. A classic example of this support is found in a pair of teachers, a twenty-seven-year-old woman and her twenty-nine-year-old husband, serving as SEP-appointed teachers in a remote village.

Rosa Ocampo and her husband Bernardo were both college graduates, both members of the SNTE teachers' union, and were sent together by SEP to teach in a rural village. She was a teacher and nurse, and served as a community youth counselor and health officer. He was a teacher, soccer coach, and something of a social director. In a 1944 interview, Rosa declared that she and her husband were "practical idealists" who entered teaching to be "guides and mentors" for a people undergoing revolutionary change. She noted that much that had been traditional in culture had been swept away in the postrevolutionary period. She believed that there was a need for the state to direct the development of modern culture since a danger existed that "otherwise youth might become rootless and degenerate." The nation's young people, she observed, "need to be put at the head table for the feast of Mexican culture and learning."[28] Bernardo taught in Nahuatl and Spanish, Rosa in Spanish. They represented the best of avilacamachismo: young, well-prepared, moral, idealistic, hard working, honest, respectful of the cultures and peoples of the past while serving as role models for the culture avilacamachismo envisioned for the future.

In a report to SEP for the period 1942 to 1946, Guillermo Bonilla y Segura affirmed that the work of SEP in the countryside went well beyond the classroom. He listed eight objectives for the culture mission schools, condensed here:

1. To better economic conditions in the communities by improving occupational techniques and practices, introducing new crops, stimulating the raising of better livestock, and improving both production and marketing procedures;
2. To improve conditions of health and sanitation;
3. To awaken a desire on the part of the inhabitants to live in better homes, with at least a minimum of desirable household equipment for the enjoyment of a satisfactory domestic life;
4. To stimulate improvement in diet and dress;
5. To organize and develop social, cultural, and recreational activities in the various communities;
6. To stimulate interest in cultural enhancement;
7. To encourage love of country and to combat all foreign influences that tend to undermine patriotism;
8. To upgrade the professional preparation of in-service rural teachers and to help improve the rural schools.

The best way to comprehend the objectives of the cultural mission teachers is to examine the duties of each as set forth by SEP guidelines. Here we can see SEP's central role in the full range of culture, and the contribution of women should be noted. The lead teacher of the mission, usually a man, organized, guided, and supervised projects. He promoted a wide range of projects including the construction and improvement of municipal roads, highways, telephone lines, and post office. To lower living costs he organized cooperative associations for the production of livestock, agricultural, and industrial goods. He built a supply warehouse to make available at cost the tools, machinery, and raw materials people needed in their daily work. Every recourse available that might raise the professional standard of rural teachers and improve school facilities was utilized.

The social worker-teacher, almost always a woman, through tactful work in homes encouraged family industries and the production of agricultural products sufficient for domestic needs. This teacher taught the women how to make wearing apparel and emphasized cleanliness, the extermination of vermin and parasites, and the use of furniture and utensils. The social worker acquainted people with their constitutional rights, advised against premature or very late marriages, and offered suggestions for the rearing and education of children. She assisted young girls about to be married to prepare for the responsibilities of home and family life and encouraged home recreation for the family through storytelling, reading, games, and songs. The use of alcohol and other social evils were constantly combated.

The nurse-teacher, again almost always a woman, took steps to ensure that water was potable and taught avoidance of disease from contamination. She also tried to maintain maximum hygiene in the markets, streets, public buildings, and meeting places, and urged compliance with the laws concerning burials. She nursed the sick, cared for expectant mothers before and during delivery, and taught the fundamentals of child care. Measures were taken to prevent and control epidemics, to establish a health and maternity clinic, and to organize a pharmacy for the community using supplies provided by SEP.

In a fully staffed SEP operation the agriculture teacher taught modern farming methods. He tried to intervene tactfully in the problems of the use of irrigation water. He instructed farmers to sell their crops to the best advantage and to secure the benefits to which they were entitled under the Farm Credit Law, thus freeing them from the obligation to pay premiums to moneylenders and profiteers. Construction teachers instructed in building materials, directed construction of new houses, and guided and assisted residents concerning the improvement of their homes. With community cooperation they built bridges, aqueducts, sewers, and other components of the local infrastructure. The trade teacher gave instruction in everything from the preservation of meats to auto mechanics.

The teacher of mechanics and operator of motion picture projectors helped interested citizens to install pumps, hydraulic rams, small hydroelectric plants, and similar equipment, and rendered service without charge to rural people who had mechanical problems. He supervised the laying of pipes for drinking water and other sanitary facilities. In addition, he operated a motion picture projector in the communities served by the mission and, whenever possible, photographed interesting aspects of community life, the work of the mission, and the scenic beauties of the region. The music teacher directed music and singing for the boys and girls of the community, instructed teachers in methods of teaching music, organized musical groups, and assisted them in obtaining the necessary instruments. The music teacher cooperated closely with the committee on recreational activities in promoting and organizing festivals and civic and social programs. An important part of his other work was to study and collect all types of regional music. The recreational teacher was the promoter of athletic activities within the community.[29]

In the rural mission program avilacamachismo demonstrated a broad spectrum of culture-state activities ranging from the practical and vocational to the higher expression of culture in music, art, and design. In these programs SEP upheld the practicability of avilacamachista idealism.

The teachers' unions responded positively to the leadership of Torres Bodet. In December 1943 he called a meeting of the two major unions, the National Confederation of Teachers and the Mexican Teachers Federation, and several smaller unions to discuss unification of all of the teachers' unions. President Avila Camacho opened the meeting with praise for the teachers and was followed by Torres Bodet, who called for all sides to compromise on the ideological issues surrounding the religious restrictions remaining in Article 3 of the 1917 Constitution. He said that Mexican education "should always be respectful of our traditions without becoming an obstacle to our progress."[30] In a resounding echo of avilacamachismo, Torres Bodet said that it was every Mexican teacher's duty to help build an internally strong, unified nation. He downplayed the need for confrontational politics and urged teachers to develop a nonpolitical consensus in the form of a professional philosophy built upon duty, respect, responsibilities, and shared goals for the nation's children. The state, he said, would build new schools throughout Mexico, and he showed the teachers plans for the construction of nearly a thousand new buildings.[31]

After six days of bitter debate in which the many years of conflict were dredged up, the teachers voted to form a union called the Sindicato Nacional de Trabajadores en Educación, or SNTE. Torres Bodet then closed the conference with a speech in which he commended the teachers for accepting the principles of national unity, progress, and professionalism.[32] In the remaining years of the Avila Camacho administration, with the help of Vicente Lombardo Toledano, the Marxist leader of the Confederación de Trabajadores de México (CTM), who supported the state during this period, SNTE was free of disruptive activities by the right or left. In the Avila Camacho sexennium, both CTM and SNTE were committed to stability and closely tied to the ever more powerful government.[33]

The administration's handling of the teachers' union exemplifies how the process of avilacamachismo worked. No other group or profession had the grassroots influence that the teachers possessed, and avilacamachismo understood that no issue in Mexican society was as potentially dangerous to national unity as public education. The successful redirection of teacher unionization along lines sympathetic to the state was an important link in the creation of authentic national unity.

Throughout this century and under several names, SEP served as a meeting house for culture and state. During the sexennium of Manuel Avila Camacho it was the central policymaking agency for cultural avilacamachismo. Many aspects of popular and high culture were influenced by SEP. In 1942, for example, SEP funded a Mexico City opera company under the leadership of the former director of the Vienna State Opera. This was the same role played by SEP in funding Mexican ballet and the Mexican Symphony Orchestra. In the performing arts the goal was to develop Mexican artists to world standards. Under Torres Bodet, SEP managed and financed every phase of public education from the smallest school in Baja California to UNAM, from professional development programs for teachers to the building of new schools, and from the translation and printing of cheap pocket classics to a comprehensive literacy program. By 1946 the principle of education for all Mexicans had been confirmed by these culture-state policies, and over half of all federal employees worked for SEP.

CHAPTER FOUR

Radio

R adio in the 1930s was changing Mexican culture and antici-pating a unique era in popular culture in the 1940s. Radio strengthened the office of the president as millions grew accustomed to listening to speeches on radio from locations throughout the nation. These speeches were not unlike the "fireside chats" being broadcast by the reform-minded president of Mexico's neighbor to the north.

At ten o'clock on Sunday evening, 25 July 1937, the Autonomous Department of News and Publicity broadcast the first edition of what was to become the most famous radio program in Latin America, *La hora nacional*. A public communications law opened the way for the state to claim significant portions of air time on both commercial and official stations. Using radio Cárdenas, and later Ávila Camacho, seized the interest of the entire nation by talking directly to the people. In 1940, there were in Mexico at least 300,000 radios, mostly in the homes of people living in small towns and cities; and group listening, popular in social or familial settings in Mexico just as in the United States, increased listenership even in isolated areas.[1] Geography made radio the first feasible means of reaching a Mexican mass audience representative of all parts of the nation. In addition, radio was generating new and innovative cultural forms.

The most popular programs featured music in what was called "the popular style," music associated with nightlife in Mexico City. By the early war years there was a building boom of cabarets and dance halls in every city and town. The most famous were in Mexico City, where musicians played before large crowds the *boleros, corridos, sones, rumbas,* and *sambas* popular on the radio. The *danzón* seems to have originated in Cuba and together with the bolero characterized Mexican urban music of the '30s and '40s, while the *musica ranchera* represented the countryside. A few other forms like the *huapango* and *sones huastecos* reflected older, regional traditions. In all, there was a wide and generous range of music.

El Salón México was Mexico City's most important dance hall in the '30s and '40s, offering a variety of Mexican popular music. Aaron Copeland wrote his *El Salón México* based upon the music of the club. Songs by famous entertainers like Toña la Negra were accompanied by orchestras like that of Noé Fajardo, and they thrilled crowds at clubs like the famous Smyrna, located at San Jeronimo Street 47. In the loud, smoke-filled clubs everyone danced and sang new songs, like Ernesto Cortazar's openly racist hit about Mexico's war against the Japanese:

> On an island among the islets
> There are also many monkeys;
> Now the father of the whole
>   Damned lot is here.
> Who mentioned fear my boys,
>   We were all born to die!
> Here's my .45 with four loaded clips.[2]

Club Smyrna became a famous venue for the radio styling of Amparo Montes, who appeared weekly on XEW,[3] the hot orchestra of Cuban-born Enrique Byron, and the more traditional sounds of Albel Domínguez and his orchestra.[4] It was here that Juan Garrido often played Agustín Lara's 1942 radio hit, *"Cantar del regimento"* (Song of the Regiment). Club Smyrna was also famous because it was built on the site of the convent that once was home to Sor Juana Inéz de la Cruz. The building had been a warehouse for years until it was remodeled in 1940 to house the club.[5] Its Spanish-Moorish decor became well known all over the world, and several film stars began their careers there. Adalberto Martínez ("Resortes"), for example, first became famous as a dancer of swing and rumba there. Everyone knew that the dance floor was over the grave of Sor Juana, and it was stylish to go to the Smyrna and "dance on Sor Juana's grave." It was André Breton who observed that surrealism was natural in Mexico!

In order to understand the cultural impact of radio in the 1940s, however, we must first look briefly at the conclusion of the Cárdenas years and observe how the creation of a relationship between the state, radio, and film came to play a critical role in the Ávila Camacho years.

When Cárdenas assumed power, the so-called "official" stations were used as production facilities for programs designed to influence the culture along the lines defined by the administration. In 1936 Cárdenas created a central agency to coordinate and develop a national radio talent pool from which the best vocalists, orchestras, nationalistic and motivational speakers, educators, poets, composers, and writers could be drawn to perform on the air.[6] In December 1936 a presidential decree created the Departamento Autónomo de Prensa y Publicidad, commonly called DAPP. This directive from the president's office referred to the state radio stations as the "cultural stations of the republic."[7] Immediately the Cárdenas government began developing more stations. In March 1937 newspapers gave generous coverage to the inauguration of two new stations and to the large number of government officials representing every federal secretariat and department who attended the ceremony. A few months later, the first DAPP report on state radio declared that from 15 March 1937 until 31 August 1937, 2,570 radio programs were produced in the central DAPP station, XEPD.[8] It is believed that most of these programs were carried on the more powerful commercial stations under the directives of the public communications laws. These guidelines, as we have seen, allowed the state to claim substantial portions of air time.[9]

The first head of DAPP was Guillermo Morales Blumenkron. A native of Puebla, he was something of a prodigy, heading up the accounting department of the Bank of Monterrey, Puebla Branch, by the time he was fifteen. In his late teens he was a successful furniture dealer before becoming the publisher of the magazine *Variedades* at twenty-one. Articulate and knowledgeable about the consequences of revolutionary violence, he believed that a new nationalism was needed for the new generation, one that would go beyond the insurrectionist era and be adequate for modern nation-building. At twenty-six he went to work for the PNR as head of the state radio station XEFO. It was the youthful Morales Blumenkron, generally referred to by Mexican historians as Guillermo Morales B., who helped Cárdenas develop the use of radio as a powerful tool in his presidential campaign. In 1938, at age thirty, Morales B. was appointed program manager of the 50,000-watt station XEW, the largest in Mexico City and one of the most powerful and influential in the nation. At XEW he repeated the youth-oriented, mass-media approach to musical programming that had made *La hora nacional* an instant success.

Morales B. developed a musical series that was picked up and rebroadcast in every section of the nation. He added dozens of up-and-coming popular music and film stars to the already popular programs featuring stars like Agustín Lara, Toña la Negra, Amparo Montes and Jorge Negrete. During the war years, XEW had the six most popular radio programs in Mexico City. These programs were *Rapsodia panamérica, Interpretación mexicana de guerra, Tributa a la libertad, La verdad es..., Radio teatro de América,* and *Historia en acción*. Morales was an example of the best and brightest young Mexican leaders who were attracted to the idealism of both Cárdenas and Ávila Camacho. It was through individuals like Morales B. that avilacamachismo was able to develop a modern, comprehensive nationalism with a powerful appeal through mass media. In later years he became wealthy, owning radio stations XEQK and XEDA, and serving the party as a consultant on radio and television issues. He served as national radio coordinator for the Díaz Ordaz campaign and owned and led the Morkron Publicity Agency until his death in 1972.[10]

After the famous first Sunday broadcast of *La hora nacional*, for the next ten years, under both Cárdenas and Ávila Camacho, Sunday at 10:00 p.m. was promoted by the state as the most entertaining and educational hour of the week. Humorists noted that it was also the only program on the air. According to the script of the first broadcast, the series began with words now familiar to every Mexican. (The program is still on the air, using basically the same opening.)

First Announcer: It is the national hour!
(Trumpet fanfare and Mexican national anthem.)
Second Announcer: XEPD and XEXA, shortwave, in cooperation with all the radio stations of Mexico, bring you this national hour of the government of Mexico. On this program you will hear important information and outstanding music by Mexican artists.[11]

Early on, DAPP organized an orchestra under the direction of Higinio Rubalcaba. For the first broadcast, compositions by Manuel M. Ponce were featured, along with short inspirational speeches about the need for education, development, national pride, and determination to fulfill the work of the Revolution. The evening concluded with the Police Band of the Federal District under the direction of composer Velino M. Pereza. The band played "Mexican Rhapsody," Pereza's own work, and once again the national anthem.

Radio was in Mexico to stay, and as the state realized its power to shape and direct culture and attitudes, broadcasting came to play an even greater role in the administration of Ávila Camacho.[12] Under Ávila Camacho the state exercised directive authority in the shaping of culture by virtue of increased levels of investment money for the creation of cultural institutions. In the radio and film industries and in the arts generally, as we shall see in later chapters, funding was carefully controlled at every level.

In 1960 Gustavo de la Garza, manager of XET in Monterrey, was asked by an American historian if over the years the government had required him to carry *La hora nacional* each Sunday evening. He replied that he had a choice. He could carry the program or "turn off his transmitter for one hour."[13] The role of the state in broadcasting was powerful from the beginning. The Constitution of 1917 had made possible either a government monopoly in broadcasting, a privately owned system, or a combination of the two. Article 28 stated that constitutional rights of monopoly were granted to the state in relation to radio-telegraphic services, but at the same time stated that "the law will punish any action that stifles free competition in any public service."[14] This strange wording seemed to imply consent for the creation of private stations, and, as noted earlier, the first commercial station went on the air in 1923. It was clear from the start, however, that the government would claim air time on a regular and nationwide basis. Legislation in the years that followed stated this clearly. In 1936 the state passed legislation that increased from ten to twenty minutes the minimum daily time each commercial station had to devote to state programming. This increase was in addition to the "spot announcements" that might be sent to a station at any time for immediate broadcast.[15] The legislation said in part, "thirty minutes daily shall be allotted, with the time of the broadcast set by the Secretary of Communications. In the case of broadcasts of national importance . . . the holders of either concessions or permits will be obligated to interconnect their stations."[16]

When Ávila Camacho took office in 1940, Mexico had ninety commercial and twelve government stations.[17] Why, then, did the state demand time on commercial stations when it owned twelve of its own?

It is important to note that while state radio stations covered many of the major urban areas of the nation, the message of avilacamachismo was rooted in the idea of a national culture that included every section of the country and every segment of society. State radio stations alone could not provide authentic national coverage, and commercial stations were needed to reach an audience truly national in scope. In 1940 much of the nation still had an inadequate infrastructure.[18] Radio was the most economical and technically efficient way of overcoming the obstacles to communication between the state and the population. Radio could leap over mountains where there were no roads, dart over arid deserts, float over muddy jungle trails, and penetrate into distant valleys and islands. Under Ávila Camacho the laws concerning the use of radio by the state were utilized in a concerted, coordinated effort to bring both the message of national unity and the creative works of national culture to all of the people.

As pointed out earlier, the agency first created to do this was called the Departamento Autónomo de Prensa y Publicidad, or DAPP. The first *jefe de radio de DAPP* was Guillermo Morales B., who responded to a request by station owners that DAPP create a program of information and culture to focus the state's message instead of continuing the short daily broadcasts. The result of this request was *La hora nacional*, which went on the air in 1937.[19] In 1939 a group of armed communists stormed into station XEW and demanded that the national Sunday hook-up for *La hora nacional* remain in place while they broadcast a message. The power was reduced, and only a small area around the station received a signal, but it was now obvious to everyone that radio was seen as a powerful communications medium.

In 1940 when Ávila Camacho came to power, DAPP had passed control of radio to a new agency called Radio Gobernación. The new head, Leopoldo de Samaniego, reported to Ávila Camacho in August 1940 that *La hora nacional* constituted the major medium whereby the government would inform the nation of what was going on in the two "most useful" areas of national life, economic development and "artistic endeavor." He proclaimed that every effort would be made to secure the most outstanding artists to perform on the program. Both popular and classical selections would be played, always "in an attempt to attain a high cultural level." He declared that the Department of Radio "has taken into the homes of Mexicans and foreigners the fruit of Revolutionary life, transformed into useful information along with the highest of artistic presentations." Samaniego reported that his goal was "to bring the Government closer to the people."[20]

In 1940 only one non-Mexican musician appeared on *La hora nacional*. The Spanish guitarist Andrés Segovia performed as "a manifestation of his feeling toward President Ávila Camacho, his government and the people of Mexico."[21] Music was the heart of the program throughout the Ávila Camacho years, as programming became progressively more sophisticated. Reflecting what is still today the style of the popular television program *Siempre en domingo*, on 7 December 1941, *La hora nacional* broadcast the first Indian State Fair in Oaxaca.[22] In this broadcast, fifty-three minutes of Indian music were shared with the nation. The music was explained and praised by Enrique Orton Díaz, one of the fair's organizers. The importance of the role of native culture and music in the development of national culture was extolled by Roberto Bonilla, an SEP representative.

During the Ávila Camacho years, four men headed Radio Gobernación. Leopoldo de Samaniego, appointed by Cárdenas, was kept on and served for two years under Ávila Camacho. He was followed by Quintin Rueda Villagrán, José Lelo de Larrea, and Gregorio Castillo. Each submitted regularly scheduled reports to the Secretaria de Gobernación, which testify to the government's use of radio in promoting national unity and national culture. It is clear that about the time Rueda Villagrán took over from Samaniego, the state decided that Mexican culture must begin to open itself up to selected influences from beyond its borders. In his annual report of 1943 Villagrán wrote:

> In order to protect the prestige that this program [*La hora nacional*] has acquired, special emphasis has been given to the selection of the artistic offerings for each concert. It is possible to present some of the most outstanding international musical fig-

ures that visit our country, thus fulfilling the objective of bringing to all segments of Mexican society the satisfaction of hearing well-selected music.[23]

Under the leadership of Villagrán, the percentage of music written by non-Mexicans included in the program increased significantly. In June 1943 not a single piece of Mexican-composed music was presented on *La hora nacional* although all of the musicians were Mexican. The program for 6 June 1943, for example, was printed in full in a large advertisement in *El Universal*. It contained the following agenda for that night's program:

Selection One: "Tancredo" by Rossini, played by the National Symphony Orchestra under the direction of Humberto Mugnai;

Selection Two: "L'Invitation ou voiyage" by DuPark, sung by Eugenia Rocabruna and accompanied on the piano by Juan D. Tercero;

Selection Three: "Una furtiva lagrima" by Donizetti, sung by Joaquín Álvarez and accompanied by the Mexican Symphony;

Selection Four: "Danza de las flautas" by Tschaikowsky, played by the Mexican Symphony;

Selection Five: "Non ti scordar di me" by Curtis, sung by Joaquín Álvarez and played by the Mexican Symphony;

Selection Six: "L'Amigo Fritz" by Mascagni, played by the Mexican Symphony Orchestra under the direction of Humberto Mugnai;

Selection Seven: "Torna a Sorriento" by Curtis, sung by Joaquín Álvarez and accompanied by the Mexican Symphony;

Selection Eight: "Luisa" by Charpentier, sung by Eugenia Rocabruna and accompanied by the Mexican Symphony; and

Selection Nine: "Cascanueces" by Tschaikowsky, played by the Mexican Symphony.[24]

What was behind this change in programming on *La hora nacional* when Rueda Villagrán took over? Program guides in 1940 make it clear that nearly every musical selection and performer on *La hora nacional*, as well as every speaker, was Mexican.

In 1943, however, a significant portion of the music on many of the programs was not Mexican, although most of the musicians were. Did this development under the leadership of Ávila Camacho's first appointed director represent a dramatic policy change on the part of the state? Was the Ávila Camacho administration abandoning its policy of shaping national culture by using radio and other forms of popular culture? No. In fact, many of the changes that took place after Mexico declared war on Germany and Japan in May 1942 can best be explained by the fact that a calculated but totally new role was developed by avilacamachismo in the international policy arena when Mexico entered the war.

In 1940 Mexico was at odds with the United States and several major European nations, inwardly directed, searching for unity and order, and still vulnerable to internal strife. By 1943, however, Mexico had become a key member of an international alliance of nations in the struggle against international fascism. The nation of Mexico was now not only a respected member of the Allies but also an industrializing nation. It was on the road toward the national self-concept implicit in avilacamachismo. As Steven Niblo has documented, by 1943, goods shortages among the poor notwithstanding, Mexico was beginning to enjoy a period of war-related prosperity that attracted thousands to Mexico City each week and turned the capital into a major international center of trade, industry, and entertainment. From 1940 until 1945, the national income tripled from 6.4 billion pesos to 18.6 billion pesos.[25] Everything was changing, and radio continued as a major agent. As José Luis Ortiz Garza observes:

> Radio was radical in that it acted as a catalyst for all kinds of change, social, political and commercial. It provoked in Mexico something that it had already provoked in some other nations. It started a new Mexico, serving everyone and reaching remote areas to satsify demands that everyone be included. [26]

These changes reflected in radio programming were moving Mexico from nationalism to internationalism and to a more cosmopolitan world view. In addition, a survey of two major Mexico

City newspapers, *Excélsior* and *El Universal*, using the first section of the Sunday editions of these newspapers on every other Sunday in 1940 and every other Sunday in 1943, reveals a change of focus not unlike the internationalization that took place on *La hora nacional*. In 1940, 75 percent of the stories in section one of *El Universal* and 70 percent of the stories in *Excélsior* were local, regional, or national in scope. By 1943, however, both papers were featuring stories in the first section of their Sunday editions that were predominantly international.[27] *Excélsior* and *El Universal* even started a section in English. The changes in *La hora nacional* and in major newspapers are similar in that each reflects not changes in domestic policy, but the emergence of Mexico as a member of the Allied international community in the struggle against fascism.

Of course, not every historian agrees with this. In his book *México en guerra*, Ortiz Garza argues that in the Ávila Camacho administration, major newspapers and magazines, with the exception of those controlled by the far right and the far left, were influenced to the point of being almost taken over by the pro-American avilacamachistas. He suggests that the wire services, financial aid, technical assistance, program advisers, and films provided by the United States played a significant role in shaping Mexican public opinion into a prowar, pro-Allied configuration. With everything from "Terry and the Pirates" and "Popeye" to several behind-the-scenes attempts to remove government officials who were not sufficiently pro-American, Mexico was flooded with posters, films, propaganda, money, and radio programs, all designed to influence the attitudes of the Mexican people toward the war. Ortiz Garza suggests that the Mexican magazine *Hoy* began to look more and more like *Life* and that *Tiempo* was a copy of *Time*.[28]

Although it is impossible to deny that these operations took place, one cannot conclude that they in any way indicate an abandonment of the Ávila Camacho domestic strategem for the shaping of an authentic Mexican national culture. In fact, one can conclude that just the opposite is the case. In the Second World War, Mexico had, perhaps for the first time, an officially friendly, mutually advantageous, and generally cordial relationship with the

United States. By 1943 Mexico and the United States were not only "good neighbors" but also Allies in a brutal world war. After declaring war, Ávila Camacho called for a voluntary reserve army of two million. The response was striking. All over the nation, according to the newspapers, in places like Tlacolula, Oaxaca and Mexico City's Chapultepec Park, the entire country resonated to the martial beat of a war drum. Newspapers carried stories of Chamula Indians drilling and women's groups organizing special courses in nursing. In May 1943 a letter was published in *El Nacional* from a young conscript named José Rosas Palafox of the 51st Infantry Battalion. Palafox proclaimed that the Mexican army was ready to fight and would show the enemy that the beloved national anthem is true when it says the words "a soldier in every son has been given you."[29]

The year 1943 was a window of opportunity for the state to hammer home its message that Mexico must be fully united in order to make common cause with the Western Alliance in a protracted war against fascism and racism. In doing so, the state's domestic policy of promoting a popular national culture by promoting film, radio, and the popular arts received strong reinforcement from international circumstances.

The Allied nations sent back to Mexico a positive perception of Mexico from abroad. As a member of the Allies, Mexico was repeatedly and publicly praised as a highly respected peer, fighting at the side of the other two nations of North America, the beleaguered Soviet Union, and what remained of free Europe. Avilacamachismo believed that Mexico's long-term role as the leader of Latin America was clear and inevitable. Mexico in 1943 was a nation honored and praised, a nation to which even the busy wartime American president, Franklin Roosevelt, paid a respectful visit. Every indication was that Mexico was leaving behind the fragmentation and violence of the old internal struggles and moving onto the world scene as a united and powerful Ally of the Western nations. Its radio industry and, indeed, its industrial development in general, was receiving widespread international recognition. It seems clear, then, that to

President Ávila Camacho, a culture moving toward world stature, a member nation in the alliance against German and Japanese aggression, a unified and courageous people, could, under these new circumstances, allow selected examples of the larger cultural heritage of the West to stand alongside the music and culture of Mexico as it was explored and celebrated weekly on the most important program on the air, *La hora nacional*.[30]

Even with the advent of foreign music on the program, the music of Mexican composers and musicians remained of central importance to *La hora nacional*. The work of Manuel M. Ponce was the centerpiece of several programs in 1943. The melodies of Alfonso Esparza Oteo and Tata Nacho appeared often. There was a stirring appearance by Los Abajeñas with Mariachi Vargas singing the 1942 corrido "El soldado mexicano." As noted, during 1943, program changes began to reflect the image of Mexico as a respected member of the world community. From the state's viewpoint, program changes on the most important hour in Mexico needed to reflect the new status of the nation. Toward this end, an advertisement of 7 March 1943 in *Excélsior* indicated that the upcoming edition of *La hora nacional* would be dedicated to "our sister Republic of Costa Rica."[31] That night, along with the national anthems of Costa Rica and Mexico, the entire nation, or at least those with radios, heard the Infantry Band of the Army and the National Symphony Orchestra, together with several soloists, play and sing eleven selections of Costa Rican music. The highlight of the program was a short speech by the president of Costa Rica, Dr. Rafael Calderón Guirdia. Newspapers the next day reported that the much-respected president of Costa Rica praised Mexico for its courage in war and its vibrant culture.[32]

As Mexican radio and film stars like Rosita Moreno, who traveled over 30,000 miles in the Pacific, and others began to tour the war zones entertaining Allied troops, Mexican popular radio music and popular culture generally began to reflect war-related and nationalist themes.[33] Ortiz Garza argues that this was totally the work of Nelson Rockefeller and his cronies. Using large amounts of advertising money and American-style programs, such as *Your Hit Parade* translated into Spanish, widespread popular support for the war was created. It is doubtful, however, that this propaganda operation had the ability and sophistication to reach so deeply into the Mexican heart and mind as to influence the corrido. The corrido is the descendant of the Spanish epic ballad called the "romance." It differs from its Spanish progenitor in that it is essentially a narrative sung about a current event or person. In the simple formula of a quatrain, corridos are a fairly accurate way of measuring the issues the poor write and sing about. The corrido was often printed on broadsides and sold at public events. During the war, corridos were still a favorite form of popular entertainment at carnivals, cockfights, traveling shows, fairs, and rural fiestas where singers often shared the stage with regional dancers. Radio enabled the state to use the corrido as a tool for national unification, but the state also used the corrido to measure the effectiveness of its propaganda. Very important was the application of the corrido to the process of radio magnification. This magnification made the patriotic corrido a valuable propaganda tool in the development of national unity. When radio came to Mexico, the corrido took to the airwaves. The Manuel Ávila Camacho files in the National Archives are filled with corridos written to honor the president by praising his wisdom and courage, lamenting his frequent illnesses, or rejoicing that he survived an assassination attempt in 1944.[34] A widely published corrido applauds Ávila Camacho and the Congress for declaring war:

Ante tal humillación	Before such humiliation
nuestro insigne Presidente	our prestigious President
firme, sereno, y valiente	firm, calm, and brave
tomó heroica decisión.	made heroic decisions.
Y en memorable sesión	In a memorable session
que trascendencias encierra	in the transcendent moment
para el Eje pidió guerra	the leader asked the Congress
al Congreso de la Unión.	for war.
Mi gran pueblo independiente	O, My independent country!

desde el campo hasta el obrero	From the farm to the worker,
el industrial y el banquero	the factory to the banker
apoyan al Presidente.[35]	We support the President.

Merle Simmons suggests that the gentle, quiet, even mild personality of Ávila Camacho may not have inspired vast numbers of corridos, but those that do exist indicate that his serene, dignified, and forthright manner of handling the war crisis, along with his success in creating a spirit of national unity, inspired songwriters to praise him highly. Simmons's research has found no evidence of a corrido in any way critical of the president or the war effort. Given the fact that this type of music was fundamentally the work of ordinary, rural people who expressed their feelings about events in this folkloric musical form, Ávila Camacho and his leadership can be regarded as having been generally popular throughout his term in office. Simmons observes that although there are historians who question the depth of Mexican support for the war and the depth of understanding among the poor for the issues involved, he sees no evidence that the war was unpopular.[36] Nor does he mention any American influence in the creation and presentation or in the distribution of the broadsheets that often were sold at a corrido's performance.[37]

Corridos were the popular mainstay of numerous radio programs in 1942 and after. One of the first to be magnified nationally was "Corrido de la guerra," first published in 1942 and sung by several stars on a number of programs in a *corrido chico*, or short version. The *corrido grande* version was written by Rodolfo Lozada and contained seventy verses. When printed as a broadsheet, it was illustrated by Gabriel Fernández Ledesma, a student of the most famous corrido illustrator in Mexico, José Guadalupe Posada. The long version tells the story of the war from the viewpoint of the Allies. It begins with the Nazis invading the small nations of Europe and suggests that they have designs on the rest of the world. It then points to the need for the peoples of the Americas to forget old differences and join together against Hitler, calling attention to the horror resulting from the sinking of two Mexican ships by the Germans. All educated people, it observes, know that Hitler is the anti-Christ of the Apocalypse, that Mussolini is a clown, and that Japan is the most treacherous nation in the world. Mexico and her people, united and strong, says the corrido, have always opened their hearts to the oppressed and to victims of hatred and barbarism. It concludes with a phrase right out of the inaugural speech of Manuel Ávila Camacho: Mexico must unite in order to prove to the entire world what it is capable of doing.[38] In a subtle but effective way, the corridos affirmed for the state that the process of magnification was effective. This popular war corrido received a great deal of air play.

As the use of corridos on the radio effectively demonstrated, radio not only measured the response of the people, but could mold opinion as well. During the war, the state developed, with the help of American funding, technical assistance, and wire service reports, a propaganda network of news and information programming that included a number of popular radio programs. The first was *Por un mundo mejor* (For a Better World), which started in 1942. It was followed in 1943 by *Europa clandestina* (Hidden Europe), which told the story of underground activities against the Nazis. The most popular, according to Ortiz Garza, were *La verdad es...* and *Interpretación mexicana de la guerra*, both hosted by a close friend of Ávila Camacho and a strong supporter of avilacamachismo, Félix F. Palavicini.

In his opening editorial broadcast on 16 November 1942, Palavicini promised to provide Mexico with truthful news and commentary about the war based on information received from United Press International, and news of the Mexican war effort from around the nation. The war, he said, was a clear struggle between "two forms of existence: freedom and slavery."[39] In a letter to his friend President Ávila Camacho, Palavicini said he was pleased with the national response to the program, which was recorded and mailed to stations throughout the nation. The president responded that he listened to the program on station XEW and thought it "the best news program in the republic."[40] Palavicini became the voice of avilacamachismo on the radio, repeatedly calling for a new Mexican spirit befitting a united people who were determined to stand by the president, the military, and the free nations of the world in the struggle to defeat the Axis powers.

It was popular music, however, that was clearly the most important ideological tool in the hands of the state. Yolanda Morena Rivas observes that the state clearly used radio and popularity of musical programs to construct an ideological framework for its views.[41] Popular singers and songwriters were able to construct lyrics supporting the war and link them to emotions that bound the people to one another and to the nation. Hundreds of songs were written to express and reflect the feelings of a nation at war. It was a fruitful era for songwriting in general. The great Agustín Lara wrote and recorded thirty-one major songs between 1940 and 1945.[42] His most popular song was "Cantar del regimento" recorded in 1942 by Julio Flores and the Juan Garrido Orchestra. Other wartime radio hits included "América unida," written by the orchestra leader Juan Garrido in 1942, and "Viva México—Viva América," written by Pedro Galindo also in 1942. Both of these songs reflect the need for unity inside the nation and the need for solidarity with the Allied nations on the international scene.

Another popular song was on the "B" side of Fernando Rosas's hit "Traigo mi .45" and was called "Corrido de los *bravucones*" (Song of the Fierce). In it the singer demands of the nation that empty words must give way to action and that Mexicans must unite again under the banner of the Virgin to defeat the enemies of liberty.[43] The most famous radio 'pianista' of the era, Challo Cervera, who often accompanied Toña la Negra and Amparo Montes, declared in 1989 that the most popular songs with Mexican soldiers and radio audiences during World War II were "Amor, amor, amor" by Gabriel Ruiz, and the controversial "Bésame mucho" by Consuelito Velázquez. He observed that when both songs became big hits in the United States, Australia, Canada, and England, it made Mexicans proud that their popular culture was at last having a worldwide impact.[44]

In the period between the middle of 1943 and the end of the war, one saw in magazines, newspapers, and on billboards, and heard in radio jingles the popular sentiments of avilacamachismo. Sentiments such as "Unidos hoy," "Con unidad: liberdad," and "Unidos para siempre" were profoundly important. Avilacamachismo took the popular, urban culture of an emerging, modern, international Mexico City and magnified it on the radio and in films, giving it a uniform shape for the masses in all parts of the nation. The styles, dances, songs, and action films used in the process appealed especially to the young, who always embrace new technology before anyone else, and who, since they had less contact with the discord of the previous era, were naturally more open to new thinking. Using film, popular music, radio, and the star syndrome, the state put mass media to work for its own ends.

The Mexican census of 1940 reveals that about 30 percent of the population was made up of *campesinos* who lived on corn, chile, and beans, almost always in a one-room house without sanitation or drinkable water. The corrido was also the music of another 20 percent of the 1940 population who lived on *ejidos*, communal villages created by Cárdenas to deal with rural poverty. The ejidos owned sixty-two million acres of land in 1940 and housed 882,000 families. Although income was only slightly higher, *ejidatarios* generally had better water, sanitation, health care, and educational centers than did the campesinos. Most villages had electricity and radios. Newspapers circulated, and from time to time a truck would arrive and set up a "moving picture." At village fairs, regional carnivals, and fiestas, campesinos and ejidatarios sang the old corridos and heard the new ones. The radio brought a new world of ideas and entertainment to this half of the population.

To the many Mexican villages at night the radio brought new kinds of music. Joining the radio audience were another 800,000 families, 20 percent of the population, who were small independent ranchers and farmers called *rancheros*. A large portion of this group was literate. Schools in these villages were adequate, and most houses had a radio. In July 1991 Amparo Montes, one of the great radio music stars of the 1940s, was interviewed by Christina Pacheco for the magazine *Siempre*. Amparo lived as a child in the typical Mexican farming village of Arboles de Tapachula. Her father played guitar and sang corridos. She fell in love with music as a child. The greatest musical gift she remembered was the coming of the radio to her home. Every night she listened to the radio. She listened to classical music and was profoundly influenced by Manuel M. Ponce, in whose work she recognized something essentially Mexican but in a newer, more challenging form. She also liked tropical music, rumbas and *merengues* from distant Mexico City clubs where the bands were Cuban or Dominican. It was seductive, powerful, and Amparo and her sister Fito felt excited and a part of something larger than their village. She remembers that everyone talked of going to Mexico City. Most seductive of all, she said, was a voice that began around eleven each night. When Agustín Lara sang *"Concha nacar"* (Shell of Pearl) and "Talismán" and *"Carita de cielo"* (Little Face in Heaven), Amparo Montes knew that she too wanted to sing for the nation on the radio.

In 1938 at age sixteen she moved to Mexico City. In those days, she said the city was *bellisima, pequeñita* (so pretty, so small). Her voice was so beautiful that she was soon sharing the stage with the biggest names in Mexican musical and variety theater, people like Chino Ibarra, Pedro Vargas, María Conesa, Toña la Negra, comedians Cantinflas and Roberto Soto, and, to her amazement, Lara himself. In the early 1940s, singing in the style of Lara, she had become famous on XEW for her interpretation of romantic boleros. Part of her success, she believed, came from the fact that when she sang on the radio at night, she knew the distant faces to whom she was singing. Later she toured the nation with pianist Juan Bruno Tarraza and with fellow radio star Toña la Negra. Looking at the crowds of young people dancing and singing her songs, she remembered that she was not always the famous Amparo Montes who now often shared an after-broadcast supper with Agustín Lara; she was also Amparo Mesa Cruz, who herself had listened to wonderful Mexican music in the village of Arboles de Tapachula.[45]

Campesinos, ejidatarios and rancheros composed 70 percent of the Mexican population in 1940.[46] This number changed rapidly as economic development and perhaps the siren song of the radio pulled large numbers of people from the land to the cities, especially Mexico City, looking for opportunity and greater contact with the national life. Participation in the music-centered popular culture, especially for young people, was one of the ways in which they sought to experience the larger nation.

Another important part of the magnification of popular culture for an eager radio audience was the development of comedy stars, of whom Cantinflas was the most famous. By 1940 large numbers of Mexican workers were literate and read newspapers and cartoon magazines. They attended the movies and appreciated the ironic humor in the uncensored comedy of Cantinflas, Tin Tan, Roberto Soto, Resortes, and Polillo. These comedians, and there were many more, were free under the Ávila Camacho government to satirize nearly any subject including politicians, the war, the United States, the church, even the president himself. Many appeared as zoot-suiters or country bumpkins. Avilacamachismo used radio and film to magnify and develop these personalities.

Most of these comedians wore the "zoot suit" fashions of the *pachuco*, the poor but very contemporary, street-smart youth of the 1940s, and most used music as a central part of their acts. Tin Tan and Roberto Soto both appeared on radio, but their prime venue was the Mexico City musical variety stage. Soto was a singer as well as a comedian, who belted out boleros, rancheros and witty corridos laced with social commentary. He was most famous for his versions of the anti-Japanese hit "Traigo mi .45." He was usually preceded on stage by beautiful female singers with strong, husky voices who sang only the most heartbreaking boleros such as "*Cita* de amor." Although not as well known as Toña la Negra or Amparo Montes, these women, among them Manolita Ariola, Aurora Muñoz and "La Torcidita," had some notoriety because they had beautiful voices, figures that were complemented by revealing dresses, and a professional stage presence. Soto's most valued assistant was Irma Villa, a beautiful young woman who sang rancheros to the cheers of the audience. When Soto came on to do his stand-up comedy, he satirized social events, movies, politicians, even the war. One of his most famous routines featured a Mexican soldier serving in the American army during the D-Day invasion. He attacked both the "black market" and the people who were profiting from the shortages. A supporter of Ávila Camacho, Soto scalded some of the conservative press who downplayed the assassination attempt on the chief executive's life in a famous routine called *"Complot de viejitos"* (Old Folks' Plot).

The more popular of the two was Tin Tan, whose real name was Germán Valdez and whose character on stage was a *pocho* (an Americanized Mexican) zoot-suiter who lived on the border and was not really a Mexican or an American. Caught between cultures, Tin Tan often dueled with his audience and when heckled, he gave as good as he got. Tin Tan was famous for poking fun at Mexican music of the sickly sweet "yo soy puro mexicano" type. Some in the audience were offended, others howled with laughter. Tin Tan often made fun of American tourists, singing popular American songs in a drunken voice, or trying to teach Marcel, his sidekick who played a guitar and dressed elegantly, to say "Los Angeles" correctly in a flat, American midwestern accent.

The most famous "bumpkin" was Polillo (Toothpick) who had a love-hate relationship with the Mexico City police and was a champion of the urban poor. Poor but unbroken, the caustic character called Polillo, like many in his audience, spoke and sang of his struggle to make a living and keep his dignity.

The Mexican musical variety stage in the era of Manuel Ávila Camacho was characterized by popular music, slapstick comedy, and honest, unflinching social satire. As a measurement of political health, this was a solid indication that avilacamachismo had the intelligence to let the culture have its head and generally refrained from direct repression. This is not to say that the state was comfortable with the artistic expression or ideas of every individual. The goal of avilacamachismo was, however, to erect a tent called popular culture, strongly built, decorated by artists of many kinds, and big enough for the whole nation.

CHAPTER FIVE

Film

As with radio, avilacamachismo used film to magnify popular culture, creating mass media stars from the ranks of musicians, singers, dancers, and comedians. It subsidized films whose characters and characterizations embodied values and virtues consistent with those of the state. In this culture-state process, icons of popular culture were created and made larger than life by the electronic media; at the same time these characters were also made accessible to every person in every section of the nation because of the innate intimacy of the media.

As it has been noted, José Vasconcelos founded the modern Mexican education system and used the state to develop the arts. But as Carl J. Mora points out, Vasconcelos failed to see the importance of film.[1] It was not until the 1930s, therefore, that the Mexican film industry got a solid start. Mora cites Ávila Camacho as the man who made the "golden age" of Mexican movie making possible. Ávila Camacho put the industry on the map by giving state money to private film producers and directors. A good film industry in 1940

87

became outstanding by 1943 when the supply of raw celluloid was cut back to the other Latin American film giant, Argentina. *Excélsior* reported in the spring of that year that the Argentine film industry was "wounded unto death" by the lack of raw film stock and facing "cessation of operation in a number of days."[2] Argentina's posture in the war was very unpopular in the United States, and as a result virtually the entire Latin American supply of raw film stock was given to Mexico.[3] In the late 1930s Mexico scored a major international success with *Allá en el rancho grande* (On the Big Ranch), a film with a pronounced Mexican theme. In 1941, with film supplied by the United States, money offered by the state through the Banco Cinematográfico—over two million pesos available in 1942—and the talent of the Mexican people, films began to be produced that projected the image of a united culture to foreign as well as domestic audiences.

Government statistics reveal that in 1940 there were 446 licensed motion picture theaters in Mexico. By 1946 the number had grown to nearly 1,100. In 1938 the Mexican people spent some thirty-nine million pesos on entertainment, and by 1946, more than one-hundred million. A breakdown of these figures reveals the changes that took place in the culture as Mexico urbanized and industrialized in the Ávila Camacho years. Of the total entertainment figure for the year 1946, 80 percent was spent on tickets to movie theaters. Ten percent was spent on a more traditional pastime, the bullfight, while another 9 percent was spent on plays, concerts, and operas. Officially, only 1 percent was spent on sporting events, and no records are available on how much was spent on nightclubs and dance halls. Of the total amount, 54 percent was spent in Mexico City. It is clear from these figures that by 1946 the cinema was playing a significant role in the lives of many Mexicans.[4]

In 1942 it was reported that radio and film personalities were growing so popular that candles were being lit in churches in honor of Mario Moreno ("Cantinflas"), Agustín Lara, and singer María Luisa Landín.[5] Thanks to the 1940 film *Ahí está el detalle* (Here Are the Details), the irreverent, street-wise Moreno became a star all over Latin America playing a *pelado* (nobody) with all of the dignity and candor that avilacamachismo could have desired for a "typical" representative of the nation's poor but spirited people. In quick succession in 1941, Moreno spoofed Hollywood in *Ni sangre ni arena* (No Blood, No Bullring) and made his most popular film, *El gendarme desconocido* (The Strange Cop). Emilio García Riera observes that seeing one of their own—a charming everyman—appear in the uniform of a policeman—a generally detested figure among the poor—gave the audience a thrilling sense of freedom. The public identified with his dignity even as he appeared ridiculous. The weapons employed by this ordinary man to flout authority suddenly appeared to be within the reach of even the most humble and ignorant of the poor.[6]

Another cultural icon produced by the film industry and radio was the quintessential Mexican singing cowboy, Jorge Negrete. Born in Guanajuato in 1911, Negrete was one of the first singing stars on Mexican radio. In 1941 Negrete made his ninth feature-length film, a box office success called *¡Ay, Jalisco, no te rajes!* (Don't Give Up, Jalisco!). Directed by Joselito Rodríguez, Negrete was, in Alejandro Galindos's words, the most faithful embodiment of the Mexican ideal. He was "tall, dark complexioned, proud, romantic, pistol packing, and willing to sing of sorrow as well as joy."[7] Negrete was a favorite of the Mexican people as well as of the Ávila Camacho administration.

In 1944 he joined his friend Mario Moreno in leading a faction of the actors union away from the left-leaning leadership of Enrique Solis and toward more strongly pro-Ávila Camacho positions.[8] In 1944 all film workers, from top actors to candy vendors in theater lobbies, were represented by the Sindicato de Trabajadores de la Industria Cinematográfia (STIC). Actors were in a group called Section Two of STIC, along with technicians and lesser-skilled studio employees such as carpenters. Negrete and Moreno at first wanted to form a section only for actors. They were supported by the National Committee of the CTM headed by Fidel Velázquez. The rest of the union then went on strike, and all filming was halted in April 1944. The threat of a forced takeover by STIC was met by an equally militant response led by Negrete, Moreno, Arturo de Córdova, and other actors who were armed.[9] In September 1945 Ávila Camacho stepped in and settled the dispute by issuing an executive order that created two unions. Two smaller unions could more easily be directed, which worked in the interest of the state. STIC would oversee distribution, production, and exhibition of short films and newsreels, while the new union, Sindicato de Trabajadores de la Produccion Cinematográfica (STPC), would make full-length films.

After the strike, Moreno, in the role of Cantinflas, remained a top box-office personality and never lost his appeal to either the ordinary person in the street or to the state. If Moreno was the appealing, everyman image the state sought to encourage, Negrete was the compelling, heroic image the state sorely needed. As *el gran charro cantor* (the great gentleman cowboy singer), he conveyed a nationalist demeanor as well as traditional virtue and charm, making him the romantic dream of Mexican women of every class. As the national image of the Mexican male, strong and courageous, Negrete embodied *machismo*. According to Luis Buñuel, Negrete was "a real Mexican charro who sang the blessing before every meal and never appeared without his groom."[10]

Movies came to the village of San José de Gracia in 1944 and were shown twice a week in a four-hundred-seat theater built by a local businessman. According to Luis Gonzáles, the local priests forbade attendance and told their parishioners that movies were schools for immorality, but gradually the people began to disobey. Gonzáles says that whenever the movie house showed films featuring singing charros like Negrete, stories about nightclubs, or comedians like Cantinflas, the house was packed for every feature. He adds that war films and Westerns in English were also very popular and that people especially enjoyed the advertisement that preceded the features. According to Gonzáles, this experience gave them access to "an imaginary other world."[11]

The great popularity of film personalities who represented the image of the nation pleased the state, and favored stars and production companies received generous financial backing.[12] Another popular star was Pedro Armendáriz. Along with Dolores del Río, Armendáriz made two important films in 1943, both directed by Emilio "El Indio" Fernández, who was also an actor of great popularity. *Flor Silvestre* and *María Candelaria* are considered two of the best films ever made in Mexico. *María Candelaria* won international acclaim at Cannes in 1946.[13] The film is a strong affirmation of the dignity and beauty of Indian life in Mexico. Although the story is tragic and somewhat outlandish, the style and grace of the direction, the natural beauty of the photography, and the honesty and emotional power of the acting make it a noteworthy film. The film calls out with the tenderness of an *alabado*, a hymn sung by workers entering and leaving a field,[14] for Indians to see themselves as a valuable segment of the national community. Fernández found backing for these two films from Films Mundiales and its president Agustín Fink. Fink and his company were among nine small production companies that were supported by the state through Banco Cinematográfico. Established by Ávila Camacho in 1942, the Banco Cinematográfico was supported by state agencies like the Banco de México and Nacional Financiera, which held 10 percent of its stock.[15] The largest of the nine was Grovas, which produced eight films in 1942.[16] Most of these films, while not overtly propagandistic, were subtle affirmations of nationhood or gentle reminders of the advantages of national unity.

In 1943 Films Mundiales produced Julio Bracho's film noir classic *Distinto amanecer* (Distinctive Dawning), starring Armendáriz and Andrea Palma. Armendáriz plays an honest labor leader who comes into conflict with a regional cacique after discovering that the corrupt governor had been taking bribes from a foreign, probably German, power. While hiding from several hired killers, Armendáriz seeks safety in the symbolic sanctuary of newfound Mexican modernity, a movie theater. In the darkened movie house he encounters another symbol of the new modernity, a sophisticated, stylish Mexican woman named Julieta, played by Palma. They discover that they had once known and loved each other years before while both were university students. Julieta

helps Armendáriz to escape, and together with her husband Ignacio, who had also been a friend in the old days, they attempt to
take possession of some material evidence that will expose the corruption in the regional government offices.

The film has two interrelated plots, both reflecting the dramatic changes in Mexican culture. In the main plot, three individuals, in the course of a single night, act with existential courage to
oppose the traditional, corrupt forces of Mexican regionalism and
disunity. Julieta, playing the role of a strong, modern, idealistic
although somewhat disillusioned Mexican woman, is forced to kill
one of the hired gangsters. In this persona, she becomes the modernized version of the Revolutionary *soldadera*, wearing a magnificent evening gown instead of a *manton*. In the second plot, a more
intimate and complex set of conflicts among three old friends is
explored. Julieta must choose between her husband and her former lover. *Distinto amanecer* was very popular with audiences
throughout Mexico. Its spare, film noir feeling captured the urban
sophistication of a changing culture while reflecting both traditional Revolutionary values and the pragmatic nationalist values of
the Ávila Camacho era.

Art, popular or learned, rarely flourishes in an atmosphere of
long-term violence and disorder. When artists emerge from the
chaos of war and revolution, they must seek out places of quiet and
safety in order to work. Manuel Ávila Camacho brought both quies-
cence and unity to Mexico. Using the Second World War as a window of opportunity, he turned the nation outward to the task of
defeating an international threat to Mexican sovereignty. Looking
inward, he promoted the idea of mass culture, an essentially modern
concept. All the while, avilacamachismo permitted some dissent in
order to allow a significant modicum of authentic and free expression. In this regard it differed from the totalitarianism of Spain,
Germany, Italy, or the Soviet Union. There was no direct censorship
of scripts. Clearly, the entire system rested on the economic incentives provided both directly and indirectly by the state. Thus it
rejected overt repression, building instead on the momentum of a

nation coalescing around personalities and creative minds. This was a state-directed popular culture, youthful, uncritical, less obsessed with the past, and encouraged to be "at home" with radio, popular music, dance, film, technology, industrialization, and internationalism.

In supporting films like *Distinto amanecer, Flor Silvestre,* and *María Candelaria*, the state exercised a formative and directive authority in the creation of national culture. By virtue of increased levels of investment of money in the creation of popular culture, the state determined and defined desired patterns in national opinion and attitude. The Mexican state in 1940, after thirty years of conflict, saw clearly the need to assert its authority in the direction of the national culture. Serious opposition had been destroyed for the most part, and the party of their president firmly controlled the state. National and regional politics had been synchronized, and according to Luis Gonzáles, the creation of a truly unified national culture was under way. It is significant that when Gonzáles lists in *San José de Gracia* what he considers to be the five fundamental goals of avilacamachismo, he puts as the first goal, "national unity."[17]

It should be noted, however, that just as Hollywood has never accurately reflected the totality and complexity of culture in the United States, so the Mexican film industry has never defined reality in Mexico. It is also true that Hollywood, without question, has played a role in the creation of America's self image and national identity. The evidence indicates that the goal of the state under Ávila Camacho was to create a similar role for the Mexican film industry. The financial interests of the state helped shape a new mythos for Mexico as the nation saw itself in its films. At the same time, the state also wanted to know how Mexico and Mexicans were viewed in foreign films.

When American filmmakers switched from silent to talking films in the late 1920s, they failed to enlist the talents of internationally famous silent film stars who spoke Spanish, such as Lupe Vélez, Dolores del Río, or Gilbert Roland. This had repercussions in Mexico. Hollywood soon lost a part of its market as the generally racist, stereotypical treatment of Mexican characters in Hollywood movies became unacceptable to Mexican movie audiences.[18]

American historians who have studied the image of Mexico and Mexicans in the literature, and later in films produced in the United States, have uncovered an ongoing use of stereotypes that Mexican film audiences found offensive. Cecil Robinson in *With the Ears of Strangers: The Mexican American Literature* (1963) and later in *Mexico and the Hispanic Southwest in American Literature* (1977) highlighted the racist nature of these stereotypes by looking in great detail at the physical characteristics of almost every Mexican personage to appear anywhere in American literature. Later, using Robinson's work as a point of departure, Arthur Petit and Dennis Showalter demonstrated in *Images of Mexican Americans in Fiction and Film* (1980) that, save for a time in the 1940s, if a Mexican appears in an American film, it is almost always within the bounds of a stereotypical image that does not allow for a full range of human characteristics or traits. This same theme is explored in Allen Woll's book *The Latin American Image in American Film* (1980). The roots of this racism are explored by Arnaldo De León in *They Call Them Greasers: Anglo Attitudes toward Mexicans in Texas, 1821–1900* (1980). The title reflects a long series of silent films that used the word "greasers" to refer to Mexicans. Film historians Petit, Showalter, and Woll clearly agree with Robinson, De León, and most of the historians and sociologists of the borderlands region beginning with Carey McWilliams in *North from Mexico* (1941), that, starting with the prevailing attitudes of the early American republic, a warped and excessively negative view of Mexicans predominated in North American literature and film.

Carl J. Mora argues in *Mexican Cinema* (1982) that it was in the administration of Ávila Camacho that very important changes took place both in Mexican film and in the American treatment of Mexicans. This important era in Mexican filmmaking began when a series of wartime problems in America and Argentina allowed Mexico to develop a strong national film industry. Clearly, the

Mexican audiences wanted to see films about Mexico and come away with positive feelings about themselves and their nation. Since this was also one of the goals of the state, Mexican films from 1940 to 1946 became more popular in Mexico than American films. Hollywood, seeing the loss of the Mexican market and not wanting the loss to become permanent, began to change.

Film critic Bosley Crowther wrote in the *New York Times* in 1941 that Hollywood was embarking on a campaign to "woo Latin America."[19] In response to the need for propaganda to counter German efforts in Mexico and, later, in response to criticism of American films with negative depictions of Mexicans and Mexico, the United States government created in October 1940 the Office of the Coordinator for Inter-American Affairs (CIAA) under the leadership of Nelson Rockefeller. CIAA had as its first director John Jay Whitney, vice president of the New York Museum of Modern Art and director of the museum's film library, the "largest film repository in the United States."[20] Whitney was determined to change the negative Mexican reaction to American films about Latin America by changing the content and quality of the films. The last attempt by American filmmakers in the decade, the 1939 Warner Brothers release *Juarez*, had somehow demonstrated everything that the Mexican audiences disliked about American films on Mexican subject matter. One critic called it "a commercial proposition made for fools and for those who have no love for Mexico."[21] The general reaction of the press in Mexico City was that the film was naive.[22]

The failure of American films to make money in Mexico captured the interest of the major Hollywood studios because a significant part of their income came from the Latin American market. For example, United Artists received 34 percent of foreign income from Latin America in 1940. While Argentina was the strongest market, Mexico was traditionally one of the weakest.[23] Whitney convinced the United States Interior Department to suggest to Hollywood producers that "Mexicans should not be portrayed as villainous, ridiculous, or poverty stricken."[24] Whitney's organization came to have great influence with the Ávila Camacho administration and tried to respond to the demand in Mexico for a more positive interpretation of Mexico and Mexicans in American films.[25] This was no easy task in a nation where a Gallup poll in 1942 ranked Mexicans sixteenth in a group of twenty nations whom Americans "respected." The Japanese ranked seventeenth and the Germans seventh![26]

Despite the obvious prejudices of most Americans regarding Mexico, Hollywood was lured by the prospect of growing markets. Encouraged by Whitney and the CIAA, Hollywood discovered Latin American themes in a new way. By early 1943 the American film industry had produced thirty films with Latin American themes, some featuring the biggest names in Hollywood, and had announced the production of another twenty-five.[27] With the dramatic decline in European markets during the war years, it is clear that money was at the heart of the American interest in Latin America. It is also clear that Hollywood was enjoying a genuine interest in all things "south of the border." As a location, Brazil topped the list of Hollywood films with Mexico following just behind. Music featured prominently in many of these films, and one, *Song of Mexico*, produced by MGM in 1945, was even bilingual.[28] In *Mexicana*, also produced in 1945, American star Constance Moore shared the screen with Mexican star Tito Guízar.

These films, which were advertised in Mexican newspapers, found an audience in Mexico especially among the young, and young women in particular, who were pleased that Mexican music and fashions were receiving attention in the United States.[29] Paramount teamed Dorothy Lamour with former Mexican radio star Arturo de Córdova in *Masquerade in Mexico* in 1945, and MGM produced a colorful and well received musical called *Holiday in Mexico* in 1946. The film starred José Iturbi and a young American star, Jane Powell, who became a sensation among young people all over Mexico.[30] Directed by Joe Pasternak, *Holiday in Mexico* received much praise in Mexico for its portrayal of Mexico as a nation of high culture and learned people, and not just a quaint place for tourists to see the folkloric arts.[31] The films that received the most positive response in Mexico, however, were those produced by the successful relationship of CIAA and the Walt Disney studios.

Whitney, Walt Disney, several of his leading associates, and several executives with CIAA toured Latin America in the summer of 1941 to listen to what people wanted to see in films about the region.[32] The short, colorful film that resulted was released in Spanish-speaking countries in August 1942 and was an instant blockbuster. Called *Saludos Amigos*, it was a technicolor combination of animation and live action. In 1943 RKO, Disney, and CIAA released *Los Tres Caballeros*, again a combination of live action and animation. The film starred Carmen Miranda and featured Donald Duck as an American involved in a subtle but telling conflict with a cocky and confident Mexican duck named Panchito. In this charming film, Donald is outwitted repeatedly by his Mexican cousin, to the delight of José Carioca, the Brazilian bird, but more to the point, to the delight of audiences all over Mexico. *Los Tres Caballeros* set records in ticket sales in Mexico City, grossing more than $120,000 in eight weeks.[33] Newspapers featured large advertisements, and nearly everyone talked about the film. In 1943 President Ávila Camacho bestowed his country's highest award, the Aztec Eagle, on the CIAA for its work in developing a more positive view of Mexico in the United States. Also honored were Louis B. Mayer and Walt Disney. Speaking for President Ávila Camacho, and reflecting his thinking that film and radio penetrate to the heart of the masses, Foreign Relations Secretary Ezequiel Padilla said that film was a medium that could penetrate "directamente en el corazon de las masas."[34] Disney alone made twenty short educational propaganda features that were well received in Mexico. These included films on the treatment of malaria, the cultivation of corn, and hemispheric defense. Several were designed to give Mexico a look at itself as seen by Americans. Ávila Camacho was pleased by *México pintoresco* (Picturesque Mexico), *Politica mexicana en desfile* (Mexican Politics on Parade), *El camino a Monterrey,* and *México exotico.*

In addition, CIAA provided the Mexican film industry with assistance in all areas of production. Expert cameramen Alexander Phillips and Rush Fisher trained individuals and crews in technical areas, and the sound expert Howard Randall trained sound crews at the Mexican studios CLASA and AZTECA.[35] This technical assistance, teamed with large-scale state financing, adequate supplies of raw film stock from the United States, and a supply of good directors, actors, technicians, and producers, including one of Latin America's first women producers, Diana Somerville, allowed Mexico to develop a film industry of great influence at home and abroad. Perhaps the outstanding cinematographer of the era (and later eras) was Gabriel Figueroa, whose use of light was unique and essentially Mexican.[36]

Looking at the film industries of Argentina and Mexico between 1940 and 1945, one sees a reversal of fortune. José Luis Ortiz Garza points out that in 1940 Argentina produced twice as many films as Mexico. A short four years later, in 1944, Mexico was producing four times as many films per year as Argentina. By 1943 Mexican films were becoming as popular abroad as they were at home. That year fifty-nine feature-length Mexican films were released in Venezuela. Cantinflas was a hit that year in Argentina in *Los tres mosqueteros*, and the religious film *Jesús de Nazaret* had been booked into three hundred Argentine theaters. Jorge Negrete was the biggest star in Argentina as well as the rest of Latin America. These films, supported directly by the Mexican state, exported images and national cultural values that, as we have seen, were strongly connected to the ideals of avilacamachismo.[37] By 1943 Mexican films were becoming so good that *Variety* suggested they be thought of as "arty" replacements for French films, unavailable because of the war. Nearly two hundred American theaters took the suggestion and showed Mexican films like *María Candelaria* and *Distinto amanecer* with English subtitles.[38] While serious shortages of film and equipment began to appear in Hollywood, American and Mexican trade papers noted the generous policy of Washington and the support of CIAA that made the best of equipment and plenty of film stock available to favored Mexican film companies.[39]

The image of Mexico in the United States was important to Ávila Camacho because he knew that a positive national self-image in Mexico would be impossible without fundamental changes in American attitudes toward Mexico. On a number of occasions Ávila Camacho himself made symbolic gestures to the other side of the border that were widely reported on radio broadcasts and published in newspapers in both nations. These gestures affirmed the new spirit of cooperation and mutual esteem between the two Allied neighbors. An editorial in the *El Paso Times* strongly praised Ávila Camacho as a friend of the United States and a man who understood and supported the importance of a nation's culture.[40] On 15 January 1945 the American consul general in Juárez, William P. Blocker, reported to the secretary of state in Washington that President Ávila Camacho not only supported culture in Mexico, but also sponsored it in the United States by providing sixty new uniforms for the Bowie High School band in El Paso.[41]

Under Ávila Camacho, the state used film as a formative influence in the reorientation of Mexican culture along lines that were supportive of avilacamachista goals. Avilacamachismo strengthened the president's power while undercutting the popular base of traditional regionalism both within party and beyond. Right- and left-wing elements in the nation's life—as well as the army, which Ávila Camacho dropped as a sector of the party—and the church were all reduced in power as avilacamachismo became the literal heart of the system. This could not have taken place without the use of film by the state to influence and direct culture.[42]

CHAPTER SIX

Art and
Architecture

Jean Charlot believed that painting in Mexico was different from
painting in Europe. The "Amerindian cultural subsoil," as he
called it—the planting of the cross in the new world a thousand
years after it arrived in Europe, the bivalent racial structure, and
the potential for violence—all worked to create a unique atmosphere for art in Mexico.[1] Yet in spite of, or because of, the rich
mixture that is Mexico, art has been one of the most dynamic
aspects of its culture. To understand how avilacamachismo related
to Mexican art between 1940 and 1946, we must look at the development of art in Mexico in the postrevolutionary period.

Bertram Wolfe suggests that to understand the postrevolutionary art world one must begin, as we have so often here, with José
Vasconcelos. Wolfe asserts that Vasconcelos, while serving as education secretary under Obregón, believed that he could "forge a
fatherland" (forjando patria) by placing culture at the heart of
political structure. He planned to do this, as we have seen, by planning publications, fomenting popular arts, teaching art in public

places, warring on illiteracy, teaching trades, building schools, opening libraries, and supporting classical music. In this process, Wolfe
observes, "within a few years almost every painter in Mexico was on
the payroll of SEP."[2] After the Revolution artists emerged as a sin-
gularly important group of influential national personalities. Beginning in the early 1920s muralists were paid by the state to decorate
the walls of schools, railroad stations, post offices, and every type of
public building. These large and spectacular paintings of egg tem-
pera on wet lime plaster, a complicated and ancient process, created
a worldwide sensation. Colorful and nationalistic paintings were
executed by individuals who became the most famous painters in
the world in their day. Among the early muralists were José
Clemente Orozco, Diego Rivera, Roberto Montenegro, Fernando
Leal, Xavier Guerrero, Fermín Revueltas and Ramón Alva de la
Canal. Later David Alfaro Siqueiros and Rufino Tamayo joined the
distinguished list. The number of artists hired on these projects was
unprecedented, and their murals were seen by the state as a visual
language useful in forging a new national consciousness.

The cultural mysticism-cum-idealism of Vasconcelos provided
the philosophical foundation for the early mural movement. Vasconcelos saw Mexico as inspiration for a war-exhausted world as
she created a race of painters and poets, all the while mixing the
blood lines of the world into what he called "the cosmic race."[3]
Soon, however, the artists began to espouse individual ideas of
their own. In 1922 they organized the Union of Technical Workers, Painters, and Sculptors, and many members wanted to tie
their work to international socialism. When repressive government returned to Mexico under Calles, the most outspoken artists,
including Leal, Alva de la Canal, and Revueltas, were no longer
given commissions by the state. Siqueiros worked in political
movements and painted little during this period. Others, including
Guerrero, Rivera, Kahlo, and Orozco, left the country. This was a
difficult, bitter period, especially for Vasconcelos. According to
Lucienne Bloch, Rivera and Kahlo were not surprised by the
repression. Bloch suggested that they were "far too realistic" about
government in Mexico to be greatly surprised by anything.[4]

In 1934, when Cárdenas came to power, the mural movement came back to life, but at this point the strong personalities of the painters led to internecine struggles over political issues and over the direction of art in Mexico. Groups were formed around Rivera on one hand and Siqueiros on the other. Something of a compromise was struck in the form of a general self-criticism issued by all parties renouncing any early murals that might have served the demagogic interests of the Mexican government more than the interests of the working class or the campesinos.[5] By 1940, despite the work of LEAR (Liga de Escritores y Artistas Revolucionarios), a union led by Leopoldo Méndez, Pablo O'Higgins, and others to unite antifascist artists and intellectuals, unity in the Mexican community of artists was a thing of the past, and many of the artists carried guns to the meetings.[6]

Mexican art during the administration of Ávila Camacho was thus divided into camps resulting from personality conflicts, political ideology, old-fashioned Mexican xenophobia, nationalism versus internationalism, the war, the state's role in financing art, and the introduction of new ideas about art by European refugees.[7] These conflicts weakened the art community. In addition, the dangerous world situation, the dramatic and rapid movement in Mexico toward industrialization,[8] the improved relations with the United States, the rise of new elements in popular culture, and the fact that the major artists were growing older, reinforced the atmosphere in which Mexican artists looked to the state for support. In response, the avilacamachista state willingly provided regular income, stability, recognition, peace of mind, and protection to a large and active community of artists. Many of the artists had political views contrary to those of the state, but as already seen, cultural avilacamachismo was tolerant as well as generous because it served the government's purposes to be so.[9]

The state was liberal with commission and salaried positions for artists it favored. During the Ávila Camacho years, Orozco, for example, painted murals on the National Supreme Court Building (1941)[10] and on the Church of the Hospital of Jesus (1942–1944), painted canvases, wrote several ballets, and designed sets for them

(1943–1945). In the remarkably busy year of 1940, he even found time to write a pamphlet for his exhibition at the Museum of Modern Art in New York City.[11] Between 21 June and 30 June 1940 he painted a six-panel portable mural for the MOMA exhibition in New York. In these six murals Orozco attacked the marriage of technology and war and the resulting birth of mass destruction. The work was hailed as a "vivid, accurate report of the fear and spiritual state of mankind."[12] Orozco's busy creative life, with financial support from the public and private sectors, exemplified the artist supported by the culture-state philosophy of avilacamachismo. Orozco was, in fact, more independent than most.

In 1940, about the time he began an affair with Mexican ballet star Gloria Campobello, and nine years before he died, Orozco created a paneled mural in the Gabino Ortiz Library in Jiquilpan, Michoacán, the birthplace of Lázaro Cárdenas. In his pocket Orozco had a commission to go to New York and paint a mural for the Museum of Modern Art, but first he had a Mexican government commission to endow a mural on the walls of a building that had once been a small church and was now designated a community library, a gift from President Cárdenas.[13] Orozco had accepted the challenge of binding the bare lunettes and apse of the old building into a mural that would be his commentary on the nation as it entered a new decade and the new administration of Manuel Ávila Camacho. It would be a statement about confusion and order in a time of change.

Today, as one leaves the bright Mexican sunlight and enters the cool darkness of the building, one sees a powerful statement of the nation in 1940. The painting is divided into two parts. One is the memory of a bloody and cruel Revolution just passed; the other, the anticipation of an uncertain but potentially bright future. Indeed, the memorial portion of the work depicts the Revolution stripped of idealism, reduced to brutality and anarchy. One feels death and the evils of militarism in the stark, primary black and red slashes and the raw ugliness of the masses. As Orozco brings the painting to 1940, however, it changes. In the panel entitled "Allegory of

Mexican Nationalism" he returns to color, movement, definition, and symbolism to create an expectant, interrogative mood. Although the work is often seen as a universal statement, reaching beyond the provincial as all great art must, one cannot but feel that Orozco created this work to say that in 1940 Mexico was entering a new era. Orozco seems to raise questions about the survival of the Mexican soul in this age of dictators, technology, and warfare.

Near the center of the mural one finds the traditional symbol of the Mexican eagle and snake, but the eagle is being crushed by the snake. Here is Mexico, corrupt, disconnected, and discontented, crushing itself. Below and to the left of the struggle, one sees a serious, almost elegant female figure astride a fierce and massive tiger. Mexico—beautiful, dignified Mexico—is riding a tiger. Nearby, another panel holds a rumpled angel, perhaps the last vestige of the innocent soul of the people, looking disoriented beneath a banner of the national colors. It was 1940, and Orozco portrayed his culture searching for itself among the internal and external dangers of the new and dangerous era. Standing in the long Mexican mural tradition, Orozco painted what he felt in his heart.

The culture-state philosophy of avilacamachismo was multiform in nature. Although it was generally directed by SEP, it also functioned in other ways. By 1941 art dealer Inéz Amor served as a connection between avilacamachismo and the art world. In her autobiographical essays she recalls a story that may serve as a metaphor for the relationship of dependency between the artists and the state. In the second year of his term, Ávila Camacho telephoned Amor's secretary, Luz Velázquez, and asked her to arrange a time when he could meet with Amor and some of the artists whose work she sold. Tamayo and Siqueiros were out of the country, but Amor, delighted by the request from "don Manuel," arranged a special showing of works by Rivera, Orozco, Ruiz, Montenegro, Covarrubias, Kahlo, Izquierdo, and O'Gorman. At seven o'clock, as the Ávila Camacho group arrived to begin the tour, a fuse caused the lights to go out. There was no panic, but Amor's associate, Alberto Misrachi, kept shouting, "Luz, la luz!"

(Light, the light!).[14] Nothing could be seen until an electrician
came to repair the system. Meanwhile, Amor formed a procession
with herself and the president in front, followed by Rivera, Orozco
and others. Going from room to room, Ávila Camacho asked
questions, while the two famous artists competed for his attention.
In the end, it turned into a great party, with the president cracking
jokes and taking notes.[15]

The role of Inéz Amor in Mexican art in the 1940s was that of
broker, dealer, and owner of important neutral ground. In 1940,
working directly for the state, Amor helped organize the largest
exhibition of Mexican art that had ever been mounted in the
United States, the New York Museum of Modern Art's *Twenty
Centuries of Mexican Art*. That same year she was also involved in
André Breton's exhibition of surrealism, an event that brought
officials of the state and artists together when it opened in Mexico
City on the night of 17 February 1940.[16]

With her sister Guadalupe, Amor opened a small gallery on
Argentina Street in 1934. By the advent of Ávila Camacho the
gallery had moved to larger quarters on Milan Street, and she was
displaying and selling works primarily by Mexican painters. In
addition, as the refugee community grew in Mexico City, she
became a dealer for many European-born artists who came to
Mexico seeking a safe haven.[17] It is not surprising, then, that when
Ávila Camacho wanted to meet the great artists of his nation, he
turned to "Inesita."[18] Selden Rodman recalls that when he wanted
to meet a painter or see a work of art, the only easy way was to call
Amor, who quickly made the arrangements.[19] She was especially
close to Siqueiros, with whom she shared a childhood friendship
in Chihuahua.[20] Much of the artistic conflict was among the four
major muralists: Rivera, Orozco, Siqueiros, and Tamayo.

In the 1930s and 1940s, Siqueiros and Rivera created a running
debate on the nature of revolutionary art. Anger and discord
among Mexican artists followed. Siqueiros believed that by 1940
the fresco medium was passé. He wrote that continuing to paint in
the folkloristic style of the past was like "playing revolutionary

songs on the organ."[21] For awhile in the 1930s, he even abandoned murals and the state commissions that went with them. Unlike Rivera—whom Rodman believes eventually pushed his personal concept of the revolutionary mural as far as it could go and, after 1943, allowed his work to become a parody of itself—Siqueiros continued to search for new ways of painting murals.[22] He began to experiment with new paint media, three-dimensional forms, synthetic lacquers that gave new power to his canvas works, and lithographs. He traveled to Spain, where he was commissioned as an officer in the Republican Army, and when he returned to Mexico in 1938, he reclaimed his role as a leading muralist while using only fresh materials and ideas.

In his "Trial of Fascism," painted on the wall of the Electrical Workers Union in Mexico City, he featured a demagogue, a vicious animal-man standing before a radio microphone above an endless sea of machine-like humanity. The design, texture, chemistry, and movement of the mural is a dramatic departure from what had gone before. It was the beginning of his "neo-realism." Unfortunately, by the end of 1940 Siqueiros was again in exile, having played a role in the first armed attempt on the life of Leon Trotsky. Amor kept his works selling briskly, while Siqueiros, with the help of Pablo Neruda, moved to Chile.

In 1944 he returned quietly to Mexico, lived on his income from Amor's gallery for awhile, and then received a major commission from the Ávila Camacho administration to paint one of his most powerful murals, "The New Democracy," in the Díaz-era performing arts center, Bellas Artes. His vision of a world suffering from the madness of fascism dovetailed well into the national identity, national unity, and war themes of avilacamachismo, even if Siqueiros's political ideology did not. After his return, he continued to paint in the "neo-realism" of the mural at the Electrical Union Hall, although his Ávila Camacho-era murals suffer somewhat from his constant experimentation with new paints.

In 1944 he painted a bold mural called "Cuahtemoc against the Myth" on a concave surface joined to a plane surface and the ceiling.

It was painted with materials that Siqueiros considered "industrial" in the sense that workers might also use them in their jobs. Rufino Tamayo, the youngest of the four major muralists, joined the confusion by attacking Siqueiros's use of new materials. Tamayo said that there was nothing revolutionary about using new paint in the same way as the old oil paint, especially when it meant a sacrifice of the traditional Mexican colors used in popular culture since pre-Columbian times. Tamayo, who lived in New York during most of the Ávila Camacho period, was highly critical of the three other major figures in the Mexican mural school during these years. His chief criticism of Rivera was that he painted Mexican objects in a style that was essentially French or Italian. This enraged the followers of Rivera. Conversely, he saw himself as executing his works in a universalist theme but with an underlying nationalist spirit.[23] Oddly, he was the most financially independent of the muralists, yet the most overtly progovernment. The jealousy and rivalry among the great artists was partly responsible for the atmosphere of discord in the Mexican art world.[24]

During these years Rivera consciously chose not to change his technique or to react to the world crisis, as had Orozco and Siqueiros. His 1943 murals in the Institute of Cardiology are attractive but indicate a failure of imagination. It has been suggested that his many affairs, his complex relationship with Frida Kahlo, health problems, conservative affection for the past, and the general confusion about the direction of Mexican art might have kept him wed to "universal myth" themes at a time when the world situation called for more than picturesque statements.

During the Ávila Camacho years, other artists were also attempting to maintain a creative edge in the Mexican mural movement amid the aesthetic confusion and were receiving state support to do so. In 1941 Juan O'Gorman received a commission to paint a large mural in the Gertrudis Bocanegra Library at Patzcuaro, a lakeside village in Michoacán not far from Jiquilpan. Artists who were paid commissions by the state continued to work in the time-honored style of the early days, which was favored by avilacamachismo. Alfredo Zalce painted several murals on the walls of schools and in 1945 painted a beautiful mural at the Museum of Morelia. José Chávez Morado painted a mural on the walls of the Hidalgo School in 1945.[25] In the early days of the Ávila Camacho administration, another traditionalist who returned to painting murals after a fifteen-year interruption was Xavier Guerrero.

Guerrero left Mexico, and his lover Tina Modotti, to go to the Soviet Union in the late 1920s. He returned quietly to Mexico during the Cárdenas years but did not paint again until 1939 when the Chauffeurs' Union of Jalisco agreed to raise a fund to decorate their new union hall. This fresco, one of the first in Mexico ever paid for by private subscription, was so well received that in 1941 the state hired Guerrero to go to Chile as an official representative of Mexico to lecture on the technique of wet lime mural painting and to paint two murals as gifts to the Chilean people from Mexico. At the "Mexico" school in the city of Chilan and in Santiago at a recreation center for workers, he executed brilliantly colored murals in the old style.

Why did the avilacamachista state support the return of a communist to the art world? The answer is that it supported art for both ideological and political reasons. The former emanated from individuals within the state, including the president himself, who were influenced by the fusion of politics and aesthetics advocated by Vasconcelos. They believed that high culture, even when it was critical of the state, was central to the culture-state relationship. This is a most important distinction between the cultural avilacamachistas and the political pragmatists. Avilacamachismo was willing to tolerate cultural expression that was critical of the state because it respected and valued the creative act of the artist.

Two areas of art found new support from the state during this period: posters and cartoons. Poster art emerged shortly after Mexico declared war on Germany and Japan in 1942. The Ávila Camacho government issued commissions to individual artists and to artists' cooperatives to create war posters. José Luis Díaz, who was a teenager in Monterrey during the war, remembers these posters everywhere: on walls, in the schools, on buses, even in shops.[26] The Ávila Camacho files in the national archives are filled with them.[27] Some of the most popular and most famous were done by the Taller de Gráfico Popular (workshop of popular graphic art), whose membership included Leopoldo Méndez, Alfredo Zalce, Pablo O'Higgins, and Ángel Bracho. Another group producing posters was the Artistas Libres de México. Membership in this professional group included José Chávez Morado, Miguel Covarrubias, Gabriel Fernández Ledesma, and Julio Prieto.

The posters are colorful and done in what has been labeled the "heroic style" of propaganda posters. Generally the posters carry a simple message that reflects both antifascist sentiment and avilacamachismo. One drawn in 1943 by Santos Balmori features a quote from Adolph Hitler: "Knowledge corrupts the young." Printmaker Chávez Morado created posters in the style of those of the Mexican Revolution. One pictures an Indian woman holding a baby and Mexican flag. It reads, "Mexican women! We need your patriotism. Work and serve in industry, in the fields, in your homes and when you are called, don't abandon liberty!" One of the most striking is by Julio Prieto. A handsome teenager with strong Indian features dominates four smaller photographs showing Mexican young people of exactly the age to which the new national popular culture was designed to appeal. The message of the poster reads, "Thus you also fight for your country!" The poster that perhaps most clearly states the goals of avilacamachismo is also by Prieto. A shovel, Springfield rifle, book, and sledgehammer are tied together with a striking red, white, and green banner proclaiming "unity."

Newspaper accounts indicate that contests were held asking students to create posters of their own, and a major exhibition was held in 1944 in Bellas Artes of the best posters. The Spanish refugee artist José Renau was honored for his work, and many refugee artists were employed, with help from the state, in the publication of propaganda materials directed at their native lands. *Alemania Libre* was filled with dramatic artwork and circulated all over Latin America. In the posters produced by Mexican artists, the people were asked to unite behind the state in a common effort to defeat an external enemy.[28]

In the magnification of popular culture, Mexican cartoon art sponsored by the state is historically the most significant yet least studied art form. In pre-Columbian Mexico, a highly respected caste of Mayan, Mixtec, and Aztec artists known as the *"tlacuilos"* preserved in picture writing the history, religion, mythology, and customs of their peoples. On bark paper or buckskin, they painted beautiful, highly stylized pictographic stories using inks made of the black oily soot of pine trees and colored with stains made from vegetables and animal fat. The codices made by these ancient Mexican artists are today among the most important artifacts owned by the major Mexican museums. The Mexican artists who brought the pictographic style back to life in this century called themselves El Circulo de Tlacuilos de México as a tribute to the ancient ones. During the Ávila Camacho years, there were many cartoon magazines in Mexico, including the only three daily cartoon magazines in the world: *Chamaco Chico* (with a daily circulation in 1944 of nearly one-half million), *Pepin,* and *Pinocho.* In fact, in 1944 the combined circulation of these three and the other Mexican cartoon magazines was greater than the combined circulation of the nation's newspapers. The important daily newspaper *Novedades,* as well as a Saturday afternoon paper published by *Novedades* called *PM,* were founded with profits from *Chamaco Chico.*[29]

Mexican cartoon art of the Ávila Camacho period, like filmmaking in Mexico in this period, is referred to as the "golden age" of cartoon art.[30] SEP was closely connected to the comic magazine industry during this period. Guillermo Cardoso is an example of the many young artists who got their start in the magazine art department of SEP, where they were employed to draw comic magazines with themes important to the state. Several of these young artists, including Jorge Carreño, studied at the state-run school La Esmerelda and later became political cartoonists or caricature artists for major newspapers or magazines. Carreño became well known for his work with *Siempre*.[31] Why were these cartoons so popular and so important? First, many of the story lines were not designed to be comic at all but popular romance or adventure. Second, most of those who bought the daily or weekly magazines were people under fifty. Third, the magazines were "permissive" in their story line in much the same way as the new popular radio music.[32] The seduction and romance scenes seem endless to the contemporary American reader, but some of their natural humor may be simply lost in the passage of time and the difference of cultures. And last, and most important for the state, the artists often printed letters from readers at the conclusion of the daily or weekly episode. Some readers were even paid if they sent in good ideas. One very popular comic was called *Adiós al colegio* (Goodbye to School) and featured drawings illustrating letters written to contact old school friends and revive memories. The readers of these magazines, which had as their themes highly Mexicanized experiences of love, adventure, and humor and still exist in various forms in Mexico today, were able to experience feelings of connectedness in much the same way the teenager Catalina felt connected to the radio songs in Ángeles Mastretta's novel of Mexico in the 1940s, *Arráncame la vida* (Take My Life).

In 1945, the romance theme of the cartoons was taken to radio and the audience was again asked to get involved. Broadcast on XEW, *Colegio de amor* became the most popular program in the nation. Young men were asked to come forward and propose marriage to their girls, or husbands to explain why they left for cigarettes four years ago and never returned. Songs from all over the country were sung; people shared regional customs and received approval and validation. Personal problems were solved. On one program a young woman came on the air to beg her boyfriend to remember to put a return address on his letters. Having gone into the army, he had written dozens of letters that she could not answer. His last letter had said that since she had not answered him, it was all over. Across the Mexican night, like the character in the romance cartoon magazine *Rutas de emoción*, she tearfully begged him to write and put a return address on the letter. While the program was still on the air, he called long distance from Guadalajara. Mexico, so vast, so often disunited, that night, through the magnification of radio and telephone, became a large caring village, weeping as these teenagers publicly reconfirmed their love.[33] Bringing together the powers of print and radio to convey cultural unity, Mexico became a village writ large.

The popularity of the cartoon magazines was the result of the efforts to eliminate illiteracy that dated back to the first educational programs of José Vasconcelos. By the late 1930s, the rise in literacy in the general public had outstripped the availability of books. In addition, the reading proficiency level of the enormous numbers of new readers was low. The cartoon magazines cost very little, thanks to SEP, and were therefore available to everyone. They had a simple story line backed up by drawings that illustrated the text, so they were perfect for new readers. They had a national focus and often printed the lyrics to popular songs or gave inside information on the lives of the new stars of popular culture and, during the war, carried the prowar, pro-unity slogans and images of avilaca-machismo. At the bottom of every page were slogans such as "The totalitarians intend to dominate the world despotically; Mexico is on the side of the democracies; to lend one's ear to enemy propaganda is treason."[34] Several of the magazines were interpretations of Mexican history. *El amor de los volcanes* took place in ancient Mexico and had as its setting the mysterious mountains Popocatepetl and Ixtaccihuatl. *El regreso de Rolando el rabioso* took place during the Mexican Independence period. The hero, Rolando, was a young Mexican soldier who, assisted by Pitoloca, an innocent who stuttered, worked to drive out the evil Spaniards.

Reflecting their close relationship with SEP, the magazines also contained a page or two of serious public service information. Several had sections devoted to science or the biographies of famous figures from Mexican history. The magazines published everything they were asked to publish and were seen, just as radio and film were, as a magnification of the new, youth-oriented popular culture. The attitude of SEP was something to the effect that people who have just learned to read are not going to begin with Spinoza. Plans were made for Spinoza to be available just as cheaply and just as conveniently when the people were ready. Luz de Lourdes Solórano points out that having cartoon fictional characters with whom ordinary people could identify was every bit as important as having "great literature." The cartoons gave them the same growth in perspective, an increase in communication skills, an exploration of values, and opportunities for escape.[35] One can add to her list that this was also an experience shared among people in every section of the nation. Young people in Mexico City were discussing the same romances, adventures, sports stories, and propaganda pieces as their peers in Piedras Negras, Merida, and Guadalajara.

Implicit in avilacamachismo was the expectation that Mexico in the postwar years would need to have a "new look" to represent her new role in the world. Another area of new state support, architecture, which brought together art and engineering, supplied the new look. As historian Rafael Loyola Díaz observed, the 1940s were a decade in which a new Mexican architecture came into being, built upon the functionalism of the 1920s:

> New designs, new concepts, new resources and technology replaced the old ideas which had dominated the early post-revolutionary period. This included much of the architecture that had been the standard and was considered modern. This led us into a newer, modern technological style.[36]

Loyola argues that the idea of creating a new, modern, united Mexico, what he calls "*construir al pais*," was made possible by the economic bonanza of World War II and the prosperity after the war.[37] Although much of the actual construction took place after the Ávila Camacho years, the new direction of Mexican architecture took shape as a manifestation of avilacamachismo. Mexico had a long architectural history, but avilacamachismo did not look to the past. Modernity, national unity, international relationships, and the new popular culture all honored the past but also implied the future. Seminal architectural changes occurred during this period in the development of new building materials, new ideas about the use of space, new ideas about the relationship of buildings to the environment, new ideas about the role of profit, and discussions of Mexico as an international leader whose architecture should reflect her new status among nations in the postwar world. The logic of *"costo mínimo y espacio máximo"* (lowest price and greatest space) flowed, according to Loyola, into the logic of *"inversion mínima y ganancia máxima"* (least investment and greatest profit).[38]

Mexico needed a large number of new buildings for schools and hospitals. Architects and medical doctors were brought together in a planning group called El Seminario de Estudios Hospitalarios under the direction of the secretary of public health. Architects included Mario Pani, Carlos Tarditi, Enrique Guerrero, Alonso Mariscal, Raúl Cacho, Antonio Pastrana, Enrique de la Mora, Mauricio Campos, Enrique Yáñez, Enrique del Moral, and José Villagrán. Medical doctors included Pedro Daniel Martínez, Alejandro Aguirre, Bernardo Sepúlveda, Ignacio Mora, and Jesús Loyola. The result of this pioneering work, in which architects listened to the insights, ideas, innovations, and special needs of the medical community, was the construction of a number of well-lighted, functional, and beautifully designed hospitals in the Mexico City area.[39] The most famous of these were the Mexican Institute of Social Security, designed by Enrique Yáñez, the National Cardiological Hospital, designed by José Villagrán, and the Hospital Manuel Gea Gonzáles, also by Villagrán.

The architects for these hospital projects and those that followed in other sections of Mexico were paid by the state and encouraged to explore innovations in style, building materials, and design. Murals decorated the walls of the new hospitals, including the previously mentioned work by Diego Rivera at the National

Cardiological Hospital. The use of open space and natural light made the buildings distinctive. Intelligent and functional style, natural light, and use of steel-reinforced concrete, as well as relatively low construction costs, made these buildings prototypes for hospitals in Mexico and the world in the decade that followed.[40]

In 1944 Jaime Torres Bodet created a similar committee to work in public school construction. School administrators as well as teachers were invited to give ideas to the architects. Membership in the Comite Administrador del Programa Federal de Construcción de Escuelas included Mario Pani, José Luis Cuevas, Enrique Yáñez, and José Villagrán. Model schools built with suggestions from teachers and containing designs that featured better lighting, new uses of glass, concrete, and steel, but with continued use of the mural tradition, included the Escuela Costa Rica designed by Villagrán in 1945, and the National Conservatory of Music designed by Pani in 1946. These buildings were early examples of the designs later associated with the Mexican School of Architecture that would receive, in the late 1940s and early 1950s, worldwide recognition for their innovation and modernity.

Under the leadership of Torres Bodet, schools were designed and built all over Mexico in the final years of the Ávila Camacho era. One of the most famous is the school named for Squadron 201, the Mexican air force squadron that fought the Japanese in the Pacific. Built in the village of Tepoztlán, the school was opened in 1945 with President Ávila Camacho and his entire cabinet present. *La hora nacional* featured the event on its weekly program. Designed by Yáñez, the school was bright, large, modern, and functional.

The American anthropologist Oscar Lewis was living in Tepoztlán in 1944 while the school was being built, preparing to write his famous study of the village. Lewis noted the school's influence in making the village children aware of the larger world and of their national identity. Tepoztlán, studied by Robert Redfield in 1926 in his pioneering work *Tepoztlán, A Mexican Village*, was still isolated when studied by Lewis in 1944.[41] Lewis explained that the changes in Tepoztlán were accelerated during the Ávila Camacho years and that radio, an occasional film, and the promotion of literacy, art, health, agriculture, sanitation, architecture, and national culture by individuals working for the state were major factors.[42] Lewis saw the school as a center of *mexicanidad*, a place where national holidays were commemorated, children wore the national school uniform, government slogans were seen on the walls, and visiting government doctors gave free medical service to the community.[43]

In 1990, modified and enlarged, the original school design was still visible. It is built of whitewashed concrete and native stone around a large patio, which extends into a large, walled playground. Situated at the base of a mountain, the view from the playground is magnificent. With its flat roof and long, low lines, it has a look that hints presciently of contemporary shopping malls. Along the patio and playground side of the school there is a covered area where the children often have class at tiny tables on fine days. One imagines that this might have been the idea a teacher shared with Yáñez and the other architects in a meeting long ago at SEP. Sylvia Martin, who interviewed the teachers in the school in 1945, found them to be nationalists and idealists who saw their work as "gathering children into the great Mexican family."[44]

A married couple was appointed by SEP to teach at the school during the war years. In addition to their teaching responsibilities, they organized neighborhood meetings of mothers to study health and hygiene, lobbied SEP for a breakfast program in the school, put up war posters, and allowed the first school-sponsored socials where young people danced to the boleros they listened to on the radio. Coca-Cola came to Tepoztlán in 1942.[45]

Here, then, in a village where most of the population spoke Nahuatl, one can see avilacamachismo reaching out to bring isolated areas into national life. Here was a new school named for Mexican war heroes who were flying fighter planes alongside British and American pilots in an international war against the Japanese. Here was a new school designed by Mexican architects pioneering with new materials and new approaches, and who were being noticed by the international community of architects. Here was a new school with new teachers who were nationalists in the image of avilacamachismo, but who were not teaching the divisive "godless socialism" of the recent past. Here was a new school where social dances were allowed and the music and dress were not unlike those of Mexico City youth, illustrating a practical national unity where urban and village youth were responding spontaneously and similarly to an irrepressible popular culture. Here was a new school where the walls were covered with murals and war posters, national holidays were celebrated, and the national flag flew on a flagpole on the playground, a flagpole tall enough to be seen from the village. Here was a new school whose opening was important enough for the president and his staff to attend. Rafael Loyola calls what happened in Mexican architecture during this period "modernización de la sociedad, modernización de la arquitectura," pointing up the parallels between the new architectural style and the modernization of Mexican society.[46] Aspiring to be unified, functional, clean, modern, and internationally respected were goals that could easily be applied to both Mexican architecture and the Mexican state's vision of Mexican culture in 1945.

Much of the new design was expressed in the construction of public buildings such as the previously mentioned hospitals and schools. Equally impressive were the office buildings, such as the headquarters of the Secretariat of Hydraulic Resources built by Mario Pani on Paseo de la Reforma in 1945, and the new post office buildings, museums, public parks, markets, and streets. Some of the most creative work was done to provide new housing for the growing middle class. The gross national product grew by a steady 6 to 8 percent during the war years, and the need for new housing was acute.[47]

Architecture, like music, reaches many people, and the use of space is a powerful medium of expression. The architecture of the Mexican neighborhoods created during this historical conjunction of need and artistic expression is important for understanding avilacamachismo, and the name most closely associated with this architecture is Luis Barragán.

His genius was to unite the clean, functional lines of the international style with the interiority of things Mexican. Using the memories of his childhood in Mazamitla, Michoacán, Barragán attempted to bring to his work the essence, but not the romanticized style, of the Mexican village. He wanted to re-create the serenity, peace, colors, and muted sounds, such as water and wind, of the Mexican village in the congested and noisy metropolis. He built his homes on an ancient lava bed in southern Mexico City called El Pedregal, and used technology to gently mold and shape the environment, not to overwhelm or destroy it. Just as the architects of the new hospitals and schools learned from teachers and doctors, so Barragán conversed with the terrain of El Pedregal. The state, rejecting the past, had not accepted a number of proposals featuring the handsome but tired cliché of colonial and neo-colonial styles. Instead, it proposed to finance a project reflecting the avilacamachista principles of modernity, unity, and internationalism. It was Luis Barragán's vision that was chosen as the best representation of these.

In his original 1944 plan, Barragán proposed three nature gardens to demonstrate that what he wanted to build, although new, would work. In 1945 he built the three gardens, joined them with paths cut gently into the lava, and built stone walls to both unite and divide the landscape. Here, in the core of his design, was its modernity and power. High stone walls and spaces that bound together sky, light, deep shade, and water captured anew the eternal character of Mexico. The movement from indoor to outdoor living was subtle and gentle, punctuated with sounds of water dripping, splashing, or falling into fountains, artificial streams, dark stone pools, swimming pools, or the coolness of a water garden. It is not surprising that Barragán, with his use of small natural gardens, walls, natural wood, water, shade, light, clean lines, white walls, and stone, became highly influential in the development of modern architecture around the world.[48]

Today many of the original homes built for the growing middle class of the late war and early postwar era, but soon taken over by the more affluent, still retain the pioneering beauty and modernity of the period in which they were designed. Their materials—natural rock, rough plaster, cement, glass, and natural wood—have generally aged well. The rock gardens, the small, cool patios that capture pieces of the sky, tile floors, earth colors, white walls, flowers, cacti, and variously sized walls remain profoundly modern in our age of the xeriscape, limited water, and ecological sensitivity. Emilio Ambasz praises Barragán for not forgetting that one has to *live* in comfort and dignity in a house, no matter how modern the design. Mokoto Suzuki has observed, "Barragán preserved mystery and privacy, two very Mexican elements, as he helped create a school of modern architecture that pleased the state."[49]

In her essay on the importance of Barragán's work, Elena Poniatowska quotes the famous saying of Alfonso Reyes, now somewhat ironic, that the area around Mexico City is *"la región más transparente de aire"* (the area with the clearest air) and observes that Barragán, from the time he built the first garden house for Carlos Trouyet, spiritually understood the integrative use of air, light, walls, sky, clouds, and gardens in modern Mexican design. Where others saw lava as a sign of death and nothingness, Barragán saw it as holy space. She sees Barragán as typical of the artistic genius who has the gift of seeing life where others see nothing at all. His work is so spiritual, she observes, that it is very nearly impossible to find furniture that seems appropriate to the wonderful human space his work provides. What Orozco was to Mexican painting, Chávez to Mexican music, and Rulfo to Mexican literature, so Barragán was to Mexican architecture.[50]

Barragán believed that architecture should be for pleasure as well as for use and should be spiritual as well as functional.[51] Whether in poor or rich neighborhoods, architecture, he believed, should have *"heimlichkeit,"* or "at homeness," for the people who live in it. If it cannot provide some of the tranquility needed for living in stressful times, then the design should be reworked. Barragán believed that this quality was especially true for Mexico, where water was scarce and where by 1945 more people were choosing for economic reasons to live on less of the land.[52]

In Barragán's view, Mexican buildings should reflect the healing powers of fresh air, gardens, shadows, and the pure Mexican light. Modernity and mexicanidad were to him symbiotic and met in his clean line, earth tones, green gardens, flowers, and shade. Architecture in this style produced a synergism that was essentially spiritual, a binding of window and sky, of shadow and light, of soul and built space. This new understanding of space in the midst of urban crowding was prophetic.[53] Barragán was supported by avilacamachismo because his understanding of the fusion of the native and essential in Mexican style with the functional and modern in international style complemented the goals of the state. His work was an expression of the hopes of avilacamachismo for a prosperous, confident, unified nation.

Using presidential grants, commissions, discretionary funds, and teaching positions, the enormous SEP operation under avila-camachismo was generous to artists.[54] During the war years, for example, one of the largest programs for the construction of public statuary in modern world history was begun in Mexico.[55] Hundreds of statues, monuments, plaques, and mosaics were built in cities and villages. Although much of the work is pedestrian and unimaginative, a significant number of the pieces are exemplary. In Pátzcuaro, Guillermo Ruiz erected a statue of Gertrudis Bocanegra that is strong and original. The statue by Marín of Emiliano Zapata in Cuernavaca dominates the northern entry to the city. The most impressive work is that of Francisco Zúñiga and Rodrigo Arenas Betancourt. Zúñiga used a simplified modern style that received international acclaim and has continued to influence modern sculpture.[56]

Art is a mystery that probes heights and depths beyond the human venture itself. Art is our brave attempt to say something that will continue to speak after we are all gone. Certainly artistic activity of all types demonstrates the mysterious connection between heart and mind and has long been recognized as a fruitful index of the health of a culture. Any study of art is also a study of the culture in which it is produced. Art has always flourished in Mexico, and during the sexennium of Manuel Ávila Camacho the state embraced, supported, and nourished countless attempts to express the human spirit and to explore the vitality of the Mexican experience.

CHAPTER SEVEN

Carlos Chávez: Avatar of Avilacamachismo

In the 1940s Mexican popular music achieved worldwide recognition. In the United States, Mexican popular music was often "covered" by American singers, and Mexican music was frequently played by the Big Bands of the era. Helen O'Connell, for example, who sang with the Tommy Dorsey band, was well known for singing in both Spanish and English. American record companies also issued albums featuring cover versions of the original popular Mexican hits, while other companies issued original Mexican music. Bing Crosby had a major hit in 1945 called "You Belong to My Heart" based on "Solamente una vez" by Agustín Lara. Another success was *Mexicana*, issued in 1943 by RCA. This album contained four ten-inch records with music taken from a popular radio program called *Down Mexico Way*, which each week featured guest artists from Mexico playing the latest Mexican radio hits. Included in this album were several songs that had been hits in both the United States and Mexico like *"Perfidia,"* *"Cielito lindo,"* and "Allá en el rancho grande." Performers on the album included Tito Guízar, Juan Arzivu, Pepe and Chabela, Dora Luz, "Los Trovadores Porteños," and Lorenzo Barcelata.

There was, however, another level of music in Mexico that had both international influence and critical significance in the relationship of culture and state during this period. The international popularity of Mexican music in fact extended to high culture. One of the best-selling albums in the United States of the 1940s was Columbia's *A Program of Mexican Music.* Mexican newspapers were delighted to report that this album, directed by Carlos Chávez, was an international success. It pleased SEP especially because one of the forms of cultural nationalism most strongly supported by the Ávila Camacho government was symphonic music.

In the United States *Newsweek, Harper's Bazaar,* and *Vogue* featured stories on Carlos Chávez in 1941. His work was praised as "indispensable" for lovers of symphonic music. He was compared to Stravinsky, and his work was called innovative and "the leading edge" of the expansion of symphonic music beyond the traditional. For his part, Chávez took every occasion to make news. Between 1940 and 1946, over five hundred stories about Chávez and his work appeared in major American newspapers and magazines. He was photographed for every major American newspaper during this period. He was, in fact, a leading spokesman for avilacamachismo, which had as its most ambitious goal the establishment of international parity with the United States. In California he declared that Mexican audiences were as sophisticated as European and American. In Houston he called for a cultural exchange between Texas and Mexico. As the leading Mexican public personality for the American press during the era, Chávez consistently demanded respect for himself, Mexico, and Mexicans.[1]

Chávez, like his friend Ávila Camacho and many leaders of his government, was entering his forties as the decade began. He was the leading figure in symphonic music in Mexico before, during, and after this period as a conductor, composer, scholar, pianist, and a cultural entrepreneur. Carlos Chávez was a paradigm of the ideals of the culture-state process, and, like Torres Bodet, was a direct link from vasconcelismo to avilacamachismo.

Chávez composed Mexican symphonic music. He wrote about the history and philosophy of Mexican music. He was as profoundly respected internationally for his thought as for his musicianship. He observed that "musical nationalism" did not improve the work of a composer who lacked talent and explained that Mexican national music in the nineteenth century was wanting because "there were no great Mexican composers in that century."[2] Using his logic, it is fair to say that by the third decade of the twentieth century Mexico was producing noteworthy music because of its excellent composers.

Carlos Chávez was one of the best composer-directors in modern musical history. After study in Europe, he returned to Mexico and in his late twenties became director of the National Conservatory of Music. With his understanding of Mexican Indian music, he composed *Sinfonía india* in 1935. Using the folk themes and rhythms of life, he composed *Llamadas* in 1934 and *Overtura republicana* in 1935. His following was strong among the learned as well as among the unsophisticated but highly musical populace. Again using Aztec and other indigenous instruments in 1940, the same year the Campobello sisters published *Ritmos indígenas*, he introduced *Xochipili-Macuixochitl,* named for the Aztec God of War, at a concert at the Museum of Modern Art in New York City.

One of the major outlets for the mass presentation of the work of Chávez and others, such as Manuel M. Ponce and Silvestre Revueltas, was the previously discussed radio program *La hora nacional*. In the 1930s and 1940s, *La hora nacional* always opened with the national anthem, which was generally followed by a march played by a military or government band. There was a long tradition of civic and military bands in Mexico, of which Manuel Barajas wrote, "Military bands have a mission in serving as a vehicle for spreading culture. Providing music of a spirited type for the general public but never in the interest of just one class. Band concerts are for all classes."[3]

Part of the success of *La hora nacional* was an innovation that allowed a mixture of traditional, military, and symphonic music. For example, after starting with music that would attract campesinos, it then moved to a second selection of music aimed at a younger audience. Popular songs were often sung by personalities like Tata Nacho (Ignacio Fernández Esperón) or in the stylings of the romantic trios who sang boleros in distinctive close harmony. According to materials found in the archives, it was then commonplace to make the third selection a piece from high culture. Amparo Montes remembers that it was often a piece by Chávez or Ponce. Known worldwide as the composer of *Estrellita* and generally considered to be the father of Mexican musical nationalism, Ponce wrote dozens of compositions based upon Mexican folk melodies and introduced them to a wide audience on *La hora nacional*. Ponce and Chávez had a longstanding relationship with SEP and joined with others in the 1930s to create one of the most original national musical movements of all time.

Much of what they pioneered in the 1930s bore fruit in the 1940s. In his book *Toward a New Music* (1937), Carlos Chávez argued that all music, no matter how learned or advanced, had to be rooted in a geography and in a culture. Chávez compositions in the 1940s were, like the architecture of Luis Barragán, simultaneously abstract, modern, even scientific, but also fundamentally Mexican.[4] Under the leadership of Chávez, in 1940 three major Mexican symphonic works made their international debut. These were *Música para orquestra sinfónica* by Salvador Contreras, *Ferial* by Manuel M. Ponce, and *El renacuajo pescador* by Silvestre Revueltas, who died tragically just as it premiered.[5] In 1940 Chávez also supported the efforts to develop ballet in Mexico, working with all three companies, two led by immigrants and one by the Campobello sisters.

In the Ávila Camacho administration, most of the major composers in Mexico, like most major painters, worked in one way or another for the state or for an agency supported by the state. The young intellectuals who created avilacamachismo loved music. As president, Ávila Camacho attended concerts at the Bellas Artes regularly and often invited Chávez to social gatherings at his residence. Chávez enjoyed the fame and opportunities presented by the culture-state relationship, and was quite willing to be a "star." He was an avatar of the idealism that went from Vasconcelos to Torres Bodet. Chávez developed and maintained two areas in his work that may be regarded as perfect examples of the avilaca-machista vision of culture and state. One was an alternative con-cert series which had two public outreach dimensions. For many years Chávez took the Mexican Symphony Orchestra to city parks and held free concerts for workers, peasants, the elderly, and chil-dren. He also held Friday concerts at Bellas Artes for half the reg-ular price. These concerts were crowded each week with students of all kinds. On one of the park concerts Chávez wrote:

> It was a bizarre and heterogeneous public for a symphonic concert—mostly workers and peasants. They were old and young, some were shabbily dressed and many wore faded blue overalls. They brought their children with them and the little ones moved about during the concert.
>
> As we start the new season of the Orquestra Sinfonica de México next Friday we look back on our pioneer work and real-ize that we have come a long way. We played then at the central Social y Deportivo Venustiano Carranza, a park for culture and recreation on the outskirts of Mexico City. We made no prelimi-nary fuss about the launching of our experiment. The Orquestra gathered and played in the theatre of the park. There was no admission charge, and no invitation was required. Any one could come, and people swarmed to listen.[6]

The idealism of vasconcelismo resonates in these state-sponsored concerts for working people. Providing high culture to the masses was the essence of the vasconcelista idealism here expressed in the culture-state milieu of avilacamachismo.

Another area of Chávez's work supported by the state was international touring through which he represented Mexico in every major city of the United States and later the world. He con-ducted the top American symphonic orchestras and received high praise from American critics and from the avilacamachista state who saw his work as leading Mexican culture onto the world stage. Olin Downs wrote in the *New York Times* during the summer of 1940:

> The Museum of Modern Art has put its public under a new debt because of the pains it has taken, in presenting a panorama of "twenty centuries of Mexican culture," to include music as an indispensable part of the exposition. The Museum has been extremely fortunate in securing for this purpose the services of Carlos Chávez, the authoritative Mexican composer, conductor and educator, who, with the aid of Eduardo Hernández Moncada has made a wonderful contribution to the museum's exhibition. The program, given by an orchestra of some twenty-five, with a small chorus, was prepared with care and scholarship.[7]

Chávez reflected avilacamachismo in his leadership, along with that of Manuel M. Ponce, in the birthing of what has been called by Latin American music historian Gerald Behague "the Aztec Renaissance and consequent Indianist movement in the arts in Mexico."[8] In October 1928 Chávez delivered a lecture at the National University praising the virtues of pre-Columbian music as expressing "what is deepest in the Mexican soul." He called the music of the Indians "the most important stage in the history of Mexican music."[9]

Another music critic and historian observed that Chávez's basic concern was to link the history of Mexican music together, finding and exploring the missing places. He did this in a sophisticated way that provided a model for others who followed him in the exploration of pre-Columbian music in Latin America. He thus fulfilled the avilacamachista desire to provide postwar Mexican leadership for the Spanish-speaking world. It seems likely that Chávez's goal was to incorporate into his compositions previously assimilated folk elements through the use of representative formulas, whether of melody, harmony, rhythm, or instrumentation, that could confer on a piece a "distinctive national flavor."[10] With this work Chávez began an evolution from nationalism to internationalism that anticipated a similar change in avilacamachista attitudes from nationalism to cosmopolitanism. Chávez moved well beyond nationalism in composing, and, in fact, a number of American critics suggested that much of his most important work, including his orchestral masterpiece *Sinfonía de Antigona*, was so highly original that it represented the cutting edge of symphonic music at that time.[11] Chávez created pieces for John Cage, wrote for Martha Graham, and discussed "swing" with Harry James and Benny Goodman.[12]

Chávez's free concerts took high culture to the masses. His international travels brought world recognition to Mexico. His use of Amerindian themes and musical instruments inspired musicians throughout Latin America. His movement from nationalism to internationalism and cosmopolitanism was influential in helping form state policy during the war years. His life was a link between the postrevolutionary idealism of the vasconcelista period and the neo-vasconcelista idealism of the forties.

Perhaps the most remarkable years in modern Mexican classical musical history were 1940 to 1944. In 1941 the Mexican Symphony Orchestra, supported generously by SEP, introduced seven new symphonies by Mexican composers. These were *Noche en Morelia* by Miguel Bernal Jiménez, *Corridos* by Salvador Contreras, *Sones de mariachi* and *Concierto* by Blas Galindo, *Sinfonía numero 1* by Eduardo Hernández Moncada, *Norte* by Luis Sandi, and one of the most internationally successful Mexican symphonic suites of all time, *Huapango* by José Pablo Moncayo. On 8 September 1941 the Ballet Theater of New York premiered *Alecko* by Leonid Massine. The busy Mexican Symphony Orchestra played Tchaikovsky's music, Marc Chagall provided the costumes and staging, and four of the best dancers in the world at the time—George Skibine, Alicia Markova, Hugh Laing, and Anthony Tudor—performed the leading roles. On 4 October 1941 Manuel M. Ponce's *Concierto del sur* premiered in Montevideo, Uruguay, with Andrés Segovia, to whom the work was dedicated, as soloist. On 29 November of that year, another touring ballet company looking for new audiences in safer parts of the world gave the first performance in Mexico City of David Lichine's *Helen of Troy*, with costumes by Marcel Vertes and music by Jules Offenbach. The leading dancers included Irina Baronova, André Eglevsky, Jerome Robbins, and Simon Semenon. Chávez, with the help of Salvador Novo, director of the National Theater, worked with Mexican officials throughout 1942 to establish a Mexican Opera Company, which introduced its first season in 1943.

On 18 March 1941 the groundbreaking opera *Tata Vasco* by Miguel Bernal Jiménez was staged. Bernal Jiménez was the only major Mexican composer who did not live in Mexico City. He turned thirty-one as his opera premiered. The text of *Tata Vasco* was written by Manuel Muñoz and was based on the life of Don Vasco de Quiroga, first Bishop of Michoacán. Although a Spaniard, Quiroga was respected throughout Mexico for his creative efforts to serve the people and better their lives. To commemorate the fourth centenary of Don Vasco's entry into Patzcuaro, Bernal Jiménez aspired to create a totally Mexican symphonic drama reflecting the traditional styles of Indian, Spanish, and mestizo music.

There are four main themes in the opera, all reflecting ideology that was compatible with avilacamachismo. The first theme is that of *la raza* (the people) and emphasizes Indian rhythms and instruments and shows the influence of Chávez. The second theme, love, features the close harmony and sentimentality of mestizo songs. The third theme is faith, a highly appropriate theme for a nation at war. The final theme is reconciliation and harmony. Don Vasco is celebrated as a person in whom there was a confluence of three cultures. In this way, the bishop was not unlike Ávila Camacho himself, a caring leader who sought economic development for his people, harmony in their identity, and respect from all who dealt with them. Ávila Camacho attended the opening of *Tata Vasco* and afterwards sent Bernal a congratulatory message.[13]

Chávez deeply appreciated the work of Bernal Jiménez and introduced his first symphony, *Noche en Morelia* in the 1941 season. In developing and supporting opera, Chávez continued to play the role of cultural entrepreneur as he had throughout the period in his manifold music and education activities.

In 1941 the Spanish refugee Rodolfo Halfter's *Violin Concierto* was premiered by Chávez and the increasingly acclaimed Orquestra Sinfonía de México. Samuel Dushkin, an American who joined an increasing number of foreigners who came to play with the orchestra, soloed. There were, in fact, so many events going on in Mexico City that the press struggled to keep up with them, often printing photographs of the musical personalities performing in the city. Ávila Camacho opened the season with words of praise for his friend Chávez. He declared to the newspapers that the work of Chávez and the other great Mexican composers was of great value to the nation.[14] The 1941 classical music season contained fifty-seven original compositions by twenty-two Mexican composers.[15] Carlos Chávez had become by 1941 the most respected Mexican personality active in world culture. He had transcended the national and emerged on the world stage.

Media stars are vital to the culture-state process, which consists of elevating personalities whose creative work is favored by the state. Culture stars are not normally associated with high culture; however, high culture creators and performers in the twentieth century from Caruso to Picasso have embodied the phenomenon because their careers also created popular adulation. The culture star phenomenon was accelerated in Mexico because of radio, and Carlos Chávez became such a star. Frequently featured in photographs and stories in the press, he was one of the best-known public personalities in Mexico.

In 1942 the symphonic season slowed but still included the debut of *Sinfonía numero 4* by Candelario Huízar, *Concierto* by José Rolón, and *Arroyos* and *Sinfonía y sexteto* by Blas Galindo. On 13 April 1942 Ávila Camacho delivered a major policy speech at the opening of the Benjamin Franklin Library in Mexico City. In it he pointed out that all over Europe libraries, schools, universities, and temples were being destroyed by hatred, while in Mexico and the United States friendship was producing culture that was creating civilization. The Mexican government, he said, "was committed to learning, culture, music, and international friendship." This, he said, was the "very heart of our political agenda."[16] In this speech he summarized the culture-state policy of his administration and its idealist heritage.

In 1943 Radio Gobernación began placing large advertisements in the Mexico City newspapers for *La hora nacional* listing coming programs and performers. The programming by this time clearly reflected avilacamachista internationalism. In 1943 music was played from all of the Allied nations, and the programming included patriotic salutes to the Mexican armed forces as well as to the other hemispheric and Allied nations. The only Mexican symphonic work to debut that year in Mexico City was a Manuel M. Ponce violin concerto. In New York City, however, there was another opening important to Mexico. Mexican newspapers noted with pride that on 11 March 1943 *El Salón México* by Aaron Copeland was performed for the first time at the Studio Theatre by the José Limón Dance Company.

The young poet Jaime Torres Bodet, now secretary of public education, supported all forms of high culture, especially the symphony, the ballet, and the opera. Leadership of the opera came from the refugee community, but most of the singers and stage designers were Mexican. Carl Alwyn, who had been director of the Vienna Opera for eighteen years, and Franz Steiner, former director of the Vienna State Opera, were hired to assist in productions. On stage in the first four productions, only seven refugees performed, and the entire cast and chorus were Mexican. The newspapers were thrilled by the voice of a young Mexican singer named Irma González. Stage sets and costumes were designed by the Mexican artists Julio Castellanos, Roberto Montenegro, and Agustín Lazo.

There were, of course, elements in the nation who rejected the culture-state policies of Ávila Camacho. They were especially critical of all forms of Mexican music and ballet, which they deemed inferior to European productions. In spring 1945, for example, there were numerous attacks on the Mexico City Ballet. The attacks implied that it was poorly done and "pagan." José Clemente Orozco responded in an open letter to the press. He began by pointing out that the best proof of the success of the Mexican Ballet was the violence of the attacks upon it. This, he said, was typical of a segment of the population who could not see the value of anything purely Mexican. He praised the efforts of the Campobello sisters and pointed out with bitterness that the ballet was not the hastily improvised affair it had been called, but the result of ten years of scholarly research and preparation. Orozco challenged the critics on the issue of European superiority. The Russian, French, and Italian ballets, he said, were "antiquated" and held together only by "the insatiable greed of impresarios." Those who held the idea that "since the Ballet de la Ciudad de México is the product of Mexicans it is necessarily inferior" were stupidly out of date in their thinking. Those days have passed, he added, and it was Mexican art, Mexican music, and Mexican ballet that represented the best and most creative dimensions of world culture.[17]

The large amounts of money involved in supporting high culture made it an area of considerable political infighting and made Chávez a controversial figure for some. The first secretary of public education in the Ávila Camacho government was Sánchez Pontón, who was replaced in September 1941 by a conservative, Véjar Vásquez. Véjar was unsympathetic to what was being called the Mexican renaissance in the arts, fearing that it was being directed by "communists." Véjar served a short term, leaving the post on 22 December 1943, but in his time in office opposed everything Chávez did. Véjar personally hated Chávez, and while secretary of public education, he attempted to destroy Chávez by cutting off funds to the Mexican Symphony Orchestra. He failed, and although he was removed from office after two years, it is clear that Véjar was one of many who opposed the idealism of avilacamachista culture-state policy. Véjar did not, or would not, understand avilacamachismo, and his failure to grasp the goals of the administration led him to make destructive and counterproductive decisions. This explains in part why only one symphony was premiered in 1943. Much of the damage was repaired by Torres Bodet, who served in the position for the last three years of the Ávila Camacho administration.

Even with only one symphony debut, and in spite of the obstructionist and dissembling tactics of Véjar, the 1943 season was a success. It opened on 4 June at Bellas Artes and was divided into three sections. First, there was a fourteen-week subscription series with concerts on Friday and Saturday nights. It was this series that was broadcast on the Mutual Network in the United States, and it was during this series that Manuel M. Ponce's *Concierto para violin y orquesta* was introduced for the first time. The Friday night concerts were half-priced for students and workers. Guest conductors for the 1943 season included Sir Thomas Beecham of the British Royal Philharmonic Symphony Orchestra and Eugene Goosens of the Cincinnati Symphony Orchestra, both of whom praised Chávez and his orchestra. In August pianist Claudio Arrau introduced a piano concerto written by Chávez; and that month pianists Miguel García and Salvador Ordóñez also made solo appearances with the orchestra. The second part of the season began in October when the Orquestra Sinfonica included a low-priced series with an emphasis on popular music. The symphony went on a national tour in late autumn.

In truth, even Véjar's repressive edicts were unable to stop the momentum building in the fine arts. In 1943, for example, a UNAM violin professor, Luis G. Saloma Núñez, was funded to start the Orquesta de Música de Cámara of UNAM. This orchestra is still performing. In summer 1991 at Sala Xochipilli, located in Mexico City at 126 Xicoténcatl, Colonia del Carmen, a concert of chamber music was held in honor of Saloma, who served as founder and director from 1943 until 1946. At this performance sponsored by the UNAM School of Music, some of his former violin students played and spoke of the exciting era in which this orchestra, now under the direction of Daniel Saloma Córdova, came into being.[18] Several of the artists spoke of the multiform influence of Chávez during that period.

In 1944, with Torres Bodet firmly in charge of SEP, full funding was restored to the Mexican Symphony. In that season, three major works by Mexican composers were introduced to the public.

They were *Sinfonía numero 1* by José Pablo Moncayo, *Tema y variaciones* by Luis Sandi, and *Sinfonía numero 2* by Eduardo Hernández Moncada. Chávez traveled to Washington in 1944 to conduct the National Symphony Orchestra. His first international success had been in the United States in 1932 in Philadelphia, where, under the direction of Leopold Stokowski, he had introduced *H.P.* (Horsepower), a musical interpretation of the troubled economic relationship between the United States and Mexico. *H.P.* contrasts the easygoing rhythms of the South with those of the hectic, industrialized North. In the last movement, the workers take over their machines in a symbolic triumph of the sensuous and lyrical over the unfeeling and mechanical. In Washington, Chávez performed *H.P.* and Moncayo's popular *Huapango Suite* to an appreciative audience.[19]

Another landmark year for the Mexican Symphony Orchestra was 1945 with four original symphonies by Mexican composers, one more than in 1944. A cultural chronology written for the seventy-fifth anniversary of the Mexican Revolution indicates that of the 110 symphonic works written and premiered in Mexico between 1906 and 1986, 22 were during the Ávila Camacho years. In other words, 20 percent of Mexican symphonic works written and premiered so far in this century occurred in the sexennium 1940–1946. In programs like *La hora nacional* or in symphonic pieces by Bernal Jiménez, Chávez or Revueltas, it is possible to see the Ávila Camacho state creating high culture and the economic environment that consistently supported the work of composers and musicians.

The record also indicates that in the administrations following Ávila Camacho, the number of symphonies composed and presented in Mexico began to decline. Before his sexennium, in the years from 1906 to 1939, there were numerous symphonies composed and performed in Mexico, the largest number while Vasconcelos was head of SEP and in the years shortly thereafter. After the Ávila Camacho sexennium, in the nearly four decades between 1947 and 1986, only thirty-six full symphonies were written and performed. In several periods in the 1950s and 1980s, no symphonic music at all was written or introduced in Mexico.[20] In assessing the overall success of symphonic music in Mexico in the productive years, one must conclude that the single individual who most nearly embodied the idealism of the vasconcelista postrevolutionary cultural nationalism and who most nearly fulfilled the amendments to that policy by the avilacamachistas was Carlos Chávez.

In 1945 the four Mexican symphonies introduced by the National Symphony Orchestra were *Nocturno* by Blas Galindo, *Sinfonía numero 1* by Carlos Jiménez Mabarak, *Sinfonía* by José Pablo Moncayo, and, posthumously, *Colorines* by Silvestre Revueltas. Revueltas, not yet thirty, well known and well liked in Mexico City cultural and intellectual circles, died suddenly on the night of the premiere of his best work. A few days before his sudden death, Revueltas attended a dinner party given by Pablo Neruda in honor of several of the Mexican intellectuals who had traveled to Spain in support of the loyalists. Guests included Octavio Paz, Juan de la Cabada, and Elena Garro. This group, which also included María Asúnsolo and Silvestre's sister, actress Rosario Revueltas, gathered often at Neruda's home. Most were at the concert in Bellas Artes and had joined in the cheering crowd calling for the composer to come forward, when the dramatic announcement of his death was made. An open coffin was placed in Bellas Artes two days later, and silent mourners, many of them young people, joined government officials and hundred of citizens to view his body. Neruda was asked to say a few words. In his eulogy he said that the name Silvestre Revueltas would come "to soar as a bell in the tolling of the country."[21] Revueltas, who shared with Chávez and Bernal Jiménez the belief that high culture could be derived from popular and indigenous music, was missed terribly by the creative community of Mexico.

In 1946 only one new Mexican symphonic work was introduced by the Mexican Symphony Orchestra. It was composed by the thirty-six-year-old organist and composer from Morelia, Miguel Bernal Jiménez, whose earlier works *Noche en Morelia* and

Tata Vasco have been mentioned. Bernal was a scholar, a teacher, a director of a school choir, and the editor of an SEP-funded journal of colonial Mexican church music called *Schola Cantorum*. A brilliant composer, Bernal studied for five years at the Pontificial Institute of Sacred Music in Rome and then returned to Morelia to teach and direct the choir at the Escuela de Musica Sagrada. As pointed out in the earlier discussion of his lyric drama, *Tata Vasco,* Bernal's work fused the rhythms and musical themes of traditional Mexico with the form and discipline of symphonic European composition.

Avilacamachismo itself was strongly influenced by Carlos Chávez, especially by his view of the role of music in society. In supporting the Mexican Symphony Orchestra or promoting the careers of popular musicians, avilacamachismo sought to use culture as a cord to bind the nation together at high as well as popular levels. Chávez argued that all Mexican music was worthy of world respect. In order for indigenous music to be appreciated, it had to be treated as though it were high culture—that is, it had to be studied. Yet constant, small irregularities of time and tempo, notation and structure, and unfamiliar sounds, made it hard for European-trained minds to understand or appreciate it. The standard Western reaction was to demean it. By 1946, however, Chávez had attained a stature in the international music world of such magnitude that he could give the nation a voice to defend its indigenous music. Mexican symphonic music, Chávez believed, could revitalize European symphonic music by the infusion of new sounds and a naturalness that indigenous music provided.[22]

Chávez saw the value of developing the technology of sound reproduction and the need for broadcasting and phonographic record quality. He was prescient in his vision of the future. He predicted the advent of electronically produced music and the rise of "world music" when African, Asian, European, and New World music began to grow toward each other because of the coming communications revolution. This, he believed, would someday bring all humanity together, just as music could bind his nation together.[23]

Because he understood the power of technology and the importance of the audience, Chávez received funding for broadcasting the Mexican Symphony Orchestra and for developing other music programs. He encouraged avilacamachismo to use the power of radio to magnify the appeal of symphonic music. Affirming the work of Chávez, Ponce, Bernal, Revueltas, and others, the state attempted to create new audiences for symphonic music in the way in which it presented musical selections on *La hora nacional*. Martial music often led to mariachi music followed by Ponce and ending with Chávez. Amparo Montes was not alone in recognizing cultural fusion in the work of Ponce, whose short variations on Mexican folk themes were a regular feature on the program. She saw in them something that was both Mexican and symphonic. Chávez believed that all concerts should be broadcast, noting that the word is derived from the action of a farmer who casts his seeds over a wide area. Planting concerts in the land, Chávez held, would bring a harvest for the nation. In 1943, along with Diego Rivera and José Clemente Orozco, he was selected as a member of the prestigious El Colegio Nacional.

The youthful Ávila Camacho administration was influenced by the thinking of Carlos Chávez and between 1940 and 1946 tried to develop some of his ideas into public policy. Chávez asked Ávila Camacho to assist the orchestra in making an appearance in El Paso, Texas, in 1944. The president, who that year gave band uniforms to an El Paso high school, as noted earlier, supported the idea of a Mexican orchestra playing concerts in the United States. Here was a concrete realization of the goal of avilacamachismo to place Mexico on equal footing with the leading nations of the world. Here was the role he wanted to see Mexico playing in the community of nations, and he was pleased when the Mutual Radio Network decided to broadcast weekly evening concerts from Mexico City in the summer of 1944.[24]

The years from 1940 to 1946 are remembered as outstanding musical years in Mexico. Radio, film, musical theater, ballet, and symphonic music produced thousands of original works in the styles of boleros, corridos, rancheros, swing, jazz, romantic, tropical, and regional sounds as well as dozens of original ballets and symphonic compositions. Mexican music was heard all over the world, had an influence on world popular music and dance, and gained respect in the concert halls of Europe and the United States. The role of music in avilacamachismo was manifold. It acted as a force for cultural unification, a musical catalyst with such appeal to the nation's youth that regionalism faded in its presence. It acted as a change agent, allowing the best of the old and new to act as thesis and antithesis and generate musical symbols for a new Mexico. Radio magnified these new cultural emblems, which could be songs or the stars who sang them, or symphonic music and the composers who created them. All of Mexico's music from this period brought new respect for the nation. Bing Crosby, Helen O'Connell, and Tommy Dorsey performed the music written in Mexico. An American radio network broadcast the Mexican Symphony live, and foreigners came to Mexico to hear the orchestra because it was, at least in 1944 and 1945, judged to be among the best in the world.[25]

Avilacamachismo, as it searched for ways to implement its goals, supported composers of international stature like Chávez, Bernal Jiménez, Ponce, and Revueltas in their exploration of the organic connections between the symphonic music of the New World and the Old. Avilacamachismo believed Mexican music to be significant in establishing Mexico's role in world culture, welcomed new types of music for national audiences, and provided for the distribution of films, records, and radio transmissions by subsidizing the development of new technology. The result was what historians have called the "golden age" in Mexican film, radio, and popular music. Young people were provided pop stars like Toña la Negra, Amparo Montes, or María Félix, and dance music by Alberto Domínguez, whose arrangements of "Perfidia" and "*Frenesí*" for Tommy Dorsey and Artie Shaw were giant hits in both Mexico and the United States. The nation was also provided with stars from high culture, like Chávez. The working

poor were provided dance music and plenty of laughter from Cantinflas, Tin Tan, and Roberto Soto. As we have seen, they were
also provided opera and ballet. The entire nation enjoyed the films
and records of Jorge Negrete, Lucha Reyes, and Pedro Infante.
Equally important, however, was the role of high culture. One
California music critic, impressed by the audience at a Chávez
concert, wrote:

> Audiences at these concerts, held in the theater of the sump-
> tuous Palace of Fine Arts, are curiously intent. The only pro-
> gram-rustling is done by casual tourists who come to the con-
> certs in the vain hope of seeing the Tiffany curtain, and is
> quelled by one icily-inquiring glance from under Chávez's eye-
> brows. His own countrymen need no such glances. From the
> frugal student in the top row of the gallery to Manuel Ávila
> Camacho in the presidential box, your Mexican knows his music
> and takes it seriously.[26]

CHAPTER EIGHT

Female Archetypes
of Change

The role of women in Mexico has long been of interest to historians, sociologists, and psychologists. Frederick C. Turner pointed out that the word *malinchismo* has come to stand for the betrayal of all things Mexican to invasive foreign powers. It is a powerful word taken directly from the name of Cortes's mistress (Malinche) who, as the original Mexican "bad woman," deceived her people and opened the way for the violent European conquest.[1] Samuel Ramos connected a perceived inferiority complex in Mexico as a nation to this crushing betrayal of the indigenous culture. Ramos suggested that the Europeans' taking of native women as wives and mistresses left the native males confused, impotent, and angry at their women. In the hundreds of years that followed, the mestizo children of this union have felt ambivalent and guilty about their unique heritage.[2] According to Ramos and others who have written on the subject, Mexican culture has come to resent as well as idealize the European father figure, while at the same time hating and feeling inferior to him.

141

This scenario has meant that the female is both denigrated and worshiped. Psychologist Michael Maccoby observed that the traditional role of a Mexican woman has been defined as "good" when she is a mother running a traditional home. In this context she is esteemed for loving unconditionally, never being unfaithful to husband or family, and always protecting, nurturing, and providing a safe haven. As a "good" woman she may be the virgin Sor Juana, La China, Valentina, Adelita, or just the eternal "María" brimming with hope and dreams and willing to produce strong sons whom she can nourish on the old traditions. As a bad woman she is a "*puta*," a Malinche, a woman who is untraditional, unfaithful, or sexually promiscuous.[3]

This complex relationship between the sexes has produced in Mexico over time, according to Ramos, Maccoby, and others, a profound sense of national confusion and an alternately authoritarian, worshipful, and exploitative attitude toward women called "*machismo*." Contemporary feminist writers on Mexico, such as Claudia Schaefer, Anna Macías, and Rosario Castellanos, have explored the reality and tragedy of Mexican women. Macías has challenged but not refuted Howard F. Cline's observation that the ability of women to earn a living before and after marriage was a phenomenon which began in Mexico during the Second World War and brought significant changes in the status of women.[4] Macías has suggested that the struggle for equal rights began with the Revolution and that the Mexican women's struggle was valiant but lost strength in the years that followed.[5]

The next two chapters explore these issues by examining the role played by seven important women during the years of the Ávila Camacho administration. In looking at the personal and professional lives of these artists we see, as Cline suggested, the symbolic beginning of change in the status of women in modern Mexico. These chapters maintain that before large numbers of Mexican women could become accountants, lawyers, government officials, and bankers, a few became, with the help of the state in the 1940s, photographers, actors, painters, cultural entrepreneurs, and writers. The women presented in these chapters emerged, in a culture dominated by men, as significant creative personalities in the interaction of state and culture during avilacamachismo. This chapter focuses on Tina Modotti and Frida Kahlo as archetypes of change in Mexican society.

After thirty years of internal conflict, the state in 1940 began to assert its dominance as the single authoritative apparatus guiding every aspect of Mexican life including culture. Serious opposition parties were under wraps although some opposition was tolerated, even encouraged. As Ávila Camacho took office, national and local politics had been synchronized, with state and party operating in a symbiotic harmony. In the 1940s, it was in Mexico City that movies were filmed and released, and radio programs produced for nationwide broadcast. Money and talent came together in this cosmopolitan and national city.

In 1940 Pablo Neruda was sent to Mexico City as a diplomat from his native Chile. In his memoirs he recalls the "flowery and thorny" beauty of the city, the clean air, the extraordinary light, the color, and the atmosphere of excitement and intrigue.[6] His succession of homes became beehives of activity, filled with the comings and goings of Mexican intellectuals and artists. They were also a haven for some of the hundreds of European intellectuals who were welcomed into Mexico first by Cárdenas and later by Ávila Camacho. Neruda mentions long visits by poets like León Felipe, Constancia de la Mora, Juan Rejano, José Morena Villa, and José Herrera Petera. He speaks of entertaining painters like Miguel Prieto and Antonio Rodríguez Luna. He reflects upon conversations with Gaulist leaders, representatives of Free France, and Republican leaders from Spain, such as Wenceslao Roces from Salamanca, who translated Marx into Spanish. There were many others, including the anti-fascist German writers Ludwig Renn and Bodo Uhse. Neruda thus describes Mexico City in 1940 as bursting with exiles, including many from Guatemala, El Salvador, and Honduras, who joined those from Europe to make the city one of the intellectual and political centers of the world.

But there were danger and violence in the air as well. Volodia Teitelboim has written of an afternoon outing in 1942, shortly after Mexico declared war on Germany. Neruda and his wife, Delia, joined his fellow Chilean consul, Luis Enrique Dálano, and his wife and child, along with Clara Porset, for an afternoon in Cuernavaca's Amatlan Park. In the course of the afternoon, they spoke loudly of their hatred of fascism, at one point raising their glasses in a "euphoric" toast to the courage of President Ávila Camacho. Shortly thereafter, they were attacked by a band of Germans who were drinking at a table near enough to overhear them. Neruda suffered a four-inch cut in his head and was rushed to an emergency room in Cuernavaca. Teitelboim says the attack was the inspiration for Neruda's prologue to Ilya Ehrenberg's book, *Death to the Invader*. The attackers were never arrested or punished.[7]

In those days of sunlight, dust, and intrigue, among the frequent guests at Neruda's home was one of the most talented women in Mexico, Tina Modotti. This remarkable woman is a prototype for the emergence of women in twentieth-century Mexican culture. She was in her lifetime a gifted photographer, ardent revolutionary, nude model for one of the world's finest photographers, nurse and fighter in the Spanish Civil War, Hollywood film actress, and nonconformist who demanded an equal standard of morality for men and women. She was a feminist and internationalist who deeply loved her adopted nation, Mexico. Accused of murder, however, she was deported in 1930 as an undesirable character, only to return in 1939 on a false passport with the tidal wave of European refugees. Who was Tina Modotti? We are given an image of her by Kenneth Rexroth in *An Autobiographical Novel*. His description of Modotti captures something of her mystery if nothing of her creative ability. Rexroth says he saw her just before the murder of her Cuban revolutionary lover, Julio Antonio Mella, at a cafe where "they all hung out with heavily armed politicians, bullfighters, criminals, prostitutes, and burlesque girls." In this avant-garde crowd, he says, "the most spectacular person of all was a photographer, artist's model, high class courtesan, and Mata Hari for the Comintern, Tina Modotti." Rexroth adds that he was "terrified of her."[8]

She was born Assunta Adelaide Luigia Modotti in Udine, Italy, on 16 August 1896, one of six children born to a mason and his wife. Udine is located at the foot of the Alps, not far from the Austrian border, a peaceful village that was poor during Modotti's childhood. Looking for a better life, her father joined several thousand northern Italian craftsmen working in San Francisco, California. One by one, he brought his family to America. Tina arrived in 1913 and went immediately to work at age seventeen in a textile factory not unlike the one she left behind in Italy. She worked hard and was loyal to her family, taking extra jobs to help make ends meet. At twenty-one she married Roubaix de L'Abrie Richey, a colorful poet and painter. One observes that it was here that the working-class leftist views of her family united with the world of the artist.[9] Exactly how she was "discovered" by Hollywood is not known, but in the early 1920s she made several successful silent films playing a gypsy or one of Hollywood's "Latin" women.

In 1921 Modotti and her husband, whom she called Robo, met several visiting Mexican officials who had come to California to study the film industry. In the group was anthropologist Ricardo Gómez Robelo, whom Vasconcelos had appointed undersecretary of fine arts. According to Modotti, Gómez Robelo spoke compellingly of the Mexican Revolution as a cultural as well as political event, capturing the imagination of the youthful and radical film actress and her artist husband.[10] Richey was especially intoxicated with the images of Mexico as the land of a cultural revolution. He decided to go there and later send for his wife. It was at this time that Modotti met Edward Weston, thirty-five, married, and the father of four boys. He was working primarily as a commercial photographer. Later he would record in the first of his famous *Daybooks* that Modotti was a woman of extraordinary beauty who would "shatter and then reconstruct" his life.[11] Modotti and Weston fell into a rapturous love affair.

Tina Modotti's introduction to Mexico was tragic. A few months after his arrival, her husband contracted smallpox and died suddenly. In grief as much as anything else, Modotti and her mother-in-law journeyed to Mexico to see the land that had so entranced Richey. Discovering the light, the spirit of the Revolution, the vital nation being born under the warm sun, Modotti stayed on for several weeks, renewing her friendship with Gómez Robelo and arranging a showing of Weston's photographs at Bellas Artes.[12] The exhibition was a sensation and was praised by Mexican artists who had not paid much attention to photography as a serious art form.

In July 1923 Modotti, Weston, and his eldest son, Chandler, then thirteen years old, moved to Mexico.[13] Renting a ten-room home in Tacubaya, Modotti introduced Weston to Gómez Robelo, the young muralist and communist Xavier Guerrero, then working with Diego Rivera, and his sister Elisa. They also met Jean Charlot, who mentions Weston but not Modotti in his *The Mexican Mural Renaissance, 1920–1925*, and, of course, José Vasconcelos, the tutelary spirit of the cultural revolution. Guided by Modotti, who spoke good Spanish, Weston's eyes were opened to Mexico.[14]

In his *Daybooks* Weston indicates that both he and Modotti had sexual affairs with others almost from the time they arrived.[15] Others picture Modotti as beautiful but austere and somewhat introverted. That Modotti was a modern woman cannot be doubted. She demanded equality in morals, conversation, and especially in artistic respect. Weston's attitude toward her was as much one of a perplexed American from the Midwest as it was that of an aspiring Bohemian. He wrote in the *Daybooks* that "there is a certain inevitable sadness in the life of a much sought after, beautiful woman, like Tina especially who, not caring for associates among her own sex, craves camaraderie and friendship from men as well as sex love."[16]

Photographer Anita Brenner thought Modotti's photographs were softer and more emotional than Weston's. At work Modotti wore blue jeans. In fact, she became famous as the first woman— Rivera and other Mexican male artists had worn them for years—to wear blue jeans in Mexico. She worked hard in the darkroom on her own photographs and on Weston's; she also printed photographs from older, unknown Mexican photographers for Anita Brenner's book, *The Wind That Swept Mexico*. In December 1924 Weston and Chandler returned to California. While he was away, Modotti posed for Diego Rivera's murals in the chapel at the Chapingo Agricultural School. Weston was openly negative about Modotti's bent toward radical political action groups. In Rivera, Modotti found a mentor who embodied the fusion of art and radicalism that she had come to Mexico to imbibe.[17] Shortly after Weston left, Modotti became an active leader in the "Hands off Nicaragua Committee."[18] As she became more politically active, her photographs were increasingly of Mexican women.

Modotti searched for a new photographic expression that could capture authentic female beauty. Throughout her lifetime, she resented her treatment as a "beauty" by the press. She hated the idea that modern women were going to be "measured by a motion picture standard."[19] As a result, she approached photographing women in a different way than Weston, who in 1924 created a series of famous photographs of Modotti lying nude on an *azotea*. Weston claimed that it was "the formal quality of the shape of the female nude" that interested him and any erotic motive was "suspended in the photographic work."[20] He wrote in the *Daybooks* that his approach was aesthetic but that "others must get from them what they bring to them," implying that he was aware that some viewed his photographs in order to be sexually stimulated.[21] His work is striking but also conventional. Taken from above, the photographs are somewhat voyeuristic, since Modotti is seemingly asleep or otherwise unaware of the camera. Modotti had no interest in this view of women.

Tina Modotti sought out and photographed working women, mothers, and grandmothers. The context for her photographs is not a lithe female body isolated and posed for the camera, but the sometimes pregnant, sometimes stooped, always active bodies of the eternal women of Mexico. These are women simply attempting to survive a hard life. Laura Mulvey and Peter Wollen have observed that Modotti photographed these women from below head height with their bodies not isolated, idealized, or on view, but connected to their children and everyday artifacts.[22]

After Weston left Mexico, Modotti began an affair with muralist and communist organizer Xavier Guerrero. Modotti joined the Mexican Communist Party in 1927, a logical step in her progression from garment worker to revolutionary artist. Anita Brenner wrote of this group of Mexican artists that for them art for art's sake was an aesthetic fallacy. "Art," she said, "is necessarily a thing of the people, not an abstract concept, nor a vehicle for exploiting whims."[23] In Modotti's photographs of men, men and women, and everyday objects, one finds the provocative, intuitive comprehension of people in the midst of poverty and human suffering but also in their spiritual environment. In one famous photograph, the long straight lines of a guitar neck intersect the crooked kernels of an ear of corn, while both lay atop the menacing, metallic precision of a bandolier of rifle bullets.[24] In another, a group of field workers gather in the shade of their own sombreros, as shadows intersect the creases of *El Machete*, the communist newspaper that holds them together for a moment in time.[25] During this period Modotti encouraged the work of Manuel Álvarez Bravo, soon to become Mexico's leading photographer. According to him, she sent some of his work to Weston who arranged to include the photographs in an exhibition in Germany.[26]

Modotti was by now the second successful female professional photographer in Mexico, the first being María Santibáñez, a self-trained artist and photographer for *El Universal Ilustrado*. Modotti received commissions from numerous sources, including a magazine published by Gabriel Figueroa and Gabriel Fernández Ledesma, and France Toor's magazine, *Mexican Folkways*. She also worked with Jean Charlot in photographing sections of José Clemente Orozco's murals so that Charlot could show them to individuals in New York.[27] In addition, she photographed the works of Diego Rivera and of her lover, Xavier Guerrero. She had numerous exhibitions in Mexico City and her work sold well. During this period she also did some pioneering work in the area of restoration photography. George R. Leighton points out that Modotti did the restoration on a number of photographs that he assembled for the 1976 edition of Anita Brenner's *The Wind That Swept Mexico*. She had become an expert in the technical side of the art form.[28] Her private and professional lives became hallmarks for Mexican feminists looking for role models.

In 1927 Guerrero left Mexico for the Soviet Union. Modotti seems to have understood his zeal to see the great scientific, communist experiment firsthand, but she herself had no desire to leave Mexico. Never long without a man in her life, by September 1928, at thirty-two, she was living with a young Cuban law student who worked as a journalist for *El Machete*. This relationship led indirectly to Tina Modotti's deportation from Mexico. Julio Antonio Mella was a youthful Cuban revolutionary who had to leave a wife behind when forced to flee from the anger of the government of General Gerardo Machado. In Mexico, Mella found Modotti in the full bloom of her beauty. Soon a shared belief in social revolution bound them as *compañeros* and lovers. Mella's zeal in the cause of social justice provided a vital and needed element for a maturing Modotti. On the night of 10 January 1929, Mella was ambushed and murdered as he and Modotti walked together toward their apartment. The Mexican press made the story a sensation by attempting to prove that Modotti herself or perhaps an agent for Xavier Guerrero murdered Mella. There was much talk of nude photographs, love triangles, and communism. In the press, Modotti became a "puta" and a "Malinche."[29] After a long and painful investigation, Modotti was cleared.

In grief, she returned to the work she loved and for which she was in great demand. She sold photographs to old sources such as *Mexican Folkways* and new ones like the *British Journal of Photography,* the *Pacific International Salon of Photographic Art*, and *Creative Art*.[30] She continued to have exhibitions, and one, entitled *The First Revolutionary Photographic Exhibition in Mexico*, included a lecture on her work by David Alfaro Siqueiros. In this lecture Siqueiros claimed an honored place for Modotti in the development of art in Mexico.[31] Modotti remained active in the Communist Party and became a frequent story item in the increasingly conservative Mexico City press. She was not, however, a Mexican citizen. On 5 February 1930, the newly elected Mexican president, a close associate of Plutarco Elías Calles named Pascual Ortiz Rubio, was taking his family for a Sunday drive in Chapultepec Park when six shots were fired at him by a young radical. The newspapers smelled a plot. Modotti was accused of conspiracy to murder the president and arrested. Imprisoned for two weeks, she was told she could remain in Mexico only if she abandoned her revolutionary views. She refused. A few days later, with the help of Manuel Álvarez Bravo, she slipped out of Mexico on a Dutch steamer. She was bound for Holland, Germany, Russia, and, within a few years, Spain.

In 1931 Modotti was living in Moscow. It was there that she decided to abandon photography for reasons not altogether clear. Perhaps confronting the problems of the Soviet Union overwhelmed her. She traveled in the Soviet Union and in parts of Europe on behalf of the Soviet International Red Aid Society. In 1934 she went to Spain to join Vittorio Vidali, a friend and lover of several years whom she first met in Mexico. Together they worked first for the Spanish Communist Party and then moved to Paris for awhile. By now she was known in Europe as a Communist organizer. Her photography was almost forgotten. When the Spanish Civil War started, she joined the famous Fifth Regiment, founded by Vidali under the nom de guerre Carlos Contreras. She served as a reporter for *Ayuda*, the newspaper of the Spanish Red Aid Society, and was now called simply "María." One wonders if this name indicated a continued identification with the poorest women of Mexico. In Valencia she attended a meeting called "The Congress for the Defense of Culture Against Fascism." Here she met Pablo Neruda and made connections with a group of Mexican intellectuals and artists including Octavio Paz, Fernando Gamboa, and the composer Silvestre Revueltas.[32] Exhausted by now, she was given a false passport as she joined thousands fleeing Spain for Mexico. She arrived in Veracruz in April 1939, not quite ten years after she had been deported.

In Mexico again, Modotti worked at first as a translator and lived with Vidali, who worked as a reporter for *El Popular*. Together they lived in the midst of the large and complex exile community that brought to Mexico a wealth of philosophers, artists, writers, and other people of outstanding ability. Their closest friends included Hannes Meyer, an architect who had once directed the Bauhaus in Germany, and Pablo and Delia Neruda. After some work, friends in the government helped her clear her name and overturn the deportation order. "María" once again became Tina Modotti, and Modotti, who had almost abandoned photography in Europe, began taking photographs in Mexico once again. Like Neruda, Modotti believed that Mexico's heart could be found in her markets.[33] The Spanish writer Constancia de la Mora, whose book *In Place of Splendor* was a best seller in the United States, asked Modotti to photograph the people of the markets around the city to illustrate a book she planned to write. Modotti began the work with enthusiasm, but death, never far away in Mexico, overtook her.

Some of the Mexican newspapers reported that she had been poisoned.[34] In fact, the years of struggle in Europe had taken a heavy toll on her health. Pablo Neruda reported that Modotti had suffered heart problems in Spain.[35] Nearly everyone who saw her in her last month of life—Neruda, Manuel Álvarez Bravo, Fernando Gamboa, and others—all said she was very tired. Gamboa said that "her skin was grey and she looked ill."[36] After a dinner party at the home of Hannes Meyer, Modotti took a taxi home. She died of a massive heart attack in the back seat of the taxi on 5 January 1942.[37] Her funeral was attended by several thousand people, including delegations from the Communist Party, labor unions, women's organizations, intellectuals, and exiles. A large retrospective of her work was staged by Inéz Amor at her Galería de Arte Mexicano. Modotti was buried in the Pantheon of Dolores, and her simple headstone contains only the words of Neruda's poem "Tina Modotti is dead." It ends with the words:

Pure is your gentle name
Pure is your fragile life

Bees, shadows, fire, ice, silence and foam
Combine with steel and wire and pollen
To make up your firm yet delicate being.[38]

Tina Modotti openly defied the traditional Mexican di-
chotomy between "good" and "bad" women. With her camera she
honored the aspirations of Mexican women. As a woman artist she
was obsessed with what was human about Mexico. In her unique
and pioneering way, she saw and captured the tragic as well as the
beautiful in ordinary Mexican life. Her importance goes beyond
her art, however. From the wearing of blue jeans to a very public
life of economic, political, artistic, and sexual independence, Tina
Modotti was a role model for many modern Mexican women, one
of the most important of whom was Frida Kahlo.

According to Hayden Herrera, author of *Frida*, the award-
winning biography of Kahlo, from the moment they first met in
1923, Modotti was an inspiration for Kahlo. It was through Modotti's influence that Kahlo joined the Communist Party. Herrera
adds that "it is almost certain" that Frida met Diego Rivera as an
adult for the first time at a party at Modotti's home which, she
points out, was for a number of years a location where the movers
and shapers of Mexican culture gathered to discuss "the latest
ideas" about art and revolution.[39] Herrera missed, however, an
important influence. One can argue that what Kahlo admired
most in Modotti was her quest to be seen as a human being, a revolutionary and artist, and not just as a beautiful woman. In fact,
both women based their art upon a lifelong struggle with their
bodies. In Modotti's case, an accident of beauty created a scenario
that led ultimately to her rejection of the traditional isolation and
idealization of the female form. Kahlo, because of her early struggle with polio and then a terrible bus accident in her youth that
forever after shaped both her life and her art, also struggled with
the issue of the female body.

Coincidentally, another woman was struggling with this issue
at exactly the same time as were Modotti and Kahlo, although

from a different perspective. She was Ana Soledad Orozco de Ávila Camacho, wife of the president. A supporter of the arts, she influenced numerous commissions given to Mexican artists hired to decorate or create art for public buildings. On two occasions señora Ávila Camacho asked for changes in or rejected the work of an artist because she felt uncomfortable with its anatomical implications. In 1943 the president's wife ordered the sculptor Olaguíbel to drape the lower section of an enormous nude he was creating using Diana Cazadora as his model.[40]

Earlier in 1942, señora Ávila Camacho rejected a painting she had commissioned Frida Kahlo to do for the presidential dining room. The painting, *Still Life*, which is today on display in the Frida Kahlo Museum in Mexico City, contains an astounding but subtle collection of Mexican fruits and vegetables that "hint disquietingly at human anatomy."[41] Painted on a round piece of tin, it has a focal point of a halved cassava melon with the fleshy meat of the fruit toward the viewer. The fruit contains a hollow, uterine-shaped lower section with several seeds inside. Above, part of the pear-shaped fruit tapers to a shoulder-like form and into a stem containing a small likeness of Kahlo's head and face. The heavy black brows are clearly identifiable. The center piece is flanked by a smaller fruit on the right side that has been sliced open as to resemble female genitalia. To the left of the large cassava is a vegetable with a stalk containing filaments similar to fallopian tubes. At the base of the painting, near the rim, is a representation in fruit of the "crowning" of a baby's head in the birth canal. One cannot know exactly what bothered señora Ávila Camacho about the painting, but she felt uncomfortable in having this "still life" on her dining room wall. In several ways the painting rejected by señora Ávila Camacho is characteristic of Kahlo's work during this period. It is a statement containing the imagery of fecundity and the life cycle. It is also emblematic, a section from a long narrative slowly revealed over time: the female body, suffering and pain, fallen nature, longing for love, veins, hearts, vines, thorns, bindings, blood, and thorny crowns, a visual feast pointing the viewer to the broken body of this Mexican woman. It is very personal art, something almost unheard of in Mexico before Kahlo. She said of her art that "they thought I was a surrealist, but I wasn't. I painted my own reality."[42]

Kahlo's life has been explored extensively. It can be argued that she did her best work as an artist in the 1940s, and this chapter will deal with her life primarily during the Ávila Camacho period. In 1940 Frida was thirty and struggling somewhat in a sexually open marriage to the flamboyant Diego Rivera. She lived some of the time in her childhood home at the corner of Londres and Allende in Coyoacán, but most of the time in their famous home in San Ángel. Her relationship with Rivera was one of deep love and stormy conflict. On several occasions she abandoned him altogether but always came back. Lucienne Bloch said that in 1935 Kahlo was inspired almost to divorce by observing the independence demonstrated by her friends, painter María Izquierdo and photographer Lola Álvarez Bravo. These two women rented an apartment and lived on incomes derived from the sale of their works.[43] Later, Kahlo and Rivera did divorce, but by 1940 they were reconciled and, after remarriage, were members of the large community of writers, painters, radicals, actors, refugees, poets, and intellectuals who gathered in Mexico City from all over the world.

Kahlo entertained her guests dressed in her famous "Tehuana" style. By all accounts, she presided over wonderful meals, great conversation, and lots of drinking, but no shootings as there had been at the parties in the 1920s. Parties often ended in outings to nightspots like the Salón México and Club Smyrna for dancing and conversation with working-class Mexicans. Kahlo was bisexual and had affairs with men and women.[44] One of her most unusual affairs was with Leon Trotsky. Trotsky and his wife came to Mexico in 1937 and were invited to move in with Kahlo and Rivera in her Coyoacán house. The affair between Trotsky and Kahlo was short and not very sweet. Kahlo thought Trotsky old-fashioned, especially in his view that "women should not smoke."[45] Before long the Trotskys took a place of their own a few blocks away, where Leon was murdered in 1940. Another important houseguest, who set the stage for Kahlo's growing recognition as an artist in the 1940s, was André Breton, the "pope of surrealism." Breton was astounded by Kahlo's work and arranged a show for her in Paris.

In 1940 Kahlo received major attention from the art world when she was exhibited with Rivera, Montenegro, Merida, Picasso, Klee, Ernst, Miró, and others in the *International Exhibition of Surrealism* at Inéz Amor's Galería de Arte Mexicano. This event captured the imagination of the Mexico City press in a year that also included the opening of Orozco's mural in Jiquilpan, Michoacán,[46] and the inauguration of the first full Mexican ballet season featuring eleven ballets, all with at least some music, scenery, or choreography created in Mexico.[47] A number of government officials attended the opening of the exhibition, and the undersecretary of the treasury, Eduardo Villaseñor, praised the role of art in Mexico and noted that in New York, at the Museum of Modern Art, an exhibition called *Veinte siglos de arte mexicano* would soon open, showing the world the range of Mexican art from the most ancient to the most modern. Everyone who was anyone in the Mexican infrastructure of culture and government was at the surrealism exhibition, and all "elegantly dressed," according to the press.[48] In a long article on the Mexican arts in 1940, Luis G. Basurto spoke of a "new renaissance" taking place.[49]

For several months in 1940, Kahlo worked urgently on the only large canvas she ever painted, *The Wounded Table.* Her goal was to have it ready for the opening of the surrealist exhibition. Hayden Herrera believes that although Frida was more a surrealist's discovery than a true surrealist, she was profoundly influenced by surrealism. She points out that Kahlo's work changed in a more clearly surreal direction after the 1940 exhibition.[50] It is also clear that the Marxist Rivera was uncomfortable with Kahlo's interest in the fantasy and absurdity of surrealism.[51] In 1943 he wrote rather awkwardly that Kahlo's work represented "monumental realism" using "occult materialism" and was so real, in fact, that it was the only painting "that was at the same time painting the exterior and interior of herself and the world."[52] Art critics have easily seen Kahlo as a surrealist. Peggy Guggenheim wrote that "having included her in my women's shows, I realized how gifted she was in the true surrealist tradition."[53]

On 24 May 1940 the gloomy and heavily walled house where Trotsky was living in Coyoacán, a few blocks from Kahlo's house, was attacked by machine-gun fire. Rivera went into hiding because he was a suspect, and he soon left quietly for the United States. David Alfaro Siqueiros was arrested, spent a year in prison, and was exiled to Chile. Three months later, when Trotsky was brutally murdered, Kahlo also came under some suspicion. After a long interrogation in which she admitted knowing the accused murderer and having him once to dinner in Coyoacán, she was released. She flew to San Francisco and on 8 December 1940 Kahlo and Rivera were remarried. Together they returned to Mexico City and began a fruitful period of painting, partying with the international community, and for Kahlo, suffering the pain of physical disintegration.

During the next five years of the Ávila Camacho administration, Kahlo received substantial financial support from the avilacamachista state. In 1941 she received a commission to paint portraits of the five most important women in Mexican history for the dining room of the National Palace. Unfortunately, these paintings were never finished. A second, smaller commission resulted in the previously mentioned anatomical still life that señora Ávila Camacho rejected.[54] In 1942 Kahlo was named a founding member of the Seminario de Cultura Mexicana, an organization created by SEP to allow selected cultural leaders to have broader social influence through lectures, exhibitions, and publications. In 1943 and 1944, Kahlo organized exhibitions in the Palace of Fine Arts and was repeatedly asked to lecture and teach around the city. But her most important professional relationship, personally and perhaps financially, was her contract to teach at the new SEP-sponsored school for painters and sculptors known as "La Esmerelda." During the remainder of the Ávila Camacho years, La Esmerelda provided leading artists support from the state in the form of a steady income. These artists included Jesús Guerrero Galván, Carlos Orozco Romero, Agustín Lazo, Manuel Rodríguez Lozano, Francisco Zúñiga, and María Izquierdo.

Kahlo's life was entering its last stage when she took the faculty position alongside Izquierdo and the others at La Esmerelda. Kahlo remained a powerful artist and personality until the end, however, and her painting and teaching activities during the war years are seen by some as her best work. For three years Kahlo worked three days a week as an employee of the state, teaching art and receiving the equivalent of about fifty 1943 dollars a month as a salary.[55] She soon moved her classroom to her home in Coyoacán, and officials at the school did not seem to mind. It was a long bus trip, but at Kahlo's famous house her students spent time with artists and intellectuals from all over the world. Down the street from her house, at the corner where a small grocery store now stands, there stood in 1943 a small bar called La Rosita. On the front wall of the bar, Frida Kahlo's students painted a mural. According to newspaper accounts, the worlds of politics, film, art, music, and literature all came to the unveiling of the mural on 19 June 1943. Concha Michel, one of the most famous folksingers in Mexico, sang duets with Kahlo, bands played, and the neighborhood children joined the famous guests in street dancing. The poet and diarist Salvador Novo, soon to become director of the School of Drama of the National Institute of Fine Arts, and at that moment writing his notes for what would become his history of the war years in Mexico, *La vida en México en el periodo presidencial de Manuel Ávila Camacho*, spoke in glowing terms of Kahlo's value to the nation as a teacher.[56]

At about age thirty-eight, Kahlo's final struggle with her broken and failing body began. Although she never actively supported the government, and often was critical of it, after she returned to Mexico and during the last four years of Ávila Camacho's sexennium, she received numerous commissions, a steady, if not large, state salary, and much "official" respect. Recognized and valued by the state, her painting during this period is complex and intriguing to art historians. Duality, egocentrism, betrayal, pre-Columbian motifs, religious motifs, wounded animals, the jungle, eroticism, pain, torture, death, androgyny, and color characterize the work of this gifted person who worked for SEP as a change agent for an emerging generation of Mexican women.

Bodies, Visions, and Sounds:

The Emergence of Mexican Women in Culture

On 1 January 1940 the yearly review of art in Mexico printed in *Excélsior* contained the photograph of a dark-eyed woman of natural beauty looking directly at the camera. Her photograph was placed between two light-skinned, blond European women, the ballet mistress Waldeen and a now forgotten actress named Orista Hecia. The effect is striking. María, whose name is synonymous with native Mexican womanhood, looks powerful, beautiful, everything the state wanted in an ideal woman. María Izquierdo was born in the village of San Juan de los Lagos, Jalisco, in 1908. She lived there, an area rich in associations with the Mexican circus industry, folk art, fairs, and religious events, until she was forced, at fourteen, into an arranged marriage. In some ways she never left her village, for her work is filled with domestic and religious odds and ends familiar to every Mexican. In the 1940 article, she leads the section on painting, no small feat for a woman in a nation and a field dominated by males. By 1940 along with several film stars and singers, María Izquierdo was one of the best-known women in Mexico.

After leaving her village and her husband, she had a studio for a while in Torreón. Wanting to learn more about painting, in 1927 she moved to Mexico City and entered the famous Academy of San Carlos, where she studied under Germán Gedovius. In 1929 she met and began a lifelong association with Lola Álvarez Bravo and Frida Kahlo. During this period, she also had an affair with Rufino Tamayo, whose influence is strong in her work. In her first exhibition in New York in 1933, when she was twenty-five, her vibrant paintings of the Virgin, still lifes, house altars, children's portraits, and landscapes received a positive review from Mexico's leading art critic, Justino Fernández.[1] From the middle of the 1930s to the late 1940s, María Izquierdo was doing something few Mexican women were able to do: She lived off her earnings as an urban professional artist. Anna Macías points out that the 1921 census lists fewer than 10,000 women in Mexico exercising a skill or profession. A few hundred were teachers; a few dozen were doctors, dentists, or lawyers. Most were telephone operators or secretaries.[2]

In the 1940s when they were joined together on the faculty of La Esmerelda, the two most famous women artists in Mexico, Kahlo and Izquierdo, were sometimes unfriendly.[3] They approached art from different perspectives, but there were similarities. Like Kahlo, Izquierdo's work is often dreamlike, though less personally revealing or tragic. Although Kahlo held that the revolutionary artist should, in the words of Bertold Brecht, strike like a hammer with the truth, neither she nor Izquierdo were overtly political in their work. As faculty of La Esmerelda, both women received the support of the Ávila Camacho government, which valued them as artists and teachers from whose creations the nation could benefit. Records indicate that they were each paid 252 pesos a month for teaching three days a week. This was about fifty United States dollars a month at a time when the average Mexican urban worker was making about twelve dollars a month.[4]

Kahlo, unlike most Mexican artists, was totally personal and self-revealing in her work. Izquierdo, although sometimes personal and always inventive, was more traditional. Her art is an act of memory and imagination, almost an idealization of the ordinary elements of Mexican life. Like Kahlo, Izquierdo painted herself and her family. But the similarity of subject matter is only superficially the same. Kahlo tore herself open in her art, as life had torn her open in the bus accident. She revealed her inner organs and her profound pain. Izquierdo, on the other hand, in *My Aunt, My Playmate and Me,* painted in 1942, reveals only an idealized memory of a tall, attractive woman with two squat children. Although the scene is pleasant enough, it is almost devoid of emotion, or perhaps designed so that the viewer could see in it his or her aunt, childhood friend, or childhood self. Despite her communist views, Kahlo received commissions and support because of the quality of her work. Izquierdo received support because of the nationalist theme in her work. Her houses are Mexican, her horses are Mexican, and her circus themes celebrate an event that was an exhilarating experience for most people in this period.

In the Mexico of the 1940s large and animated crowds attended art exhibitions. S. Walter Washington, first secretary of the United States Embassy in Mexico during the Ávila Camacho years, told of the opening of an exhibition by education secretary Jaime Torres Bodet on 22 July 1946 at Bellas Artes. He observed that "Mexicans of all classes" crowded the event in numbers much larger than one might see at a similar event in the United States. He saw "young men in mechanic's or workmen's overalls, girls who might have been schoolteachers, girls who might have been debutantes, whole families of obviously poor people and a fair sprinkling of campesinos in white shirts and trousers and wide sombreros in their hands."[5]

In Izquierdo's work there is a unity of visual objects that often includes Mexican religious iconography. Kahlo's work also often includes the crown of thorns, the wounded side, the sacred heart, or the suffering of the crucified. Such visual imagery is subliminally powerful in a culture that is steeped in religious language and images. Suffering, a crown of thorns, and a cross are everyday similes in Mexican conversation and home life. In conversation one might hear, *"Llevo la cruz a cuestas"* (I am carrying a cross) as a way of saying that one is burdened with worry. In response to the age-old question "How are you?" one might hear *"Aquí con esta cruz"* (I am near the cross), meaning that one is suffering from some serious problem. Aging parents make the sign of the cross in the air in the direction of where their children live as an act of unseen parental love. Paper, wood, candles, stone, and wire are used to make devotional objects for the home. This visual milieu was the context for the work of Kahlo and Izquierdo, neither of whom cared much for the Catholic faith as an institution but understood its role in the soul of the nation. Both shared the Mexican sense of ironic humor. Just as the characters played by Cantinflas were works of cinematographic art because they presented a careworn and impoverished individual who, becoming empowered by the love of his community, discovered ways of standing up against injustice, so Kahlo and Izquierdo explored the tragic sense of life with dark humor. Kahlo at her most broken remains dignified and brave.

In the 1940s Izquierdo's work turned more to the things she remembered in her village home. With skill that kept her work fresh and away from cliché, she painted landscapes filled with objects and figures decidedly Mexican.[6] Her 1946 painting *Red Snapper* represents this high level of originality. The background for the painting is a mountain skyline, modernized with telephone poles and recognizable to anyone who has driven in northern Mexico. In the foreground is a plain wooden table, covered by a bright tablecloth upon which rests a cornucopia of Mexican fruits, cheeses and peppers. A large red snapper anchors the center of the painting, which is a savory union of dry desert air and salt air, mountains and coasts, coconut and chili, of Mexico coast to coast. One can see why Izquierdo's work was appreciated by the builders of avilacamachismo. It reflects what they saw in themselves and their culture, hundreds of small Mexican objects that, unified, become a visual expression of the country.

Izquierdo entered with gusto into the life of the partly Mexican, partly refugee intellectual and artistic community of wartime

Mexico City. She was a central figure in the previously mentioned camarilla of Pablo Neruda; in 1938 she met and began an affair with a Chilean painter named Raúl Uribe.[7] In 1945 she received a commission to do a large mural but, for reasons that today we could only call sexist, was forced to abandon the project because of severe criticism from Rivera and Siqueiros. They claimed that she was too inexperienced in the medium of fresco painting to do a good job and orchestrated her removal.[8] In 1948 she suffered the first of a series of strokes that would kill her in 1955. She was so ill that at the time of her last visit to see Kahlo, she had to be assisted to the bedside of the dying painter.[9] From 1940 until 1946, however, with fair health and support from the state, she painted at least 150 works. Between 1948 and her death, only 20 are known to have been finished.[10]

Hailed by *Excélsior* as the "most important living symbol" of the era, film star María Félix is another woman who played a major role in the great and lasting social changes taking place in Mexico in the 1940s.[11] In spring 1992 one of the largest television audiences ever recorded in Mexico tuned their sets to watch *Movida*, a nightly variety show hosted by Veronica Castro. The following day every newspaper in the nation carried stories of the program that had featured the rare personal appearance of "La Doña," as Félix was called by the press ever since her 1943 film *Doña Barbara*. The seventy-seven-year-old film star was still as controversial as ever.[12]

Many of the newspaper accounts of the program centered on Félix's contemporary life as a wealthy international star who demanded that the entire set of Castro's show be rebuilt to look like the living room of her home in Mexico City, that all of the art and furniture in her living room be brought to the set, and that she be interviewed only by the famous news anchorman Jacobo Zabludovsky. The press used the occasion to recall the series of adventures and controversies surrounding Félix's long life, especially her affairs and marriages.[13] During this period she also made a cameo appearance on a popular soap opera. On the night of the *Movida* interview, she smoked a cigar and wore the most famous piece of jewelry in modern Mexico, the "regalo de amor," a spectacular necklace of diamonds and emeralds given to her by Jorge Negrete when they married in the "wedding of idols." When one speaks of the glamour and sophistication of the 1940s in Mexico, said the Argentine novelist Manuel Puig, "one speaks of María Félix."[14]

Kahlo and Félix were friends, although the entire nation knew that Rivera and Félix were having an affair while she posed for him. Newspapers carried lurid stories and published photographs of the two. According to Hayden Herrera, the three major Mexico City papers carried stories that Rivera was planning to divorce Kahlo and marry the beauty on her condition that "she could bring her twenty-year-old girlfriend, a beautiful Spanish refugee who had served Frida as nurse and companion, into the marriage as part of a ménage à trois."[15]

Feminist Debra Castillo has pointed out that public expression of alternative forms of sexual behavior are rare in Mexican culture because, whereas the male is granted permission to have many sexual partners, women who dare to do so are considered insane. "Una loca," says Castillo, is any woman "who crosses the threshold of the home and steps beyond the traditional bounds of proper, womanly behavior." This appropriate behavior is called in Spanish *pudor*, which means modesty, decorum, humility, and purity. It is also called *recado*, which means prudence, caution, shyness, and gentleness.[16] The influence of film stars on popular culture has been debated for as long as there have been film stars. Oddly, in the 1940s the Mexican press was much less inhibited in writing about the lives and relationships of individuals in the film and radio industry than was the American press. María Félix may have been the most famous woman in Mexico by 1946, and Mexico could not get enough of her. Throughout the 1940s she was portrayed breaking new ground beyond the confines of the traditional home. In everything she did, she communicated to a fascinated public that women could also live free from the existing social conventions. And she came across as anything but insane.

María Félix was born on 8 April 1914 in the northern Sonoran village of Alamos. According to Paco Ignacio Taibo, her biographer, it was the radio that first brought the voice of Agustín Lara to Félix. She has said that she was "just fourteen when I first heard Lara singing on the radio," and, though he did not sing with conventional beauty, "I was struck by his voice and said to my brother that sometime I would marry him."[17] First, however, she was married to a cosmetics salesman with whom she had her first and only child, Enrique Álvarez Félix. In 1940, when she was already twenty-six years old, Félix met the man who changed her life, the pioneer Mexican film director and cinematographer, Fernando Palacios. Félix seems to have simply walked away from her family. Paco Ignacio Taibo quotes Palacios as saying that he would make Félix "into one of the most important women in world cinema."[18] He did, but the relationship with Palacios was one-sided, and when Félix became a star after making the film *El peñón de ánimas* (The Ghost Cliffs), produced and directed by Miguel Zacarias for Grovas Films in 1942, Félix left him broken and estranged from his family.[19] Although she was now twenty-eight, Félix was nearly ten years younger than the leading star of Mexican cinema in 1942, the elegant and beautiful Dolores del Río.

Grovas Films, who signed Félix for her first film, produced eight films in 1942 with generous backing by the newly created Banco Cinematográfico, the state film financing agency. In 1942 Grovas was the largest film company in Mexico and received the most money from the Ávila Camacho government.[20] Félix had now begun a long film career that would include forty-seven pictures and a series of marriages and affairs that became the daily bread of Mexican newspapers. In 1943, also for Grovas, Félix starred in *Doña Barbara* and was directed by Fernando de Fuentes.[21] Although *Flor Silvestre* and *María Candelaria* were the two most popular films of 1943, both directed by Emilio Fernández and now considered classics, there were so many other outstanding films that 1943 is sometimes regarded as the best year in the history of Mexican cinema. In 1941 thirty-seven films were produced in Mexico; in 1942, forty-seven; in 1943, sixty-nine; in 1944, seventy-five; and in 1945, eighty-two. Direct support by the state increased film production throughout the Ávila Camacho years, and the overall quality of acting, directing, cinematography, and script was high.[22]

In 1943 María Félix married the man some call "the Irving Berlin of Mexico," Agustín Lara. It was the most famous wedding in modern Mexican history and created a journalistic firestorm. In his long career, Lara wrote the scores for nineteen films, sang on the first popular radio program, created or fundamentally influenced much of the style of Mexican popular music between 1925 and 1950, and composed and published 190 songs between his first, "La prisionera" in 1926, and his last, "A poco no" in 1968.[23] No popular singer-songwriter in Mexican history was as well known as Lara, and when he married María Félix in 1943, the press went wild as "the woman without a heart" (*La mujer sin alma*, the title of her fifth film) married the man who had written the most popular and sometimes controversial love songs of the era, such as "Te quiero" and "Solamente una vez." The press frenzy continued over the years as the Lara-Félix relationship became a spectacle.

Lara was born in Veracruz in 1897 or 1900. He was well educated and discovered as a *joven prodigio* while living in Coyoacán. He was influenced by Carlos Gardel, Rudolf Valentino films, and the piano players at neighborhood bordellos. Needing to support his family, he began writing songs while playing the piano and attending the Military College. His first hit in 1926 led him to star in the radio show *La hora azul* on XEW in 1930. This was the program that introduced María Félix to his voice in the dark Mexican night. The year that they were married, Lara wrote "Cada noche un amor" for the film *Distinto amanacer*, which starred Andrea Palma, a film previously discussed at length.[24] He said it was written for Félix, as were "María Bonita" and "Madrid." The marriage of Lara and Félix lasted less than a decade and was followed by her almost equally sensational marriage to Jorge Negrete, the co-star of her first film. Negrete was very popular with the Mexican public and with the Ávila Camacho regime. When Negrete died suddenly, Félix caused a scandal by wearing slacks to the funeral.[25]

Mexico was changing. The year Félix and Lara married, 1943, a photograph appeared in several Mexican newspapers of five young women dressed in battle dress and wearing slacks. Blanca Lastiri, Margarie Galván, Squadron Chief Enriqueta de Leal, Norah Gonzáles, and Violeta de Torres, all attractive young women between the ages of twenty and twenty-four, were the first members of the Mexican army's parachute nurses brigade, the first organization of its kind in Latin America. The leader, Enriqueta de Leal, was the first professional woman parachute jumper in Mexico. There were fifteen young women in the squadron, all trained at the Aviation School in Mexico City. Nearby, another group of young women, also wearing slacks, were working in the new airplane factory in Mexico City, turning out the "Tezuitlán," a sturdy training plane named after Ávila Camacho's birthplace.[26] Photographs of Frida Kahlo taken during this period by Lola Álvarez Bravo show her frequently wearing slacks.[27]

In an important 1970 essay entitled "La participación de la mujer mexicana en la educación formal," novelist Rosario Castellanos argued that the theoretical equality of the sexes as set forth by the Constitution of 1917 had been clearly undermined and dissipated by the powerful grip of traditional culture. She explained that Mexican culture demanded that women be controlled by men, remain silent, and embrace matrimony and maternity.[28] From the 1920s on, however, there were women who worked consciously to change the culture by living alternative lifestyles. All the women of this chapter resisted and rejected the pressures of traditionalism in their lives and in their art. Two more of these women were Nellie Campobello and her sister, Gloria.

Nellie Campobello first achieved success as a writer. Later she and her sister, Gloria, became the leading figures in the development of Mexican dance. There is a myth that they had come down from the highlands of Durango to create a revolution in dance as dramatic as the Revolution of rifles and machine guns. The myth proclaims that they wanted to forge the Revolution with the art of the ballet. Although the myth is appealing, the story of their lives is rooted in Mexican reality.

They were born during the Revolution in the midst of the fighting in the north. Orphaned and taken to live in Mexico City, they discovered ballet as schoolgirls. Gloria Campobello later said that, at the age of five, seeing Anna Pavlova dance captured her heart forever. As young women they studied under a number of teachers, including one from the Russian Imperial Ballet Company, and finally under Eleanor Wallace, who inspired the young women with dance theory and classical technique.[29] In 1929 Nellie Campobello published her first serious writing and shortly thereafter went to work for the government in the Department of Fine Arts. The following year, while on a trip to Cuba where they met Langston Hughes and Gabriel García Lorca, the sisters decided to open the first fully Mexican school of ballet.

The novels of Nellie Campobello, including the 1930 *Cartucho*, deal primarily with the upheaval and chaos of the Mexican Revolution. Nellie said that the stories of *Cartucho* are "historic truth, tragic happenings seen by my eyes as a child in a city, just as other eyes could see similar occurrences in Berlin or London during the world war."[30] In 1932 she was named honorary professor of Mexican dance at the National University and, together with Gloria, produced the first "revolutionary ballet of the masses," called *.30-.30* after the favorite weapon of the followers of Pancho Villa, Nellie's hero. Throughout the 1930s, the sisters worked for SEP. Nellie Campobello said of this period that they were "messengers of the art of the dance," traveling and "laboring for the people because the Revolutionary government needed us."[31]

In the year that Ávila Camacho became president, the Campobello sisters published the most important book in the history of Mexican dance, *Ritmos indígenas de México*. They sought to identify the indigenous sounds, movements, rhythms, and steps of the Mexicans before the arrival of European influence. They hoped to uncover an aboriginal foundation upon which they could build a Mexican ballet. Observing the dances of the Yaquis and Mayas, among others, they suggested that in these dances there was a "manner of walking," a movement in which the carriage of the body, the direction of the feet, the speed, attitude and gait, the angle of the shoulders, the flexibility of the waist, rigidity and inclination of the bust, were unique forms of dance expression.[32]

The sisters argued that these ancient dance forms contain expressions of "beauty and pain they would never dare to speak of."[33]

The large emigré community in Mexico City also had an impact on the dance. The year 1940 saw a fusion of Mexican and European talent in a season that featured eleven ballets. Several were based upon music written or directed by noted Mexican composers. These included *Entre sombras anda el fuego* with music by Blas Galindo, *Antígona* directed by Carlos Chávez, *El renacuajo* with music by Silvestre Revueltas, *Procesional* with music by Eduardo Hernández Moncada, *Danza de las fuerzas nuevas* with music by Blas Galindo, and *La coronela* with music by Silvestre Revueltas.[34] With ballet entering a new era and receiving popular and governmental support, Martín Luis Guzmán approached the Campobellos with the idea of creating, "out of exclusively Mexican elements, a ballet troupe that would practice the art with the same perfection as that of any foreign company."[35] Gaining the putative support of Octavio Véjar Vázquez, the education secretary in the Ávila Camacho administration, as well as Javier Rojo Gómez, a powerful political leader in the Federal District, the Mexico City Ballet was formed.[36] Gloria Campobello was secretary and treasurer, and the muralist José Clemente Orozco, among others, was a board member.[37]

In 1943 seven ballets were presented, including two that were written, choreographed, staged, costumed, and danced by Mexican artists.[38] The first, *Umbral*, used the music of Franz Schubert and was choreographed by Gloria Campobello, with costumes and scenery by her lover, Orozco. It was not until the second production, *Buensanta*, that Nellie Campobello reached her ideal of a totally Mexican ballet, with music by Ernesto Elorduy, Manuel M. Ponce, Felipe Villanueva, Jesús Martínez, Domínguez Portas, and Ricardo Castro. Written by Martín Luis Guzmán, the story was choreographed by Nellie Campobello, with costumes and scenery designed by Roberto Montenegro.

Gloria Campobello was apparently the inspiration for the ballet *Ballerina*. Orozco wrote the plot and designed the set and the costumes. Gloria Campobello choreographed it and was the featured dancer. The music was by Franz Schubert. In the opening scene, the ballerina puts on her stage makeup and rehearses the positions of classical ballet. Like Gloria Campobello in real life, the ballerina is intoxicated with the joy of dance. Nellie Campobello later wrote that "she loved the dance and most certainly gave her entire life for the dance."[39]

In her lifetime, Gloria Campobello had many relationships but, disregarding convention, she never married. She was famous for tragic affairs since most of her lovers were somehow killed, and for her passionate affair with Orozco. He was many years older than she and, by most accounts, he was very much in love with her.

From 1941 until 1946, the great painter, who was entering his sixties and was soon to die, spent a good deal of his time writing ballets, designing sets and costumes, and serving on the board of the Mexico City Ballet. In *Ballerina*, Orozco pays homage to his beautiful twenty-six-year-old lover, Gloriacita. In the second scene, Gloria Campobello again executes to perfection the classical style, inspiring her fellow students to a kind of dance ecstasy. But as she continues, she becomes frustrated. The other dancers leave the stage. Alone, she becomes unsure of herself. Unable to sustain perfection, she unties her hair and weeps in despair. In a fantasy, she opens herself to light and hope. The set opens as stars and fields become her arena. She dances until she is exhausted and drops on the dark stage. A strong, bright light suddenly surrounds her, and she arises again for an instant. Suddenly the light fades, and the ballerina falls to the stage, unable to rise again. Strangely, the ballet was prescient, for Gloria Campobello, whose beauty and fashion were standard fare in Mexican newspapers in the 1940s, faded as she neared fifty and died at fifty-one in 1958. Orozco wrote several ballets for his lover who, according to her sister, "seemed like an incorporeal body when she danced, floating in the air."[40] For this transparent, enigmatic creature, so Mexican, so graceful, Orozco also wrote *Carta de amor*, which was never staged. Nor was *Teoría*, his last attempt to write a ballet for his lover. He also wrote and designed scenery and costumes for a ballet called *Parvula*, based upon the childhood of the Campobello sisters, which was never produced.[41]

In 1945 Nellie Campobello choreographed two important Mexican ballets and her sister one. The first was a nationalistic work called *Obertura republicana*, with music by Carlos Chávez and scenery and costumes by José Clemente Orozco. In some ways it is a reworking of her earlier ballet *.30-.30.* The ballet tells the story of the Revolution in three parts. It begins with the popular uprising. The war spirit comes forth from the earth, yet peace and war exist at the same time. In part two, all is renewed by the cleansing flame of the Revolution. In the final part, designed for a Mexico in the midst of change, all things, the good and bad, feminine and masculine, rich and poor, unite, just as President Ávila Camacho, the "father of Mexican unity," wanted in a modern, revolutionary nation. Nellie Campobello's second work, entitled *Ixtepec*, which anticipated her 1947 masterpiece *Feria,* included music arranged by Eduardo Hernández Moncada, Alfredo Pacheco, Abundio Martínez, Salvador Morlet, A. de la Peña, L. Espinoza, Lerdo de Tejada, Juventino Rosas, Emil Waldtuefel, Johann Strauss, and Edward Strauss. Nellie designed the costumes.[42]

In *Clase de ballet*, set in a 1940 ballet class, Nellie explores in her choreography the conflict between the classical and the modern. Gloria Campobello dances the part of the teacher, beautiful and well-versed in the classical tradition, who struggles to understand the innovations of modern dance. In the end, both are celebrated with joy, suggesting that in dance and perhaps even in Mexican life, the old Hegelian notion of thesis in struggle with antithesis can, indeed, result in something newer, better and, over time, unified.

Nellie and Gloria Campobello were vital artistic and intellectual role models for the women of Mexico. In her novels, Nellie Campobello championed freedom. She demanded the right to say what she wanted to say and live as she pleased. Gloria Campobello lived to dance. In the Ávila Camacho era, they were appreciated and supported by a government that approved of what Nellie called her "cultural patriotism." Rooted in a love of Mexico, it was also authentic and existential. In her prose Nellie Campobello captured the spirit of Mexico. In *Cartucho* she described the village of

Jiménez in words as clean as Hemingway's: "Jiménez is a dusty little town. Its streets look like starving intestines. Its streetlights sing
a sad song for your eyes when, in the tearful night, they kiss your
face. Faces that are not sad nor bold, but rather washed out like
faces in a seance."[43] In Mexican literature, Nellie Campobello was
the first major woman writer of the twentieth century. In their
research on Mexican dance and in their work in the development
of Mexican ballet, Gloria and Nellie Campobello were formative
figures.

What Nellie and Gloria Campobello did for dance was part of
an explosion of artistic activity in Mexico in the Ávila Camacho
years. In fact, in the first two years of the administration, with liberal support from the government, three ballet companies were
formed in Mexico. The companies of Ana Sokolov and Waldeen,
as mentioned earlier, produced eleven ballets in 1940, with many
contributions from Spanish refugees. Rodolfo Halfter composed
two ballets for Ana Sokolov, and José Bergamín also wrote two
ballets. Mexican composers who contributed to these first two
companies included Blas Galindo and Silvestre Revueltas. And,
just as the Mexico City Ballet had from Orozco, so Sokolov and
Waldeen had sets and costumes designed by artists of the caliber of
Carlos Merida, Antonio Ruiz, Manuel Rodríguez Lozano, and
Antonio Rodríguez Luna.[44]

In June 1941 President Ávila Camacho gave a speech praising
the growth of Mexico's culture, especially in opera, symphonic
music, and dance, calling it "the fertility of peace."[45] When he
addressed Congress on 1 September 1941, he said:

> There are signs in Mexico that the moment is near when we
> shall see how the human spirit resurges in its various manifesta-
> tions. It is possible that our country, which anticipated with the
> 1910 Revolution certain reforms of a social and economic char-
> acter that were later adopted by other nations, will again be in
> the vanguard when the world begins to emerge from the dark-
> ness into which brute force has plunged it.[46]

Beginning in 1940 with the production of *La coronela* with music by Revueltas, *Procesional* with music by Eduardo Hernández Moncada, and *La danza de las fuerzas nuevas* with music by Blas Galindo, and continuing with the work of the Campobello sisters, especially the important 1945 works *Obertura republicana* with music by Carlos Chávez and *Ixtepec* with music by Eduardo Hernández Moncada, dance flourished in Mexico under President Ávila Camacho.

Another important female artist in 1940s Mexico was Lola Álvarez Bravo. Like her close friend and sometimes housemate María Izquierdo, Álvarez Bravo was born in Jalisco. A few years older then Izquierdo, Álvarez Bravo was born in 1905 in the town of Lagos de Moreno. It is interesting and perhaps even important to note that Lola Álvarez Bravo, María Izquierdo, Frida Kahlo, Nellie and Gloria Campobello, and María Félix were all somewhere in their thirties during the period 1940 to 1946. Only Tina Modotti, who died at forty-six in 1942, was older. It was Modotti who taught Álvarez Bravo the art, technique, and technology of photography.[47] By 1940 Álvarez Bravo was among the best known women in Mexico. She had been married in 1921 to the successful photographer Manuel Álvarez Bravo, who had learned from his friend Tina Modotti and from the German immigrant Hugo Brehme.[48] Divorced by the early 1930s, Lola Álvarez Bravo became close to Izquierdo and Kahlo. She photographed them frequently. Beginning in the early 1940s, after she had taken an important state position as head of the Department of Photography in the National Institute of Fine Arts, she began a series of photographs of Kahlo and many other Mexican and refugee intellectuals and artists. One of these features Kahlo looking into what appears to be a colonial-style window. The window, however, has been filled with a mirror and Kahlo sees only herself when she attempts to look out. Among other photographs in the series are those of the many individuals who helped shape Mexican culture in the 1940s, including a pensive Salvador Novo and a less than healthy looking María Izquierdo.[49]

In 1943 Lola Álvarez Bravo, Gloria and Nellie Campobello, and even Frida Kahlo and María Izquierdo (both of whom would enter a period of physical decline leading to death a decade later) were vibrant, beautiful women in their thirties. These were five of the most influential women in Mexico, and all were receiving a paycheck from the government. In addition, María Félix was beginning her long career with a film company that was almost totally financed by the state. Why? What did the Ávila Camacho government have to gain? Ávila Camacho and his leaders were careful not to emphasize the continuation of the old programs such as land reform, nationalization of foreign-owned property, or "socialist" education. Slowly moving away from the old, they set off down a new road together. In picking national unity, industrialization, international respectability, capitalism, and "modernity," they were launching Mexico into a brave new world that required a modified approach to nationalism.

This new approach to nationalism was based on what we have called " modal personalities." But it was not so much what the personalities had to say; indeed, some, like Frida Kahlo, never said much that the Ávila Camacho leadership cared to hear. Rather, it was the context in which they functioned as "national" personalities that gave them value. Linking this popular culture of personalities to the goals of the state was the genius of avilacamachismo. The state's organization of culture was characterized by the practice of bringing "personalities" into the state-party system by paying, praising, promoting, and using them for the ongoing good of the system.

The women discussed here are cases in point. They received a monthly income from the state for holding a public position, and in 1943 and 1944, María Félix received an income from a state supported film company. These women achieved a measure of personal autonomy as female role models for the youth-oriented national culture. They were all young, attractive, gifted, and independent. All were influential in areas that today are ranked as being of major importance in advertising as it seeks to influence trends among young women between the ages of twelve and twenty-five. These areas are fashion, cosmetics, lifestyle, music, and personality.[50] In addition, these women were of value to the state because they were nationalistic in outlook. Lola Álvarez Bravo, for example, photographed Mexican people and found not misery, but vitality. Just as Tina Modotti had done, Álvarez Bravo photographed markets, daily work, prayer, and play. Like Frida Kahlo, she embraced the fantastic in Mexican life, playing with the grotesque and laughing at death in the style of the Mexican poor. María Félix was a perfect counterpoint to the state. As the administration led the nation into an alliance with the United States, Félix publicly rejected Hollywood.[51] Fiercely proud and independent, Félix, like Cantinflas, represented exactly what the state needed, a way of having it both ways. Félix represented modernity and self-determination, while at the same time she was a part of a measured plan for the development of national personalities.

In 1985, in what one can argue represents an interesting corroboration of the thesis that the Ávila Camacho administration created popular culture as a tool for the creation of national unity and national identity, Ángeles Mastretta published the internationally acclaimed novel, *Arráncame la vida*. In this work Mastretta explores the formation of Mexican culture in the 1940s by writing from the perspective of a young Mexican woman named Catalina Guzmán, who is obsessed with radio music and film stars like María Félix and Jorge Negrete.

Her account begins with her marriage to an older man, Andrés, who supports a regional political boss. Mastretta wrote the novel at several levels: the individual story, the national story, and what Claudia Schaefer calls the aesthetic level. Schaefer observes that "in the interstices opened up" by the use of dozens of verses from the popular music of the era, one encounters an intersection of opposing views of history and social relations, one being "official and dominant (the state)" and the other "representing individual dissent."[52] Although Schaefer understands the role of popular culture in Mastretta's novel, she does not understand the role of the

state under Cárdenas and Ávila Camacho in the creation of popular culture in Mexico in the 1940s. Schaefer suggests that Catalina
discovers herself in a kind of Mexican *"Bildungsroman"* in relationship with and escape from her family and husband.

What Schaefer does not seem to see, however, is the way in
which Catalina is given a new voice by the state through the lyrics
of the songs that play such an important role in her emergence as a
woman. In the novel Catalina, like Amparo Montes and María
Félix, listens every night to the voices of the stars on XEW. One
can argue that these lyrics represent, in the case of one young Mexican woman (who represents the youth culture of the era), the con-
vergence of the national and the personal; thus Catalina reflects lit-
erally the goals of avilacamachismo. Toña la Negra, Pedro Vargas,
Jorge Negrete, and Agustín Lara become role models to young
Catalina and link her private search for identity to the broader
national search. The radio becomes for Catalina a release of energy
through a new, exciting medium. The radio programs of this era
represent a moment in Mexican history when desire, hope, expectation, memory, and national and sexual identity united in what
Schaefer has called "configurations with new connotations."
Although she misses the role of the state, Schaefer is quite right
when she picks up on the idea that the radio music of the era
"linked two centers of power that concurrently exercise a certain
erotic seduction: music and politics, the most compelling sites for
individual assertion."[53]

One can observe that Catalina has much within her life story
that resonates with the stories of the women in this chapter. In the
novel Catalina marries, like María Izquierdo, at fourteen. She
marries an older man who is unfaithful, and, like Frida Kahlo, she
has an affair with a woman. Later, at the funeral of her husband
she desires to "wear red," not black, like María Félix, and wants to
turn men's heads.[54] Like Álvarez Bravo, Kahlo, Izquierdo, and
Gloria and Nellie Campobello, she falls in love with a great artist,
a composer named Carlos Vives (Carlos Chávez?), whom she
meets at Bellas Artes. His music is richer and more difficult than

the simple melodies of the radio. After she takes her powerful, aging husband to a Vives concert, the old man observes something that Ávila Camacho would have found ironic. The old general remarks that "this young man has political talent, no one without such talent can get so much applause from an audience. Just look at him, it is as if he has just given the speech of a lifetime."[55] Catalina is often prevented from listening to the radio by her husband. It is too loud, too modern, too out of his control. The aging general represents the older Mexican nationalism as well as repression, regionalism, discord, and corruption. He also embodies the most conservative elements within the PRI who want to hold on to the old ways. He has no idea why his wife, like María Félix once had done, listens to the voices of the radio stars, who fill the dark Mexican night with their songs.

CHAPTER TEN

The Legacy of Avilacamachismo

How do we best understand and describe this bold culture-state experiment? As we approach the close of the century, what can we say came of the culture-state policies of avilacamachismo? Was this unique joining of culture and state a failure? Was it an unrealistic set of notions easily subsumed by the massive infusion of North American capital? Were the culture-state modal personalities replaced by a new power elite whose economic success stories reduce culture to the cold footnotes of a period of transition? Is the language of the materialist historians (that is, the language of classic economics and politics) the best way to tell the Ávila Camacho story? Have any of the culture-state policies had lasting or measurable impact?

The building blocks for this study of the history of Mexico during the Ávila Camacho sexennium have been cultural rather than economic or political. This is not to say, however, that materialist approaches are discounted. Materialist approaches, such as that of Marvin Harris, attempt to demonstrate how physical elements

179

from climate to industrial and banking organization are formative in the shaping of the cognitive dimensions of culture.[1] This is akin to Marxist approaches which hold that relationships of economic production are always determinative of political thought. This broad family of materialist theories is particularly helpful in dealing with sudden or major shifts in a culture. Often these shifts have to do with major changes in the relationships of economic production. Shifts in these areas also often attend shifts in world view by a population. Thus, the materialist argument that the sexennium of Ávila Camacho was a transition period, best explained by classical economic and political historical materialist theory, is not wrong; it is simply not adequate. It is, in fact, misleading because it does not confront the culture-state dynamics of the era.

The challenge of culture in avilacamachista Mexico—Mexico during one short six-year period in the 1940s—requires the discipline of listening. One listens to Mexico in this golden age—a period of strong political leadership, wonderful music, dance, film, theater, and radio—and writes with what can only be described as a "listening heart." One listens in such a way as to hear the story unfolding on its own terms. One listens for the aspirations and ideals of a nation moving toward articulated goals. One resists the temptation, ever present for the outsider, the European or North American historian, to recast the story using only the tools of materialist theory, structuralism, or semiotics. One of the most telling and tragic aspects of Mexican history has been the failure of external and invading peoples to listen to Mexico.

In the last two years of the Ávila Camacho administration a group of young entrepreneurial leaders developed extraordinary influence in the PRI as a result of the influx of capital from the war. The wealth generated in the final years of the sexennium set the stage for a new series of compromises in the name of national unity that favored conservative, monied elements in the society. Cardenismo pioneered the process of coalition and compromise as a road to national unity. Avilacamachismo began with a similar orientation but moved, under the influence of the new capital, to rightist positions unsympathetic to social reform or change. Within a few years, this delimited system, which accepted partners from the left only if absolutely necessary, became a hallmark of the PRI. It led to the tilting of the system in the direction of the powerful and away from the poor and disadvantaged. Unfortunately, it meant also that industrial capitalism neglected economic development at the level where it was most needed. Ultimately, it diminished agrarian progress and did not respond to the problems of population growth, urbanization, and health care. Thus there emerged in the last years of avilacamachismo and in the subsequent administrations a system in which the powerful formed coalitions with one another and with cooperative members of the government.[2] Yet, even as these influences developed and grew stronger, the cultural avilacamachistas held the line: The Mexican national budget in 1945 allocated 171,000,000 pesos to SEP. This was an increase of 43 percent over the 1944 budget and reflected the commitment of avilacamachismo to undergird national unity with education and literacy. In 1945 public education was the second largest item in the budget, ranking just behind agricultural programs and just ahead of public works. National defense, even in the war years, never ranked higher than fourth. The entire budget for 1945 was 1,004,000,000 pesos.[3] These figures illustrate the priorities of avilacamachismo but do not reveal a fundamental political change that would take place and color the way in which historians have treated the subject.

Joining Steven Niblo, historian Ricardo Tirado has argued that the rise of the financial power and influence of the new business leaders in the party and government shaped the final years of the administration and changed the trajectory of avilacamachismo.[4] From the start avilacamachismo focused on national unity and a strong economy, but no one anticipated the massive infusion of capital from the war. For the first three years things went according to plan. A united Mexico with a solid economy produced a cohesive foreign policy that by the end of 1943 guided Mexico into partnership with the Allies. But no political system is impervious to the influence of world events. Between 1943 and 1946, the Mexican economy boomed, and the influx of capital greatly affected Mexico and avilacamachismo. The avilaca-machista plan for economic development was in place, but its results were unforeseen.

President Ávila Camacho declared in his inaugural address on 1 December 1940 that the Revolution had entered a new era that demanded a new birth of ideas, a spiritual renewal for the healing of the nation's old wounds, and an agenda for economic develop-ment and prosperity.[5] The Mexican economy grew in the Ávila Camacho years 2 percent annually, modest by the standards of the developed nations, but a major step forward for Mexico. Robert Bennett suggests that this growth was the result of five avilaca-machista policies: (1) tax incentives for those willing to invest; (2) protected internal markets and high tariffs; (3) tight money poli-cies that kept the peso strong; (4) heavy investment by interna-tional banks, and (5) increased exports to the United States.[6]

These policies reflected a disciplined, internationally minded, business-oriented government. Yet avilacamachismo's very success in the economic area may have led many historians to fail to see beyond the economic boom that took place from 1943 to 1946. Alfonso Taracena argues that the ideals of avilacamachismo simply disappeared amid the wealth generated by the war.[7] Those defending avilacamachismo see economic corruption as victimiz-ing the movement but not as totally destroying its ideals. Taking this view are Ricardo Pozas Horcasitas, Ana Camarena, and Fer-nando González. In their account of the creation of *Seguro Social*, for example, they point out that despite strong opposition from the medical community and the new capitalist groups, avilaca-machismo continued to see the social security system as a means of implementing two of the original goals of the administration, unity and prosperity. These historians conclude that *"la creacíon del Seguro Social fue, sin duda, la medida del gobierno con caracter social más importante de los años cuarenta"* (the creation of social security was, without a doubt, the act of the government with the most social importance of the 1940s).[8]

Did the dynamic economy overwhelm the cultural policies of avilacamachismo? Has avilacamachismo been neglected or misunderstood by historians because in the last two years of the war an economic boom determined a different agenda for postwar Mexico, an agenda that overshadowed cultural avilacamachismo? Did the infusion of capital create a new power elite who had little time for or interest in the idealistic cultural nationalism of the avilacamachistas? The answer to these questions is yes. Yet one can argue that avilacamachismo will never be fully understood if the economic legacy, with its emphasis on the transitional nature of the era, remains unchallenged and the relationship of culture and state remains unstudied. The purpose here has not been to prove that culture is a more important legacy than the economic one; rather it is to bring forward and elucidate a neglected theme of equal or greater importance for the understanding of this period. But how can we measure the importance of the culture-state legacy of avilacamachismo?

First, we must affirm that avilacamachismo was the quite understandable product of a historical process and not an aberration. Manuel Ávila Camacho did not invent the culture-state relationship. It was formed in the remote past of Hispanic history and has been a basic theme throughout Mexican history.

In the thirteenth century when Alfonso X, *"El sabio"* (the wise), came to the throne of Castilla and León, there was a critical moment in the formation of both the Spanish state and Spanish culture, initiating a relationship that has endured in Spain and Latin America until the present. In 1252 the struggle to drive Islam from the Iberian Peninsula paused for a 240-year period of preparation, contemplation, and consolidation before the final push at Granada ended Moslem rule. At this time, the indefatigable drive toward reconquest, fueled in part by hysterical religious fanaticism and in part by the dynamic resolve to create a Spanish nation, faltered as the Castilians and their allies began to deal with issues of culture and state as well as with strategies for the final battle. Significantly, during this period they began to rename the landscape. The Moslem Baetis River, for example, became the

Spanish Guadalquivir, even though the Spanish name still contained, according to Prescott H. Williams, the Arabic word *guade* meaning "watering hole."[9] This is a telling linguistic artifact, for Alfonso X had in mind the creation of a Spanish state and culture from the mixture of people who remained in the land. The Alfonsine era (1252–1284) was one in which a cultural foundation of Greco-Roman, North African, Hebraic, Catholic, and Castilian sources was built by this poet and statesman.

In the years between the death of Alfonso in 1284 and the union of Aragón and Castilla in 1474, Spanish culture and the Spanish state became increasingly bound to the Catholic faith. In 1480, under the rule of Isabella and Ferdinand, the Inquisition was established in Spain to purify the national religion. Fernand Braudel observes that the cohesion of Spain in the fifteenth century was that of a people who had for centuries been the underdog in relation to another civilization, had seen themselves as weaker and less intelligent, and now were suddenly liberated. Although a superior power at last, "it had not yet acquired the internal confidence nor the reflexes of a superior power. It went on fighting."[10] In 1492 the last Moslems were defeated, the Jews were expelled, and America was "discovered."

Roman Catholicism followed Spain to the New World. In Mexico the state and church fought over social issues throughout the three centuries that Mexico was a part of the Spanish empire. Concerning this long struggle Colin MacLachlan has observed that a common fund of philosophical notions facilitated political exchange and empire-building:

> [A]ll sides manipulated ideas to support their particular interests. In the end the most powerful group prevailed, yet at the same time found itself restricted by philosophical principles. The manipulation of ideas justified and legitimized but also modified and restrained. Consequently, in the Spanish world intellectuals functioned at the very heart of the sociopolitical system.[11]

In the seventeenth century, the "baroque age" came to Mexico as "a continuous polemic on the Catholic way of life with a mixture of ideals of the Middle Ages and the Renaissance."[12] José Antonio Maravall has called the baroque Spain's true form and fulfillment. The movement produced Cervantes, Lope de Vega, El Greco, Velázquez and Calderón. Maravall maintains that the "conflictive" nature of the baroque era in the Spanish world produced the first "modern" personality type, which emerged with genius from the tension and crises of baroque society.[13]

Baroque Mexico with its dual tensions of flesh and soul, solemnity and burlesque, produced a genius in Sor Juana Inéz de la Cruz, a woman who, although a member of the ascetic Order of Discalced Carmelites, wrote poems of striking modernity. An intellectually liberated woman who was well connected to the cultural elite, Sor Juana's poetry conveys an eternal theme:

> Which has the greater sin when burned
> By the same lawless fever:
> She, who has been amorously deceived,
> He, the sly deceiver.
> Or which deserves the sterner blame,
> Though each will be a sinner:
> She who becomes a whore for pay,
> Or he who pays to win her?[14]

In colonial Mexico the church functioned as a state within a state and did not hesitate to excommunicate an enemy or to ask the secular state to put to death anyone with whom it was greatly displeased. It is not surprising then that the history of Mexico in the nineteenth century became a struggle between church and state, between those who wanted a church-dominated culture and those who wanted a culture under a political state. The liberal reforms of the 1857 Constitution and later the 1917 Constitution resolved the issue in favor of the state; but following the 1910 Revolution, culture was left prostrate and had to be rebuilt in a process of which avilacamachismo was very much a part and which is still ongoing. Thus the problem of culture and state is ever present in the unfolding of Mexican history. The study of this subject could begin at any point after the conquest. The role of culture in the state is a recurring theme from generation to generation. It includes the issues of national, regional, and racial identity; the struggle for power at all levels; and a complex catalogue of economic, political, linguistic, and religious factors. Octavio Paz has observed that the history of Mexico can best be understood in the context of the culture-state conflict. He says that the history of Mexico from the conquest to the Revolution can be regarded as a "search for our own selves, which have been deformed or disguised by alien institutions, and for a form that will express them."[15]

We have yet to fully understand the long-term historical consequences of the avilacamachista era. The culture-state relationship in Mexico assumed its modern structure in the early 1920s and evolved in the 1930s through the cultural program of Lázaro Cárdenas. It reached a new plateau with Ávila Camacho, and the influence of cultural avilacamachismo has continued to the present day.

Avilacamachismo consolidated the philosophy that culture and state should interact for the advancement of the nation. The tradition of the unprecedented Museum of Modern Art exhibition in 1940 called *Twenty Centuries of Mexican Art*, planned by the state, has continued for political and diplomatic ends on an even grander scale in the 1990s by the Salinas de Gortari administration with the spectacular Mexican art exhibition *Mexico: Three Thousand Years of Splendors* in New York, Los Angeles, and San Antonio in 1990 and 1991. Attracting record crowds and intense media coverage, and generating a five-hundred-page catalogue, the exhibition represented a continuation of the use of culture by the state to promote United States recognition of Mexico and support for internationalization through NAFTA.[16] In 1992 the administration of President Salinas de Gortari sponsored a tour in the United States of a priceless collection of Aztec art,[17] and in Europe on 24 August 1992, Mexico opened a widely acclaimed exhibition of Mexican art at the Frankfurt Book Fair.[18] These are fairly typical illustrations of the culture and state process advanced by the avilacamachistas, here projected for Mexico's new global policies.[19]

The culture-state relationship remains visible domestically as well. For example, on 12 August 1992 in Xalapa, Veracruz, the president of Mexico and several members of his administration opened a state-sponsored exhibition of major artists from ten Latin American nations called *América Hoy*. The artists met with citizens and cultural leaders to discuss the future of art in the Spanish-speaking world.[20] In this meeting one can see the active role of the state in the formation of culture, as well as the avilacamachista legacy of placing Mexico in a leadership role in the international community. Another example of the enduring influence of cultural avilacamachismo was the announcement that the Fondo Nacional para la Cultura y las Artes (FNCA) would cooperate with two private agencies, Bancomer and the Rockefeller Foundation, to fund forty-two new arts projects in Mexico.[21] While the state remains the chief backer of cultural programs, it is now sharing that role with private enterprise, reflecting the neo-liberal policies of the 1990s.

Avilacamachistas worked to develop a permanent friendship with the United States. Its leaders declared often that the nation's future was tied to good relations with their northern neighbor and demanded that this friendship be one of mutual respect and reciprocity. They placed Mexican sovereignty and Mexican national culture on a footing equal with those of the wartime Allies. They demanded and received international respect as they moved Mexico into the United Nations. In the 1990s the views of the avilacamachistas appear prescient. Mexico has been joined to the United States and Canada in one of the three major world trading blocs. When representatives of Mexico signed the North American Free Trade Agreement in San Antonio, Texas, in 1992, it was symbolic fulfillment of the role envisioned for Mexico by Ávila Camacho as a respected member of the world community.[22] President Ernesto Zedillo Ponce de León, elected in 1994, has continued to work for good United States-Mexico relations.

Perhaps the most dramatic expression of avilacamachista continuity is in the resolution of old, divisive problems. In September 1992, Mexico re-established full diplomatic relations with the Vatican after 130 years. This capped a rapprochement between Mexico and the Vatican that began in 1940 when Ávila Camacho made his famous public gesture of reconciliation with the church. After 1992, all of the laws passed between 1856 and 1861 that revoked the rights of the church were rescinded. The new legislation gives the church the right to own property and conduct religious education. In language strongly reminiscent of that used fifty years ago by Ávila Camacho, President Zedillo has announced repeatedly that it is time to overcome old antagonisms that have caused pain and preserved old divisions.[23] In 1998, the PRI has begun to allow opposition parties to gain power and influence in ways that until recently would have been impossible.

Finally, the era remains "golden" in the hearts of many Mexicans, and must be honored as such. One indication of the importance of avilacamachismo is that this period, more than any other, is today remembered as a golden era of popular and high culture. This view is shared by nearly all of the Mexicans interviewed for this book who are over fifty. In addition, a great deal of energy is devoted to the period on radio and television and in magazines and newspapers in Mexico today. This is especially true when leading figures of the era die. The death of Emilio "El Indio" Fernández in 1987 generated dozens of articles and at least two television retrospectives.[24] The legacy of the era may be seen in the fact that its music and many of its artistic personalities remain popular today. Alicia Mena's 1997 play *There Comes a Time* is an example of the enduring nostalgia many Mexicans and Mexican Americans have for the era. In the play, the music of Toña la Negra and the films and songs of Pedro Infante are the cultural icons around which a beautiful Mexican American twenty-something woman builds her life. Totally rejecting the 1990s, she reads only old magazines, listens to the old music, and watches the "golden oldies" of Mexican cinema on television. Her sister, a Chicana activist, and her mother try to bring her into the modern world, and their struggle over culture and the role of women form the humorous basis for a charming musical comedy.[25]

The generally peaceful circumstances of Mexican life since 1946, partially the result of the avilacamachista commitment to national unity, continue to benefit the nation as it nears the beginning of a new century. Artists, filmmakers, songwriters, poets, dancers, television stars, and writers have a safe and honored environment for the creative process. American filmmakers have chosen to make hundreds of films in Mexico, taking advantage of both the congenial atmosphere and the wealth of talent there.

In the end, this golden age of culture and state will never find its rightful place in the history of the nation if the period is seen only as a "transition" between Cárdenas and postwar corruption.[26] It is, in fact, grander, richer, and far more complex and important than any economic or political history of the era has been able to capture. It was an era of art and creative energy that remains close to the hearts of the Mexican people.

NOTES

INTRODUCTION

1. For example, see Carlos Monsivais in *Sociedad y cultura entre la guerra y la estabilidad politica: El México de los '40s,* ed. Rafael Loyola Díaz (México: Grijalbo, 1990).

2. Peter Berger, *The Homeless Mind: Modernization and Consciousness* (New York: Vintage Books, 1973), 173–74.

3. Steven D. Morris, *Corruption and Politics in Contemporary Mexico* (Tuscaloosa: University of Alabama Press, 1991), 57.

4. E. B. Tylor, *Primitive Culture: Researches into the Development of Mythology, Philosophy, Religion, Language, Art and Customs,* vol. 1 (New York: Henry and Holt, 1877), 1.

5. Samuel Ramos, *Profile of Man and Culture in Mexico,* trans. Peter G. Earle (Austin: University of Texas Press, 1975), 26.

6. Alex Inkeles, "Some Observations on Culture and Personality Studies" in *Personality in Nature, Society and Culture,* ed. Clyde Kluckhorn and Henry A. Murray, 2d rev. ed. (New York: Grove Press, 1956), 577–90.

7. David Brion Davis, "Some Recent Directions in American Cultural History," *The American Historical Review* 73, no. 3 (February 1968): 696–707.

8. Jacques Barzun, "Cultural History in Synthesis," *The Vanities of History,* ed. Fritz Stern (New York: Harper, 1956), 387–402.

9. Ibid.

10. Especially helpful in this area is the work of David L. Raby, *Educación y revolución social en México, 1921–1940* (México: Sepsentas, 1974).

CHAPTER 1

1. Claude Fell, *José Vasconcelos: Los años del aguila, 1920–1925* (México: Universidad Autonoma de México [hereinafter UNAM], 1989), 87.

2. Enrique Krauze, *Caudillos culturales en la Revolución Mexicana* (México: Siglo Veintiuno, 1976), 101.

3. Juan Hernández Luna, ed., *Conferencias del ateneo de la juventud* (México: UNAM, 1962), 108.

4. Raúl Cardial Reyes, *Retorno a caso* (México: UNAM, 1986), 43–59.

5. Enrique Krauze, *Caras de la historia* (México: Joaquin Mortiz, 1983), 22.

6. Ibid., 162.

7. José Vasconcelos, *Ulises criollo* (México: Botas, 1936), 192–207.

8. José Vasconcelos, *La tormenta* (México: Botas, 1938), 96.

9. Henry C. Schmidt, *The Roots of Lo Mexicano* (College Station: Texas A&M University Press, 1978), 97.

10. Jean Meyer and Enrique Krauze, *Historia de la Revolución Mexicana, vol. 3, periodo 1924–1928: La reconstrucción económica* (México: El Colegio de México, 1974), 109–11.

11. Ibid., 174.

12. Ibid., 190.

13. José Vasconcelos, "El desastre," in *Obras,* vol. 2 (México: Botas, 1959), 496.

14. Luis Gonzáles, *Historia de la Revolución Mexicana, vol. 15, periodo 1934–1940* (México: El Colegio de México, 1981), 216.

15. Albert Michaels and James Wilkie, eds., *Revolution in Mexico: The Years of Upheaval, 1910–1940* (New York: Knopf, 1969), 219–21.

16. González, *Revolución Mexicana*, 204.

17. Diana Negrete, *Jorge Negrete* (México: Diana, 1989), 46.

18. *Excélsior*, 2 June 1923.

19. *Diario Oficial*, 26 April 1926.

20. Renfro Norris Cole, "A History of *La hora nacional*" (Ph.D. diss., Michigan State University, 1963), 39.

21. Negrete, *Jorge Negrete*, 100.

22. González, *Revolución Mexicana*, 293.

23. Ibid., 290.

24. Howard F. Cline, *The United States and Mexico* (Cambridge: Harvard University Press, 1983), 220–21.

25. González, *Revolución Mexicana*, 295.

26. *Los Angeles Times*, 6 December 1934.

27. González, *Revolución Mexicana, 307–9.*

28. Ibid.

29. *Hoy,* 4 January 1940.

30. Luis González, *San José de Gracia,* trans. John Upton (Austin: University of Texas Press, 1974), 204.

31. Gloria González Atkins, interview with author, 26 September 1978.

32. Jorge Vera Estañol, *La Revolución Mexicana* (México: Porrua, 1957), 630.

33. Frank Tannenbaum, *Mexico: The Struggle for Peace and Bread* (New York: Knopf, 1968), 94.

34. Howard F. Cline, *Mexico: Revolution to Evolution, 1940–1960* (New York: Oxford University Press, 1967), 224.

35. Edwin Lieuwen, *Mexican Militarism, 1910–1940* (Westport, Conn.: Greenwood Press, 1978), 118.

36. Ibid., 121.

37. Ibid., 125.

38. *Excélsior,* 14 August 1938.

39. *Excélsior,* 17 August 1938.

40. Tannenbaum, *The Struggle*, 82.

41. *Nacional,* 2 May 1939.

42. *Excélsior,* 16 July 1939.

43. González, *San José,* 56.

44. The best work on Lázaro Cárdenas and his sexennium is Marjorie Becker, *Setting the Virgin on Fire: Lázaro Cárdenas, Michoacán Peasants and the Redemption of the Mexican Revolution* (Berkeley: University of California Press, 1995).

45. Lieuwen, *Mexican Militarism*, 627.

46. Selden Rodman, interview with author, 13 June 1992.

CHAPTER 2

1. Betty Kirk, *Covering the Mexican Front* (Norman: University of Oklahoma Press, 1942), 329.

2. See the cover of *Hoy,* 17 September 1940.

3. Kirk, *Mexican Front*, 330.

4. James C. Cockcroft and Bo Anderson, "Latin American Radicalism," in *Borzoi Reader in Latin American History*, vol. 2, ed. Thomas C. Hood (New York: Knopf, 1982), 362–80.

5. Letter from Ambassador George S. Messersmith to Secretary of State, USNA, RG 59, 812.51/4-1045, 1945.

6. Yolanda Moreno Rivas, *Historia de la musica popular mexicana* (México: Alianza Editorial Mexicana, 1979), 88. Agustín Lara's lyric may be translated, I want you even though God doesn't want you. The songs may be translated as follows: "La ultima noche" (The Last Night), "Tu ya no soplas" (You've Lost It), "El hijo desobediente" (The Disobedient Son), "Pecadora" (The Nagger), "Toda la vida" (All of Life), "Frio en la alma" (Cold Heart), and "Traigo mi .45" (Bring Me My .45).

7. A most helpful study of the Avila Camacho family is the work of Wil G. Pansters, especially *Politics and Power in Puebla: The Political History of a Mexican State, 1937–1987* (Amsterdam: CEDLA, 1990).

8. Steven Niblo, *War, Diplomacy and Development: The U.S. and Mexico, 1938–1954* (Wilmington, Del.: Scholarly Resource Press, 1995), 90.

9. Ibid.

10. Ibid.

11. Ibid.

12. Ibid.

13. *Foreign Relations of the United States Department of State* (Washington, D.C.: GPO, 1944), 7:406.

14. Secretaria de Relaciones Exterior, *Seis años de actividad el nacional* (México: n.p., 1946), 80–83.

15. *Nacional*, 20 November 1941.

16. Ezequiel Padilla, "Agreement between the United States and Mexico," 25 November 1941. (English text released by the Mexican Secretariat of Foreign Relations [Mexico: International Press Service Bureau, National and International Series No. 9, 1941]).

17. Secretaria de Relaciones Exteriores, *Memoria* (México: n.p., 1943), 317.

18. George Messersmith to United States Department of State, USNA, RG 59, 812.51/3-945, 12 April 1944.

19. George Messersmith to John W. Carregan, USNA, RG 59, 812.51/3-945, 9 March 1945.

20. George Messersmith to United States Department of State, USNA, RG 59, 812.00/321-48, 26 April 1943.

21. Report of the Export-Import Task Force, *First Semi-Annual Report to Congress for the Period July to December 1944* (1945), Appendix B, 204–60.

22. José Luis Ortiz Garza, *México en guerra* (México: Espejo de México, 1989), 135.

23. *Nacional*, 20 April 1943.

24. *La Prensa,* 20 April 1943.

25. *El Porvenir de Monterrey,* 20 April 1943.

26. George Messersmith to Sumner Welles, USNA, RG 59, 812.00/1.3143, 2 April 1945.

27. *Nacional*, 17 September 1943.

28. Kirk, *Mexican Front*, 276.

29. *Excélsior*, 18 September 1943.

30. Raleigh Gibson to Secretary of State, USNA, RG 59, 812.404/4-1045, 10 April 1945.

31. John Chávez, *The Lost Land: The Chicano Image in the Southwest* (Albuquerque: University of New Mexico Press, 1984), 119.

32. Guy Ray to Secretary of State, USNA, RG 59, 862.202-10/15, 30 July 1942.

33. *El Universal,* 10 March 1943.

34. Ezequiel Padilla, *Free Men of America* (New York: Ziff Davis, 1943), 107.

35. *Nacional,* 7 March 1941.

36. Carmela Elvira Santoro, "United States and Mexican Relations during World War II" (Ph.D. diss., University of Michigan, 1967), 200.

37. *Excélsior*, 12 April 1942.

38. *Excélsior*, 6 January 1945.

39. Howard F. Cline, *United States and Mexico* (New York: Atheneum, 1963), 29.

40. *Excélsior*, 6 January 1945.

41. George Messersmith to United States Department of State, USNA, RG 59, 812.740.0011, 23 November 1943. `

42. *Excélsior*, 9 March 1944.

43. George Messersmith to United States Department of State, USNA, RG 59, 812.740.0011, 23 November 1943.

44. *Nacional*, 10 December 1945.

45. James Bigley, former associate director of the Chester Nimitz Library, Fredericksburg, Texas, interview with author, 10 April 1988.

46. Roderic A. Camp, *Mexican Political Biographies* (Tucson: University of Arizona Press, 1982), 208.
47. Ibid., 35.
48. Ibid., 145.
49. Francísco Sánchez González, *Abelardo L. Rodríguez: Obra económica y social* (México: n.p., 1954), 100.
50. *Nacional*, 15 December 1941.
51. *Excélsior*, 20 June 1944.
52. *Excélsior,* 19 February 1945.
53. Rodman, interview, 15 June 1992.
54. Camp, *Biographies*, 79.
55. Ibid., 85.
56. Ibid., 82.
57. *Excélsior,* 20 March 1944.
58. *Nacional,* 12 March 1946.
59. *Excélsior,* 15 January 1946.
60. *Excélsior,* 26 September 1942.
61. *Nacional,* 2 October 1965.

CHAPTER 3

1. Secretariat of Public Education (hereinafter SEP), *La casa de estudiante indigena* (México: Talleres Gráficos de la Nación, 1927), 121.
2. SEP, *Las missiones culturales* (México: Talleres Gráficos de la Nación, 1927), 12.
3. Ernest Gruening, *Mexico and Its Heritage* (New York: Appleton, 1928), 515.
4. Ramon Edward Ruiz, *Mexico: The Challenge of Poverty and Illiteracy* (San Marcos, Calif.: Huntington Library Press, 1963), 160.
5. *El Maestro Rural*, 15 July 1934, 13–14.
6. *El Universal*, 14 October 1936.
7. John Britton, *Educación y radicalismo en México, 1931–1940* (México: Montes, 1955), 206–19.
8. Shirley Brice Heath, *Telling Tongues: Language Policy in Mexico* (New York: Teachers College Press, 1972), 113.
9. Salvador Novo, *La vida en México en el periodo presidencial de Manuel Avila Camacho* (México: Empresas Editoriales, 1965), 11.

10. Camp, *Biographies*, 311.

11. Daniel Cosío Villegas, *Memorias* (México: Joaquín Mortiz, 1976), 178–79.

12. SEP, *Teoria y aplicación de la reforma educación* (México: Talleres Gráficos de la Nación, 1963), 17.

13. Octavio Véjar Vásquez, *Hacia una escuela de unidad nacional* (México: Discurso Editorial, 1944), 24.

14. Alberto Dallal, *El dancing mexicano* (México: Oasis, 1982), 97.

15. Jaime Torres Bodet, *Educación mexicana: Discursos, entrevistas y mensajes* (México: SEP, 1944), 90.

16. Jaime Torres Bodet, *Tiempo de arena* (México: Fondo de Cultura Económica, 1955), 62.

17. lbid., 156.

18. Ibid., 217.

19. Jaime Torres Bodet, *Discursos* (México: Porrua, 1965), 421.

20. Heath, *Telling Tongues*, 128.

21. Eric Vane, "Required Reading," *Inter-American Magazine* 5 (20 August 1945): 12.

22. Heath, *Telling Tongues*, 129.

23. Volodia Teitelboim, *Neruda: An Intimate Biography* (Austin: University of Texas Press, 1988), 144.

24. "Diez años de México," *Nuestra Musica Editorial Boletin* 11 (March 1946).

25. Jaime Torres Bodet, *Memorias: Años contra tiempo* (México: Porrua, 1969), 29.

26. SEP Departamento de Asuntos Indigenas, *Memorias, 1945–1946* (México: n.p., 1946), 125.

27. *Revista Mexicana de Educación* 1 (November 1940): 356.

28. "Communidades de promoción," *Boletin Indigenista* 5 (June 1945): 161–63.

29. SEP, "Las missiones culturales" *Memoria, 1942–1946* (México: Talleres Gráficos de la Nación, 1946), 7–57.

30. *El Universal*, 25 December 1943.

31. Jaime Torres Bodet, *La obra educativa: Seis años de actividades nacional* (México: Porrua, 1969), 133.

32. Ibid., 424.

33. John Britton, "Teacher Unionization and the Corporate State," *Hispanic American Historical Review* 59, no. 4 (1979): 674.

CHAPTER 4

1. Jose Iturriaga, *La estructura social y cultural de México* (México: Financiera, 1951), 201.
2. Documental Servicio Cultural, *La II guerra mundial: Su música* (México: Asociación Mexicana de Estudios Fonográficos 27, 1989).
3. Christina Pacheco, "Yo soy el bolero," *Siempre*, 17 July 1991, 44–47.
4. *Excélsior*, 11 November 1940.
5. Dallal, *El dancing*, 130.
6. *Diario Oficial*, 31 December 1936.
7. Ibid.
8. Phillip L. Barbour, "Commercial and Cultural Broadcasting in Mexico," *Annals of the Ancunian Academy of Political and Social Science* (March 1940): 101.
9. Ibid., 101.
10. Cole, "History of *La hora nacional,*" 39.
11. Ortiz Garza, *México en guerra*, 18–20.
12. Ibid., 25.
13. Cole, "History of *La hora nacional,*" 89.
14. Article 28, Mexican Constitution of 1917.
15. Cole, "History of *La hora nacional,*" 23.
16. *Diario Oficial*, 30 December 1936.
17. Archivo General de la Nación-Manuel Avila Camacho [hereinafter AGN-MAC] 187, "Seis años de gobierno al servicio de México" (México: Secretaría de Gobernación, 1940), Leg. 198, Exp. 268/12.
18. Ibid., 159.
19. Joy Elizabeth Hayes, "Radio Broadcasting and Nation Building in Mexico and the United States, 1925–1945" (Ph.D. diss., University of California at San Diego, 1994), 10.
20. AGN-MAC 187, Memoria de la Secretaría de Gobernación, 1945, Leg. 109, Exp. 124/2.
21. Ibid., 109.
22. On 11 December 1990, *Siempre en domingo*, a national television program hosted by Raúl Fernández, broadcast live from the State Fair of Oaxaca. The program covered two other state fairs in 1990.
23. AGN-MAC 187, Memoria de la Secretaría de Gobernación, 1943, Leg. 105, Exp. 530/2.
24. *El Universal*, 6 June 1943.

25. Michael Meyer and William Sherman, *The Course of Mexican History* (Oxford: Oxford University Press, 1983), 636.

26. Ortiz Garza, *México en guerra*, 143.

27. *Excélsior*, 1940 and 1943; *El Universal*, 1940 and 1943.

28. Ortiz Garza, *México en guerra*, 90.

29. *El Nacional*, 20 May 1943.

30. *El Nacional*, 20 June 1943.

31. *Excélsior*, 7 March 1943.

32. *El Nacional*, 8 March 1943.

33. *El Nacional*, 10 April 1944.

34. AGN-MAC 187, Ordenación Asuntos Personales, Leg. 1, Exp. 101/5.

35. Ibid., 1: 101/6.

36. An example of this view is Frederick Marks's *Wind over Sand: The Diplomacy of Franklin Roosevelt* (Athens: University of Georgia Press, 1988).

37. Merle Simmons, *The Mexican Corrido* (New York: Harper, 1956), 242.

38. AGN-MAC 187, Leg. 102, Exp. 4/118.

39. *Excélsior*, 16 November 1942.

40. AGN-MAC 187, Leg. 512, Exp. 32/146, 27 February 1943.

41. Moreno Rivas, *Musica popular mexicana*, 87.

42. Ibid., 158.

43. Documental Servicio Cultural, *La II guerra mundial*.

44. *Excélsior*, 27 April 1989.

45. Pacheco, *Siempre*, 64.

46. *El Nacional*, 13 June 1940.

CHAPTER 5

1. Carl J. Mora, *Mexican Cinema: Reflections of a Society, 1896–1980* (Berkeley: University of California Press, 1982), 20.

2. *Excélsior*, 20 March 1943.

3. María Luisa Amador and Jorge Ayala Blanco, *Cartelera cinematográfica, 1940–1949* (México: UNAM, 1982), 47.

4. Herbert Cerwin, *These Are the Mexicans* (New York: Reynal and Hitchcock, 1947), 274.

5. *Excélsior*, 26 September 1942.

6. Emilio García Riera, *El cine mexicano* (México: Era, 1963), 77.

7. Luis Buñuel, *My Last Sigh* (New York: Vintage Press, 1983), 190.

8. Negrete, *Jorge Negrete*, 172–90.

9. *El Nacional*, 20 June 1945.

10. Buñuel, *My Last Sigh*, 198.

11. Luis González, *San José*, 222.

12. Carlos Martínez Assad, "El cine como lo vi y como me contarón," in *Sociedad y cultura entre la guerra y la estabilidad politica*, 341–43.

13. An excellent discussion of these films can be found in *Mexican Postcards* by Carlos Monsivais (London: Verso, 1997). The chapter on Dolores del Río titled "The Face as Institution" is especially good.

14. *University of Chicago Spanish Dictionary*, s.v. "alabado."

15. *Diario Filmico Mexicano*, 24 January 1943.

16. Mora, *Mexican Cinema*, 59.

17. González, *San José*, 217.

18. John Chávez, "The Image of the Mexican in American Films" (Class lecture at Texas A&M University, 15 March 1989).

19. Bosley Crowther, *New York Times*, 10 March 1941.

20. Gaizka S. de Usabel, "The High Noon of American Films in Latin America," (Ph.D. diss., UMI Research Press, 1982), 157.

21. *Variety*, 12 July 1939.

22. *Excélsior*, 12 March 1940.

23. de Usabel, "High Noon of American Films," 142.

24. *Variety,* 5 November 1942.

25. Ortiz Garza, *México en guerra*, 158–77.

26. Richard R. Lingeman, *Don't You Know There Is a War On?* (New York: Putnam, 1976), 714.

27. Fred Fejes, *Imperialism, Media, and the Good Neighbor: New Deal Foreign Policy and United States Shortwave Broadcasting to Latin America* (Norwood, N.J.: Ablex Publishing Corp., 1986), 90.

28. de Usabel, "High Noon of American Films," 162.

29. Gloria Carranza Ortiz (who was nineteen years old and living in Mexico City in 1943), interview with author, Odessa, Texas, 1977.

30. Luz Gómez Villaseñor (who was seventeen and living in Puebla in 1943), interview with author, Guanajuato, Guanajuato, Mexico, June 1991. In 1946, MGM also released a color spectacular titled *Easy to Wed,* starring Van Johnson, Lucille Ball, and Esther Williams. Partly filmed in Mexico, it introduced two Mexican hit songs to Americans, "*Acerca ta más*" (Come Closer), sung in Spanish by Williams, and "Viva México, Viva América."

31. *Excélsior*, 20 November 1946.
32. de Usabel, "High Noon of American Films," 164.
33. Ortiz Garza, *México en guerra*, 172.
34. *Excélsior*, 11 January 1943.
35. *Variety*, 8 September 1947.
36. Tom Dey, "Gabriel Figueroa: Mexico's Master Cinematographer," *American Cinematographer* (March 1992): 34–40.
37. Negrete, *Jorge Negrete,* 124.
38. *Variety*, 13 October 1943.
39. de Usabel, "High Noon of American Films," 172.
40. *El Paso Times*, 13 January 1945.
41. USNA, RG 59, 812.404, 1 January 1945.
42. The best comprehensive introduction to the films of this period is Emilio García Riera, *Historia documental del cine mexicana, 1929–1976,* 18 volumes (México: Universidad de Guadalajara, Jalisco, 1976); also important is the analysis of Aurelio de los Reyes in *Medio siglo de cine mexicano, 1896–1947* (México: Trillas, 1987).

CHAPTER 6

1. Jean Charlot, *The Mexican Mural Renaissance, 1920–1925* (reprint, New Haven: Yale University Press, 1967), 315.
2. Bertram D. Wolfe, *The Fabulous Life of Diego Rivera,* 2d ed. (reprint, New York: Stein and Day, 1984), 141.
3. José Vasconcelos, *La raza cósmica: Mision de la raza iberoamericana* (México: Espasa-Calpe, 1948), 107.
4. Lucienne Bloch, interview with the author, College of Santa Fe, Santa Fe, New Mexico, 1987.
5. Ibid.
6. Rodman, interview, 15 June 1992.
7. Bernard S. Myers, *Mexican Painting in Our Time* (New York: Oxford University Press, 1956), 166.
8. Wouter von Ginneken, *Socio-Economic Group Income Distribution in Mexico* (London: Croom Hall, 1980), 140.
9. Blanca Torres, *Historia de la Revolución Mexicana,* vol. 19 of *México en la segunda guerra mundial* (México: n.p., 1979), 154.
10. AGN-MAC 187, Leg. 360, Exp. 100/1.

11. *New York Times*, 4 July 1940.
12. Myers, *Mexican Painting*, 106.
13. AGN-MAC 187, Leg. 266, Exp. 17/2.
14. Inéz Amor, *Una mujer en arte mexicana: Memorias de Inéz Amor* (México: UNAM, 1987).
15. Ibid.
16. Rodman, interview, 15 June 1992.
17. Wolfe, *Diego Rivera,* 140.
18. Ibid., 112.
19. Rodman, interview, 15 June 1992.
20. Wolfe, *Diego Rivera*, 160–63.
21. Myers, *Mexican Painting*, 167.
22. Rodman, interview, 15 June 1992.
23. Octavio Paz, *Tamayo* (México: Colección Arte Dirección General de Publicaciones, UNAM, 1958), 53–55.
24. Robert Goldwater, *Rufino Tamayo* (New York: Quadrangle Press, 1947), 94–95.
25. Myers, *Mexican Painting*, 186.
26. José Luis Díaz, interview with author, San Miguel de Allende, México, 6 June 1991.
27. AGN-MAC 187, Leg. 4, Exp. 1/10.
28. There are several hundred of these books and posters scattered throughout the Manuel Avila Camacho Collection in the national archives in Mexico City.
29. John R. White, "Mexico's Fighting Press," *Inter-American* 19, no. 8 (1944): 16.
30. Ibid.
31. Rosalua de Valdes, *Artes de México,* August 1955, 85.
32. Ibid., 64.
33. Patricia Fent Ross, "Radio College of Love," *Inter-American* 4, no. 8 (20 November 1944): 29.
34 *El Nacional*, 22 March 1944.
35. Luz de Lourdes Solórzano, *Artes de México,* August 1955, 80.
36. Rafael Loyola Díaz, *La influencia de los "democracias" durante la segunda guerra mundial* (México: Universidad Autonoma Metropolitana, 1980), 221. Author's translation of Loyola's text.
37. Ibid., 322.
38. Ibid., 322.

39. Jorge Fernández Varela, ed. "México: Setenta y cinco años de Revolucion IV," in *Educación, cultura y communicación* (México: Fondo de Cultura Económica, 1988), 466.

40. AGN-MAC, Leg. 380, Exp. 20/2.

41. Oscar Lewis, *Life in a Mexican Village: Tepoztlán Revisited* (Urbana: University of Illinois Press, 1963), 387.

42. Oscar Lewis, *Tepoztlán: A Village in Mexico* (New York: Holt, Rinehart & Winston, 1960), 15.

43. Ibid., 49.

44. Sylvia Martin, *You Meet Them in Mexico* (New Brunswick: Rutgers University Press, 1945), 175.

45. Lewis, *Tepoztlán: A Village in Mexico*, 43.

46. Loyola, *La influencia*, 322.

47. von Ginneken, *Income Distribution*, 202.

48. Emilio Ambasz, *The Architecture of Luis Barragán* (New York: Mirror Press, 1976), 8.

49. Mokoto Suzuki, "The Balance of Art and Nature," in *Modern Mexican Architecture,* ed. R. T. Monroe (New York: Vantage, 1983), 35.

50. Elena Poniatowska, *Todo México* (México: Diana, 1990), 21.

51. Ibid., 40.

52. Rodman, interview, 15 June 1992.

53. Poniatowska, *Todo México*, 24.

54. AGN-MAC 187, Leg. 612, Exp. 161/12.

55. AGN-MAC 187, Leg. 640, Exp. 120/4.

56. *New York Times*, 12 May 1949.

CHAPTER 7

1. Alberto Webb, *Carlos Chávez* (México: Ediciones mexicanas de música, 1950), 92.

2. Carlos Chávez, "La musica," in *México y la cultura*, ed. José Torres Blanco (México: SEP, 1946), 533.

3. Manuel Barajas, *México y la cultura musical* (México: DAPP, 1938), 23. Author's translation of Barajas.

4. Carlos Chávez, *Toward a New Music* (New York: Harper & Row, 1937), 88.

5. *Excélsior*, 12 June 1941.

6. AGN-MAC, Leg. 611, Exp. 24/8, 30 May 1945.
7. *New York Times*, 2 June 1940.
8. Gerald Behague, *Music in Latin America* (Englewood Cliffs, N.J.: Prentice-Hall, 1979), 130.
9. lbid., 132.
10. Roberto García Morilto, *Carlos Chávez: Vida y obra* (México: Fondo de Cultura Económica, 1960), 211.
11. *St. Louis Globe-Democrat*, 5 May 1939.
12. *Washington Star*, 1940.
13. AGN-MAC 187, Leg. 690, Exp. 134/12, copy of note from Manuel Avila Camacho to Miguel Bernal Jiménez.
14. *El Universal*, 2 June 1941.
15. Kirk, *Mexican Front*, 147.
16. *New York Times*, 12 March 1943.
17. This letter was in the three largest Mexico City newspapers in April and May of 1945.
18. Concert program for the Orquesta de Música de Cámara de UNAM, Sala Xochipilli, 126 Xicoténcatl, Mexico City, 20 June 1991.
19. *Washington Post*, 29 July 1944.
20. Varela, *Educación, cultura y communicación*, 914.
21. Volodia Teitelboim, *Neruda* (Austin: University of Texas Press, 1991), 248.
22. Chávez, *New Music*, 58.
23. Ibid., 76.
24. Robert L. Parker, *Carlos Chávez: Mexico's Modern Day Orpheus* (Boston: Twayne, 1983), 8.
25. *New York Times*, 16 March 1941.
26. Ada Page, "Mexican Orchestra," *Pacific Coast Musician* 4, no. 5 (1942): 12.

CHAPTER 8

1. Frederick C. Turner, *The Dynamic of Mexican Nationalism* (Chapel Hill: University of North Carolina Press, 1968), 175.
2. Ramos, *Profile*, 114–15.
3. Michael Maccoby, "On the Mexican National Character," *The Annals of Psychology* 370, no. 16 (March 1967): 68–72.
4. Cline, *Revolution to Evolution*.

 5. This is a main idea in Anna Macías, *Against All Odds: The Feminist Movement in Mexico to 1940* (London: Greenwood Press, 1982), 105.

 6. Pablo Neruda, *Memorias: Confieso que he vivido* (New York: Penguin, 1984), 150.

 7. Teitelboim, *Intimate Biography*, 246.

 8. Kenneth Rexroth, *An Autobiographical Novel* (Garden City, N.J.: Garden City Press, 1966), 344.

 9. Mildred Constantine, *Tina Modotti: A Fragile Life* (New York: Rizzoli, 1983), 27.

10. Ibid., 28.

11. Edward Weston, *Daybooks*, vol. 1 (New York: Hillerton, 1961), 84.

12. Constantine, *Tina Modotti*, 52.

13. Weston, *Daybooks*, vol. 1, 13.

14. Ibid., 52.

15. Ibid.

16. Ibid., 58.

17. Constantine, *Tina Modotti*, 76.

18. Ibid., 78.

19. Laura Mulvey and Peter Wollen, "The Discourse of the Body," in *New Images for Old: The Iconography of the Body* (New York: Harper & Row, 1985), 213.

20. Ibid., 214

21. Weston, *Daybooks*, vol. 2, 323.

22. Mulvey and Wollen, *New Images*, 214.

23. Anita Brenner, *Idols behind Altars* (New York: Biblo and Janner, 1957), 246.

24. Photograph by Tina Modotti, *Corn, Guitar and Cartridge,* 1928, Tina Modotti Museum, Trieste, Italy.

25. Photograph by Tina Modotti, *Man Reading* El Machete, 1924, Archivo Fotográfico Historico, Pachuca, Mexico.

26. Constantine, *Tina Modotti*, 29.

27. José Clemente Orozco, *The Artist in New York* (reprint, Austin: University of Texas Press, 1974), 85.

28. Anita Brenner, *The Wind That Swept Mexico* (Austin: University of Texas Press, 1976), 298.

29. *Excélsior*, 12 January 1929.

30. Constantine, *Tina Modotti*, 145.

31. *El Machete*, 15 December 1929.

32. Vittorio Vidali, *Il Wuinto Reggimento* (Milan: Augusto Press, 1973), 209.

33. Neruda, *Memorias*, 50.

34. *Excélsior*, 6 January 1942.

35. Neruda, *Memorias*, 255.

36. Constantine, *Tina Modotti*, 186.

37. *Excélsior,* 6 January 1942.

38. Inscription on tombstone of Tina Modotti.

39. Hayden Herrera, *Frida: A Biography of Frida Kahlo* (New York: Harper & Row, 1983), 80.

40. José Augustín, *Tragicomedia mexicana: La vida en México de 1940 a 1970* (México: Planeta, 1990), 53.

41. Herrera, *Frida*, 321.

42. Ibid., 366

43. Bloch, interview, 18 June 1984.

44. Ibid.

45. Ibid.

46. *Excélsior*, 20 March 1940.

47. Miguel Covarrubias, *Artes de México,* August 1955, 70.

48. *El Nacional*, 18 January 1940.

49. *Excélsior*, 1 January 1940.

50. Herrera, *Frida*, 256.

51. Bloch, interview, 18 June 1984.

52. Diego Rivera, "Frida Kahlo y el arte mexicano," *Boletin del semenario de cultura mexicano* 2 (October 1943): 89.

53. Peggy Guggenheim, *Confessions of an Art Addict* (New York: MacMillan & Co., 1960), 166.

54. Herrera, *Frida*, 320.

55. Ibid., 328.

56. *La Prensa*, 20 June 1943.

CHAPTER 9

1. Erika Billeter, "Frida and Maria," *Images of Mexico* exhibition catalog, ed. Ross Arms (Dallas: Museum of Art Press, 1987), 136.

2. Macías, *Feminist Movement*, 105.

3. Billeter, *Images*, 129.

4. Herrera, *Frida*, 328.

5. S. Walter Washington to the Secretary of State, USNA, RG 59, 812.403, 8-646, 22 July 1946.

6. Fernando Gamboa et al., *María Izquierdo: Essays* (México: Centro Cultural y Arte Contemporaneo, 1988), 50.

7. Ibid., 54.

8. *Excélsior*, 23 May 1945.

9. Herrera, *Frida*, 409.

10. Gamboa et al., *María Izquierdo*, 34.

11. *Excélsior*, 14 May 1943.

12. Herrera, *Frida*, 370.

13. *El Nacional*, 1 May 1992.

14. Edmond White, "Diva Mexicana," *Vanity Fair,* November 1990, 208.

15. Herrera, *Frida*, 371.

16. Debra Castillo, *Talking Back* (Ithaca: Cornell Press, 1992), 16.

17. Paco Ignacio Taibo, *María Félix* (México: Corona, 1984), 208.

18. Ibid., 207.

19. Mora, *Mexican Cinema*, 155.

20. Ibid., 59.

21. Ibid., 155.

22. Mora uses these figures in *Mexican Cinema*, p. 155; Amador and Ayala Blanco in *Cartelera Cinematográfico* suggest slightly lower numbers.

23. Moreno Rivas, *Historia*, 156.

24. Ibid., 145.

25. Taibo, *María Félix*, 65.

26. Vera McMillan, "Air Minded Mexico," *Inter-American Magazine* 2, no. 2 (December 1943): 84.

27. Lola Álvarez Bravo, *Frida and Her World*, photography exhibition, Mexic-Arte Center, Austin, Texas, May 17–29, 1992.

28. Rosario Castellanos, *Mujer que sabe latín* (1973; reprint, México: Fondo de Cultura Económica, 1984), 35.

29. D. Edmund Verlinger, "Gardens of Freedom: The Life and Works of Nellie Campobello," (master's thesis, University of Ohio, 1973), 301.

30. Nellie Campobello, introduction to *Cartucho* (1930; reprint, Albuquerque: Mesa, 1969), 17.

31. Ibid.

32. Nellie and Gloria Campobello, *Ritmos indígenas de México* (México: SEP, 1940), 7.

33. Ibid., 13.

34. Covarrubias, *Artes de México*, 70. The ballets may be translated as follows: *Entre sombras anda el fuego* (The Fire Dances between Shadows), *Antígona* (Antigone), *El renacuajo* (The Runt), *Danza de las fuerzas nuevas* (The Dance of New Forces), and *La coronela* (The Lady Colonel).
35. Verlinger, "Gardens of Freedom," 324.
36. Ibid., 314.
37. Official dance program, Mexico City Ballet, October 1945.
38. Covarrubias, *Artes de México*, 69.
39. Verlinger, "Gardens of Freedom," 301.
40. Ibid., 296.
41. Ibid., 297.
42. Covarrubias, *Artes de México*, 69.
43. Campobello, *Cartucho*, 280.
44. Covarrubias, *Artes de México,* 60.
45. Kirk, *Mexican Front*, 146.
46. *Excélsior*, 2 September 1941.
47. Lola Álvarez Bravo, *Reencuentros* (México: El Consejo Nacional Para Cultura, 1989), 5.
48. Erika Billeter, *Photographers Who Made History* exhibition catalog (Dallas: Museum of Art Press, 1987), 372.
49. Ibid., 373.
50. Murry McEdwards, *Advertising and Propaganda* (Toronto: University of Toronto Press, 1970), 50.
51. Taibo, *María Félix*, 133.
52. Claudia Schaefer, *Textured Lives: Women, Art and Representation in Modern Mexico* (Tucson: University of Arizona Press, 1992), 89.
53. Ibid., 95.
54. Ángeles Mastretta, *Arráncame la vida* (México: Oceano, 1985), 220.
55. Ibid., 131.

CHAPTER 10

1. Marvin Harris, *Cultural Materialism* (New York: Random House, 1979).
2. Sánchez Gonzáles, *Abelardo L. Rodríguez*, 25–95.
3. Lieuwen, *Mexican Militarism*, 100.

4. Ricardo Tirado, "La alianza con los empresarios," in *Sociedad y cultura entre la guerra y estabilidad politica*, 195.

5. *Excélsior*, 2 December 1940.

6. Robert L. Bennett, *The Financial Sector and Economic Development: The Mexican Case* (Baltimore: Johns Hopkins University Press, 1965), 5.

7. Alfonso Taracena, *La vida en México bajo Avila Camacho* (México: Editorial, 1976), 202.

8. Ricardo Pozas Horcasitas, Ana Camarena, and Fernando González, "De lo duro a lo seguro: La fundación del seguro social mexicano," in *Sociedad y cultura entre la guerra y estabilidad politica*, 323.

9. Prescott H. Williams, lecture, "Introduction to Archaeology," Austin Presbyterian Theological Seminary, 10 November 1970.

10. Fernand Braudel, *The Mediterranean and the Mediterranean World in the Age of Philip II*, vol. 1 (New York: Harper and Row, 1966), 825.

11. Colin MacLachlan, *Spain's Empire in the New World: The Role of Ideas in Institutional and Social Change* (Berkeley: University of California Press, 1988), ix.

12. Irving Leonard, *Baroque Times in Old Mexico* (Ann Arbor: University of Michigan Press, 1959), 29.

13. José Antonio Maravell, *Culture of the Baroque: Analysis of a Historical Structure* (Minneapolis: University of Minnesota Press, 1986), 111.

14. Octavio Paz, *Sor Juana Inéz de la Cruz* (México: Fondo de la Cultura Económica, 1983), 200.

15. Octavio Paz, *The Labyrinth of Solitude: Life and Thought in Mexico* (New York: Grove Press, 1980), 166.

16. *New York Times*, 13 June 1990.

17. *Rocky Mountain News*, 9 September 1992.

18. *Unomasuno*, 25 August 1992.

19. *Excélsior,* 25 August 1992.

20. *Unomasuno*, 14 August 1992.

21. Ibid.

22. *New York Times*, 27 September 1992.

23. *Excélsior*, 20 August 1992.

24. *Excélsior*, 22 June 1987.

25. Alicia Mena, *There Comes a Time*, performed at the Jumpstart Theater, San Antonio, Texas, 9 August 1997.

26. An excellent book on the role of corruption in Mexico is Steven D. Morris, *Corruption and Politics in Contemporary Mexico* (Tuscaloosa: University of Alabama Press, 1991).

BIBLIOGRAPHY

BIBLIOGRAPHIES AND ARCHIVAL GUIDES

Archivo General de la Nación. *Inventario de Ramo Instrucción Pública y Bellas Artes*. México, n.d.

Bibliografía historica mexicana. México: El Colegio de México, 1967.

García y García, J. Jesús. *Guia de Archivos*. México: Universidad Nacional Autonoma de México, 1972.

ARCHIVAL MATERIAL

Archivo General de la Nación-Manuel Avila Camacho 187. Leg. 1. Exp. 101/5. Ordenación Asuntos Personales.

——. Leg. 4. Exp. 1/10. Memoria de Secretaria de Gobernación.

——. Leg. 102. Exp. 4/118. Memoria de Secretaria de Gobernación.

——. Leg. 105. Exp. 530/2. Memoria de Secretaria de Gobernación.

——. Leg. 109. Exp. 124/2. Memoria de Secretaria de Gobernación.

——. Leg. 198. Exp. 268/12. Secretaria de Gobernación. "Seis años de gobierno al servicio de México," 1940.

——. Leg. 210. Exp. 141/4. Memoria de Secretaria de Gobernación.

——. Leg. 266. Exp. 17/2. Memoria de Secretaria de Gobernación.

——. Leg. 360. Exp. 100/1. Memoria de Secretaria de Gobernación.

——. Leg. 380. Exp. 20/2.

——. Leg. 512. Exp. 32/146.

——. Leg. 611. Exp. 24/8. "Copy of letter Carlos Chávez to Manuel Avila Camacho." 1945.

——. Leg. 612. Exp. 161/12. Memoria de Secretaria de Gobernación.

———. Leg. 640. Exp. 120/4. Memoria de Secretaria de Gobernación.

———. Leg. 670. Exp. 124/2. Memoria de Secretaria de Gobernación, 1945.

———. Leg. 690. Exp. 134/12. "Copy of note Manuel Avila Camacho to Miguel Bernal Jiménez."

Foreign Relations of the United States Department of State. Washington: United States Government Printing Office 7:406, 1944.

Messersmith, George. Papers. University of Delaware.

Mexican Constitution of 1917. Article 28.

Report of the Export-Import Task Force. *First Semi-Annual Report to Congress for the Period July to December, 1944.* Appendix B. Washington, D.C.: United States Government Printing Office, 1945.

United States National Archives, Department of State General Records. Record Group 59, 862.202-10/15. "Guy Ray to Secretary of State," 30 July 1942.

———. RG 59, 812.00/321-48. "George Messersmith to the United States Department of State," 26 April 1943.

———. RG 59, 812.740.0011. "George Messersmith to the United States Department of State," 23 November 1943.

———. RG 59, 812.51/3-945. "George Messersmith to United States Department of State," 12 April 1944.

———. RG 59, 812.404. 1 January 1945.

———. RG 59, 812.51/3-945. "George Messsersmith to John W. Carregan," 9 March 1945.

———. RG 59, 812.00/1.3143. "George Messersmith to Sumner Welles," 2 April 1945.

———. RG 59, 812.51/4-1045. "Ambassador George S. Messersmith to Secretary of State." Letters, 1945.

———. RG 59, 812.404/4-1045. "Raleigh Gibson to Secretary of State," 10 April 1945.

———. RG 59, 812.403, 8-646. "S. Walter Washington to the Secretary of State," 22 July 1946.

BOOKS AND ARTICLES

Almazán, Juan Andreu. *Memorias de General Juan Andreu Almazán: Informes y documentos sobre la campana politica de 1940.* México: Editorial Quintana-Impresor, 1941.

Álvarez Bravo, Lola. *Reencuentros.* México: El Consejo Nacional para Cultura, 1989.

Amador, María Luisa, and Jorge Ayala Blanco. *Cartelera Cinematográfica* 1-3. Centro Universitario de Estudios Cinematográficos, 1980.

———. *Cartelera Cinematográfica, 1940–1949.* México: Universidad Autonoma de México (hereinafter UNAM), 1982.

Ambasz, Emilio. *The Architecture of Luis Barragán.* New York: Mirror Press, 1976.

Amor, Inéz. *Una mujer en arte mexicana: Memorias de Inéz Amor.* México: UNAM, 1987.

Augustín, José. *Tragicomedia mexicana: La vida en México de 1940 a 1970.* México: Planeta, 1990.

Barajas, Manuel. *México y la cultura musical.* México: Departamento Autónamo de Prensa y Publicidad (hereinafter DAPP), 1938.

Barbour, Phillip L. "Commercial and Cultural Broadcasting in Mexico." *Annals of the Ancunian Academy of Political and Social Science* (March 1940).

Barzun, Jacques. "Cultural History in Synthesis." *The Vanities of History.* Edited by Fritz Stern. New York: Harper, 1956.

Becker, Marjorie. *Setting the Virgin on Fire: Lázaro Cárdenas, Michoacán Peasants and the Redemption of the Mexican Revolution.* Berkeley: University of California Press, 1995.

Behague, Gerald. *Music in Latin America.* Englewood Cliffs, N. J.: Prentice-Hall, 1979.

Bennett, Robert L. *The Financial Sector and Economic Development: The Mexican Case.* Baltimore: Johns Hopkins University Press, 1965.

Berger, Peter. *The Homeless Mind: Modernization and Consciousness.* New York: Vintage Books, 1973.

Braudel, Fernand. *The Mediterranean and the Mediterranean World in the Age of Philip II.* Vol. 1. New York: Harper and Row, 1966.

Brenner, Anita. *Idols behind Altars.* New York: Biblo and Janner, 1957.

———. *The Wind That Swept Mexico.* Austin: University of Texas Press, 1976.

Britton, John. *Educación y radicalismo en México, 1931–1940.* México: Montes, 1955.

———. "Teacher Unionization and the Corporate State." *Hispanic American Historical Review* 59, no. 4 (1979).

Buñuel, Luis. *My Last Sigh.* New York: Vintage Press, 1983.

Camp, Roderic A. *Mexican Political Biographies.* Tucson: University of Arizona Press, 1982.

Campobello, Nellie. *Cartucho.* Translated by Renfro Norris Cole. 1930. Reprint, Albuquerque: Mesa, 1969.

Campobello, Nellie, and Gloria Campobello. *Ritmos indígenas de México*. México: Secretariat of Public Education (hereinafter SEP), 1940.

Carrillo, Alejandro. *La revolución industrial en México*. México: Universidad Obrera, 1945.

Castellanos, Rosario. *Mujer que sabe latín*. 1973. Reprint, México: Fondo de Cultura Económica, 1984.

Castillo, Debra. *Talking Back*. Ithaca: Cornell University Press, 1992.

Cerwin, Herbert. *These Are the Mexicans*. New York: Reynal and Hitchcock, 1947.

Charlot, Jean. *The Mexican Mural Renaissance, 1920–1925*. Reprint, New Haven: Yale University Press, 1967.

Chávez, Carlos. "La musica." *México y la cultura*. Edited by José Torres Blanco. México: SEP, 1946.

———. *Toward a New Music*. New York: Harper & Row, 1937.

Chávez, John. *The Lost Land: The Chicano Image in the Southwest*. Albuquerque: University of New Mexico Press, 1984.

Cline, Howard F. *Mexico: Revolution to Evolution, 1940–1960*. New York: Oxford University Press, 1967.

———. *The United States and Mexico*. Cambridge: Harvard University Press, 1983.

———. *United States and Mexico*. New York: Atheneum, 1963.

Cockcroft, James C., and Bo Anderson. "Latin American Radicalism." *Borzoi Reader in Latin American History*. Vol. 2. Edited by Thomas C. Hood. New York: Knopf, 1982.

Cole, Renfro Norris. "A History of *La hora nacional*." Ph.D. diss., Michigan State University, 1963.

"Communidades de promoción." *Boletin Indigenista* 5 (1945).

Constantine, Mildred. *Tina Modotti: A Fragile Life*. New York: Rizzoli, 1983.

Cosío Villegas, Daniel. *Memorias*. México: Joaquín Mortiz, 1976.

Covarrubias, Miguel. *Artes de México,* August 1955.

Dallal, Alberto. *El dancing mexicano*. México: Oasis, 1982.

Davis, David Brion. "Some Recent Directions in American Cultural History." *The American Historical Review* 73, no. 3 (1968).

de los Reyes, Aurelio. *Medio siglo de cine mexicano, 1896–1947*. México: Trillas, 1987.

de Lourdes Solórzano, Luz. *Artes de México*, August 1955.

de Usabel, Gaizka S. "The High Noon of American Films in Latin America." Ph.D. diss., UMI Research Press (Ann Arbor), 1982.

de Valdes, Rosalua. *Artes de México,* August 1955.

Dey, Tom. "Gabriel Figueroa: Mexico's Master Cinematographer." *American Cinematographer,* March 1992.

"Diez años de México." *Nuestra Música Editorial Boletin* 11, no. 1 (1946).

Fein, Seth. "The United States and the Mexican Film Industry after World War II." *Texas Papers on Mexico: Pre-publication working papers of the Mexican Center, Institute of Latin American Studies.* Austin: University of Texas Press, n.d.

Fejes, Fred. *Imperialism, Media and the Good Neighbor: New Deal Foreign Policy and United States Shortwave Broadcasting to Latin America.* Norwood, N.J.: Ablex Publishing Corp., 1986.

Fell, Claude. *José Vasconcelos: Los años del aguila, 1920–1925.* México: UNAM, 1989.

Gamboa, Fernando, et al. *María Izquierdo: Essays.* México: Centro Cultural y Arte Contemporaneo, 1988.

García Morilto, Roberto. *Carlos Chávez: Vida y obra.* México: Fondo de Cultura Económica, 1960.

García Riera, Emilio. *El cine mexicano.* México: Era, 1963.

———. *Historia documental del cine mexicana, 1929–1976.* 18 volumes. México: Universidad de Guadalajara, Jalisco, 1976.

Gaxiola, Francísco Javier. *Memorias.* México: Editorial Porrua, 1975.

Goldwater, Robert. *Rufino Tamayo.* New York: Quadrangle Press, 1947.

González, Luis. *Historia de la Revolución Mexicana, vol. 15, periodo 1934–1940.* México: El Colegio de México, 1981.

———. *San José de Gracia.* Translated by John Upton. Austin: University of Texas Press, 1974.

Gruening, Ernest. *Mexico and Its Heritage.* New York: Appleton, 1928.

Guggenheim, Peggy. *Confessions of an Art Addict.* New York: MacMillan and Co., 1960.

Harris, Marvin. *Cultural Materialism.* New York: Random House, 1979.

Hayes, Joy Elizabeth. "Radio Broadcasting and Nation Building in Mexico and the United States, 1925–1945." Ph.D. diss., University of California at San Diego, 1994.

Heath, Shirley Brice. *Telling Tongues: Language Policy in Mexico.* New York: Teachers College Press, 1972.

Hernández Luna, Juan, ed. *Conferencias del ateneo de la juventud.* México: UNAM, 1962.

Herrera, Hayden. *Frida: A Biography of Frida Kahlo.* New York: Harper and Row, 1983.

Hoy. 4 January 1940 and 17 September 1940.

Inkeles, Alex. "Some Observations on Culture and Personality Studies." *Personality in Nature, Society and Culture*. Edited by Clyde Kluckhorn and Henry A. Murray. 2d rev. ed. New York: Grove Press, 1956.

Iturriaga, José. *La estructura social y cultural de México*. México: Financiera, 1951.

Kirk, Betty. *Covering the Mexican Front*. Norman: University of Oklahoma Press, 1942.

Krauze, Enrique. *Caras de la historia*. México: Joaquin Mortiz, 1983.

———. *Caudillos culturales en la Revolución Mexicana*. México: Siglo Veintiuno, 1976.

———. *La presidencia imperial: Ascenso y caida del sistema politico mexicano, 1940–1946*. México: Tusquets, 1997.

Leonard, Irving. *Baroque Times in Old Mexico*. Ann Arbor: University of Michigan Press, 1959.

Lewis, Oscar. *Life in a Mexican Village: Tepoztlán Revisited*. Urbana: University of Illinois Press, 1963.

———. *Tepoztlán: A Village in Mexico*. New York: Holt, Rinehart & Winston, 1960.

Lieuwen, Edwin. *Mexican Militarism, 1910–1940*. Westport, Conn.: Greenwood Press, 1978.

Lingeman, Richard R. *Don't You Know There Is a War On?* New York: Putnam, 1976.

Loyola Díaz, Rafael. *La influencia de las "democracias" durante le segunda guerra mundial*. México: Universidad Autonoma Metropolitana, 1980.

———. *La sucesión presidencia en México, 1928–1988*. Edited by Carlos Assad. México: Nueva Imagen, 1992.

Maccoby, Michael. "On the Mexican National Character." *The Annals of Psychology* 370, no. 16 (1967).

Macías, Anna. *Against All Odds: The Feminist Movement in Mexico to 1940*. London: Greenwood Press, 1982.

MacLachlan, Colin M. *Spain's Empire in the New World: The Role of Ideas in Institutional and Social Change*. Berkeley: University of California Press, 1988.

Maravell, José Antonio. *Culture of the Baroque: Analysis of a Historical Structure*. Minneapolis: University of Minnesota Press, 1986.

Marks, Frederick W., II. *Wind over Sand: The Diplomacy of Franklin Roosevelt*. Athens: University of Georgia Press, 1988.

Martin, Sylvia. *You Meet Them in Mexico*. New Brunswick: Rutgers University Press, 1945.

Martínez Assad, Carlos. "El cine come lo vi y como me contarón." *Sociedad y cultura entre la guerra y la estabilidad politica: El México de los '40s*. Edited by Rafael Loyola Díaz. México: Grijalbo, 1990.

Mastretta, Ángeles. *Arrancame la vida*. México: Oceano, 1985.

McEdwards, Murry. *Advertising and Propaganda*. Toronto: University of Toronto Press, 1970.

McMillan, Vera. "Air Minded Mexico." *Inter-American Magazine* 2, no. 2 (December 1943).

Meyer, Jean, and Enrique Krauze. *Historia de la Revolución Mexicana, vol. 3, periodo 1924–1928: La reconstrucción económica*. México: El Colegio de México, 1974.

Meyer, Michael, and William Sherman. *The Course of Mexican History*. Oxford: Oxford University Press, 1983.

Michaels, Albert, and James Wilkie, eds. *Revolution in Mexico: The Years of Upheaval, 1910–1940*. New York: Knopf, 1969.

Monsivais, Carlos. *Mexican Postcards*. Translated by John Kranianskas. London: Verso, 1997.

———. *Sociedad y cultura entre la guerra y la estabilidad politica: El México de los '40s*. Edited by Rafael Loyola Díaz. México: Grijalbo, 1990.

Monsivais, Carlos, and Carlos Bonfil. *A traves del espejo: El cine mexicano y su publico*. México: El Milagro, 1994.

Mora, Carl J. *Mexican Cinema: Reflections of a Society, 1896–1980*. Berkeley: University of California Press, 1982.

Moreno Rivas, Yolanda. *Historia de la música popular mexicana*. México: Alianza Editorial Mexicana, 1979.

Mulvey, Laura, and Peter Wollen. "The Discourse of the Body." *New Images for Old: The Iconography of the Body*. Edited by James Dixon. New York: Harper and Row, 1985.

Myers, Bernard S. *Mexican Painting in Our Time*. New York: Oxford University Press, 1956.

Negrete, Diana. *Jorge Negrete*. México: Diana, 1989.

Neruda, Pablo. *Memorias: Confieso que he vivido*. New York: Penguin, 1984.

Niblo, Stephen R. *War, Diplomacy and Development: The United States and Mexico, 1938–1954*. Wilmington, Del.: Scholarly Resource Press, 1995.

Norris, Steven D. *Corruption and Politics in Contemporary Mexico.* Tuscaloosa: University of Alabama Press, 1991.

Novo, Salvador. *La vida en México en el periodo presidential de Manuel Avila Camacho.* México: Empresas Editoriales, 1965.

Orozco, José Clemente. *The Artist in New York.* Reprint, Austin: University of Texas Press, 1974.

Ortiz Garza, José Luis. *México en guerra.* México: Espejo de México, 1989.

Otero, Miguel. "Vista de la esperanza." *Revista Mexicana de Educación* 1, no. 4 (1940).

Pacheco, Christina. "Yo soy el bolero." *Siempre,* 17 July 1991.

Padilla, Ezequiel. *Agreement between the United States and Mexico.* National and International Series, no. 9. Mexican Secretariat of Foreign Relations. Mexico: International Press Service Bureau, 1941.

———. *Free Men of America.* Translated by Mark Smith. New York: Ziff Davis, 1943.

Page, Ada. "Mexican Orchestra." *Pacific Coast Musician* 4, no. 5 (1942).

Pansters, Wil G. *Politics and Power in Puebla: The Political History of a Mexican State, 1937–1987.* Amsterdam: CEDLA, 1990.

Parker, Robert L. *Carlos Chávez: Mexico's Modern Day Orpheus.* Boston: Twayne, 1983.

Paz, Octavio. *Sor Juana Inéz de la Cruz.* México: Fondo de la Cultura Económica, 1983.

———. *The Labyrinth of Solitude: Life and Thought in Mexico.* New York: Grove Press, 1980.

———. *Tamayo.* México: Colección Arte Dirección General de Publicaciones, UNAM, 1958.

Poniatowska, Elena. *Todo México.* México: Diana, 1990.

Pozas Horcasitas, Ricardo, Ana Camarena, and Fernando González. "De lo duro a lo seguro: La fundación del seguro social mexicano." *Sociedad y cultura entre la guerra y la estabilidad politica: El México de los '40s.* Edited by Rafael Loyola Díaz. México: Grijalbo, 1990.

Raby, David L. *Educación y revolución social en México, 1921–1940.* Translated by Roberto Gómez Cireza. México: Sepsentas, 1974.

Ramos, Samuel. *Profile of Man and Culture in Mexico.* Translated by Peter G. Earle. Austin: University of Texas Press, 1975.

Revista Mexicana de Educación 1 (November 1940).

Rexroth, Kenneth. *An Autobiographical Novel.* Garden City, N.J.: Garden City Press, 1966.

Reyes, Raúl Cardial. *Retorno a caso*. México: UNAM, 1986.

Rivera, Diego. "Frida Kahlo y el arte mexicano." *Boletin del semenario de cultura mexicano* 2 (October 1943).

Ross, Patricia Fent. "Radio College of Love." *Inter-American Magazine* 4, no. 8 (1944).

Ruiz, Ramon Edward. *Mexico: The Challenge of Poverty and Illiteracy*. San Marcos, Calif.: Huntington Library Press, 1963.

Sánchez González, Francísco. *Abelardo L. Rodríguez: Obra economica y social*. México: n.p., 1954.

Santoro, Carmela Elvira. "United States and Mexican Relations during World War II." Ph.D. diss., University of Michigan, 1967.

Schaefer, Claudia. *Textured Lives: Women, Art and Representation in Modern Mexico*. Tucson: University of Arizona Press, 1992.

Schmidt, Henry C. *The Roots of Lo Mexicano*. College Station: Texas A&M University Press, 1978.

Secretaria de Relaciones Exteriores. *Memoria*. México: n.p., 1943.

———. *Seis años de actividad el nacional*. México: n.p., 1946.

Secretariat of Public Education. *La casa de estudiante indígena*. México: Talleres Gráficos de la Nación, 1927.

———. *Las missiones culturales*. México: Talleres Gráficos de la Nación, 1927.

———. *Las missiones culturales: Memoria, 1942–1946*. México: Talleres Gráficos de la Nación, 1946.

———. Departmento de Asuntos Indígenas. *Memorias, 1945–1946*. México: n.p., 1946.

———. *Teoria y aplicacion de la reforma educación*. México: Talleres Gráficos de la Nación, 1963.

Simmons, Merle. *The Mexican Corrido*. New York: Harper, 1956.

Suzuki, Mokoto. "The Balance of Art and Nature." *Modern Mexican Architecture*. Edited by R. T. Monroe. New York: Vantage, 1983.

Taibo, Paco Ignacio. *María Félix*. México: Corona, 1984.

Tannenbaum, Frank. *Mexico: The Struggle for Peace and Bread*. New York: Knopf, 1968.

Taracena, Alfonso. *La vida en México bajo Avila Camacho*. México: Editorial, 1976.

Teitelboim, Volodia. *Neruda: An Intimate Biography*. Austin: University of Texas Press, 1988.

———. *Neruda*. Austin: University of Texas Press, 1991.

Tirado, Ricardo. "La alianza con los empresarios." *Sociedad y cultura entre la guerra y la estabilidad politica: El México de los '40s*. Edited by Rafael Loyola Díaz. México: Grijalbo, 1990.

Torres, Blanca. *Historia de la Revolución Mexicana*. Vol. 19 of *México en la segunda guerra mundial*. México: n.p., 1979.

Torres Bodet, Jaime. *Discursos*. México: Porrua, 1965.

———. *Educación mexicana: Discursos, entrevistas y mensajes*. México: SEP, 1944.

———. *La obra educativa: Seis años de actividades nacional*. México: Porrua, 1969.

———. *Memorias: Años contra tiempo*. México: Porrua, 1969.

———. *Tiempo de arena*. México: Fondo de Cultura Económica, 1955.

Turner, Frederick C. *The Dynamic of Mexican Nationalism*. Chapel Hill: University of North Carolina Press, 1968.

Tylor, E. B. *Primitive Culture: Researches into the Development of Mythology, Philosophy, Religion, Language, Art and Customs*. Vol. 1. New York: Henry and Holt, 1877.

Vane, Eric. "Required Reading." *Inter-American Magazine* 5, no. 8 (1945).

Varela, Jorge Fernández, ed. "México: Setenta y cinco años de Revolucion IV." *Educación, cultura y communicación*. México: Fondo de Cultura Económica, 1988.

Vasconcelos, José. "El desastre," in *Obras*. Vol. 2. México: Botas, 1959.

———. *La Raza Cósmica: Mision de la raza iberoamericana*. México: Espasa-Calpe, 1948.

———. *La Tormenta*. México: Botas, 1938.

———. *Ulises Criollo*. México: Botas, 1936.

Véjar Vásquez, Octavio. *Hacia una esquela de unidad nacional*. México: Discurso Editorial, 1944.

Vera Estañol, Jorge. *La Revolución Mexicana*. México: Porrua, 1957.

Verlinger, D. Edmund. "Gardens of Freedom: The Life and Works of Nellie Campobello." Master's thesis, University of Ohio, 1973.

Vidali, Vittorio. *Il Wuinto Reggimento*. Milan: Augusto Press, 1973.

von Ginneken, Wouter. *Socio-Economic Group Income Distribution in Mexico*. London: Croom Hall, 1980.

Webb, Alberto. *Carlos Chávez*. México: Ediciones mexicanas de musica, 1950.

Weston, Edward. *Daybooks*. Vols. 1 and 2. New York: Hillerton, 1961.

White, Edmond. "Diva Mexicana." *Vanity Fair*, February 1990.

White, John R. "Mexico's Fighting Press." *Inter-American Magazine* 19, no. 8 (1944).

Wilkie, James W. *The Mexican Revolution: Federal Expenditure and Social Change since 1910*. Berkeley: University of California Press, 1970.

Wolfe, Bertram D. *The Fabulous Life of Diego Rivera*. 2d ed. Reprint, New York: Stein and Day, 1984.

NEWSPAPERS

Diario Oficial. 26 April 1926 and April–December 1936.

Diario Filmico Mexicano. 24 January 1943.

El Machete. 15 December 1929.

El Maestro Rural. 15 July 1934.

El Nacional. January 1940–March 1944.

El Paso Times, 13 January 1945.

El Porvenir de Monterrey. 20 April 1943.

El Universal. 14 October 1936 and March 1943–October 1948.

Excélsior. 2 June 1923, 12 January 1929, August 1938–January 1946, 11 December 1971, 22 June 1987, 27 April 1989, and August 1992.

La Prensa. April–June 1943.

Los Angeles Times. 6 December 1934.

Nacional. May 1939–November 1946, 2 October 1965.

New York Times. June 1940–May 1949, 13 June 1990, and 27 September 1992.

Rocky Mountain News. 9 September 1992.

St. Louis Globe-Democrat. 5 May 1939.

Unomasuno. August 1992.

Variety. 12 July 1939, 5 November 1942, 13 October 1943, and 8 September 1947.

Washington Post. May 1940–July 1944.

Washington Star. 1940.

PERSONAL INTERVIEWS

Atkins, Gloria Gonzales. Teacher. Interview with author. Odessa, Texas, 26 September 1978.

Bigley, James. Former associate director of the Chester Nimitz Library. Interview with author. Fredericksburg, Texas, 10 April 1988.

Bloch, Lucienne. Painter and friend of Frida Kahlo. Interview with author. College of Santa Fe, Santa Fe, New Mexico, 18 June 1984.

——. Interview with author. 1987.

Carranza Ortiz, Gloria. Interview with author. Odessa, Texas. 1977.

Díaz, José Luis. Teacher. Interview with author. San Miguel de Allende, Mexico. 6 June 1991.

Gómez Villaseñor, Luz. Interview with author. Guanajuato, Guanajuato, Mexico, June 1991.

Rodman, Selden. Author and collector. Interview with author. Oakland, New Jersey, 13–17 June 1992.

ART EXHIBITIONS, CATALOGUES, PLAYS,
AND OTHER PUBLIC PRESENTATIONS

Álvarez Bravo, Lola. *Frida and Her World,* photography exhibition. Austin, Texas: Mexic-Arte Center, 17–29 May 1992.

Billeter, Erika. *Photographers Who Made History,* exhibition catalog. Dallas: Museum of Art Press, 1987.

———. "Frida and Maria." *Images of Mexico,* exhibition catalog. Edited by Ross Arms. Dallas: Museum of Art Press, 1987.

Chávez, John. "The Image of the Mexican in American Films," lecture. Texas A&M University, 15 March 1989.

Documental Servicio Cultural. *La II guerra mundial: Su música.* México: Asociación Mexicana de Estudios Fonográficos 27, 1989.

Mena, Alicia. *There Comes a Time.* Jumpstart Theater performance. San Antonio, Texas, August 1997.

Mexico City Ballet. Official Dance Program, October 1945.

Modotti, Tina. *Corn, Guitar and Cartridge.* 1928 photograph. Trieste, Italy: Tina Modotti Museum.

———. *Man Reading* El Machete. 1924 photograph. Pachuca, Mexico: Archivo Fotográfico Historico.

Orquesta de Música de Camara de UNAM. Concert program. Mexico City: Sala Xochipilli, 20 June 1991.

Siempre en domingo. Hosted by Raúl Fernández and broadcast live from the State Fair of Oaxaca. Recorded by author, 11 December 1990.

Williams, Prescott H. "Introduction to Archaeology," lecture. Austin Presbyterian Theological Seminary, 10 November 1970.

INDEX

Archivo General de la Nación (AGN), 10
Alemán, Miguel, 2
Alfonso X, 183–84
Almazán, Juan Andreu, 22–23
Álvarez Bravo, Lola, 160, 173–74
Amor, Guadalupe, 106
Amor, Inéz, 105–106
Armendáriz, Pedro, 91
ateneistas, 12
Ávila Camacho, Manuel, 1, 25–28, 49, 78, 97, 182
Ávila Camacho, Maximino, 39
Azcárraga, Emilio, 34

Beecham, Sir Thomas, 134
Bergson, Henri, 11
Bernal Jiménez, Miguel, 129, 130, 135–36
Barragán, Luis, 8, 119–21
Bassols, Narciso, 12, 25, 46
Buñuel, Luis, 90

Calles, Plutarco Elías, 14, 28, 46
camarilla, 4
Campobello, Gloria, 104, 169–72
Campobello, Nellie, 125, 167–69
Canabal, Gerrido, 18
Cantinflas, 37, 84, 88, 98
Cárdenas, Lázaro, 1, 14–23, 28, 35, 48

cartoonists, 32, 33, 111–14, 55
cardenismo, 17
Caso, Alfonso, 12
Caso, Antonio, 11
Castillo Nájera, Francísco, 31
Catholic church, 17–18, 22–23
caudillismo, 14
Charlot, Jean, 101
Chávez, Carlos, 8, 120, 124–30, 133–35
Club Smyrna, 66
comedians, 84–90
Communist Party of Mexico, 9, 18, 133, 152
Constitution of 1917, 47, 185
Confederation of Mexican Workers (CTM), 21, 63, 89
Copeland, Aaron, 132
Coordinator of Inter-American Affairs (CIAA), 95–98
corridos, 79–81
Cosío Villegas, Daniel, 12
Crosby, Bing, 123, 139

danzón, 66
Departamento Autónomo de Prensa y Publicidad (DAPP), 67, 71
de Andrade, Marta, 42
de la Cruz, Sor Juana, 67, 185
del Río, Delores, 91
Disney, Walt, 97
Domínguez, Alberto, 139
Dorsey, Tommy, 123, 139

ejidos, 82
El Paso, Texas, 99
El Salón México, 66
Excélsior, 32, 36

Federal Bureau of Investigation, 34
Félix, María, 37, 139, 163–66, 174, 176–77
Figueroa, Gabriel, 98

Galindo, Blas, 129, 131, 136
Gamio, Manuel, 19
Gaxiola, Francísco Javier, 4, 29, 38–39
Generation of 1910, 12
Generation of 1915, 12
Gómez Morín, Manuel, 12, 33
Guerrero, Xavier, 102, 109
Gutiérrez, Eulalio, 13
Guzmán, Martín Luis, 11

hispanidad, 33
Hitler, Adolph, 110
Hoy, 19, 34, 75
Hull, Cordell, 30

Infante, Pedro, 140, 188
Izquierdo, María, 159–163

Jiquilpan, Michoacán, 104, 108

Kant, Immanuel, 11
Kahlo, Frida, 10, 105, 108, 152–58, 160, 174–75

La hora nacional, 65–68, 71–73, 125, 132–35
Lamour, Dorothy, 96
la Negra, Toña, 83, 176
Lara, Agustín, 27, 67, 88, 123, 166–67
League of Revolutionary Artists and Writers (LEAR), 103
Lewis, Oscar, 116–17

malinchismo, 141
Mena, Alicia, 188–89
Messersmith, George, 29–30, 31
Mexican air force, 36–37, 55
Mexican army, 20–21, 36
Modotti, Tina, 3, 9, 109, 145–152
Moncayo, José Pablo, 129, 135
Montes, Amparo, 82–83, 176

Morales Blumenkron, Guillermo, 68
Múgica, Francísco, 22

North American Free Trade Agreement (NAFTA), 186–87
National Action Party (PAN), 12, 22, 33
National Revolutionary Party (PNR), 14, 18, 20, 26
National Syndicate of Workers in Education (SNTE), 63
Negrete, Jorge, 15, 37, 89–90, 175, 176
Neruda, Pablo, 38, 107, 143–145
New York Public Library, 13
Novo, Salvador, 34, 157

Obregón, Alvaro, 3, 14
O'Connell, Helen, 139
O'Gorman, Juan, 108
O'Higgins, Pablo, 110
Orozco, José Clemente, 102, 104, 120, 132

Padilla, Ezequiel, 34–35, 37
Pani, Mario, 115, 118
Party of the Mexican Revolution (PRM), 18
Pasternak, Joseph, 96
Paz, Octavio, 136, 186
Ponce, Manuel M., 126, 128–29, 134, 139
Poodevan, Vidal, 30
Poniatowska, Elena, 4, 120
Posada, José Guadalupe, 79
printmakers, 109–11

Ramos, Samuel, 4, 12
Revueltas, Silvestre, 126, 136
Reyes, Alfonso, 11
Rivera, Diego, 30, 102, 108
Rockefeller, Nelson, 34, 95
Rodríguez, Abelardo, 14, 38
Roosevelt, Franklin D., 30, 32, 76

Saloma Núñez, Luis, 134

Sánchez Pontón, Luis, 50
Secretariat of Public Education (SEP), 40, 45, 57–59, 62, 64, 105, 111, 129, 158, 181
Shaw, Artie, 139
Sierra, Justo, 11
Siqueiros, David Alfaro, 102, 106–108
Silva Herzog, Jésus, 12, 41
sinarquistas, 33–34
singers, 82–85
songwriters, 81–83

Tamayo, Rufino, 102–105
Tepoztlán, 10, 116–17
Tin Tan, 84–85, 140
Toledano, Vincento Lombardo, 12, 25
Torres Bodet, Jaime, 2, 4, 37, 40, 52–55, 132, 133
Tylor, E. B., 4

Unamuno, Miguel, 11
Universidad Autonoma de México (UNAM), 38, 40, 42, 43, 50, 64, 134

Vasconcelos, José, 2, 3, 9, 11–14, 45, 51, 87
Véjar Vásquez, Octavio, 50, 133–134
Velásquez, Consuelo, 27
Villa, Francísco "Pancho," 13
Villaseñor, José, 115–16

Washington, S. Walter, 161
Welles, Sumner, 30

XEW, 16, 34, 66, 68, 83, 112